□ 全国高等院校商务英语精品教材
□ 全国商务英语研究会推荐教材

新编商务英语

综合教程 教学参考书 **1**

（第二版） (Second Edition)

Business English: A Comprehensive Course

XINBIAN SHANGWU YINGYU ZONGHE JIAOCHENG JIAOXUE CANKAOSHU

总主编　虞苏美　　张春柏

主　编　张　逸

编　者　全建强　　赵　刚

　　　　周　淳　　陈　翔

　　　　高惠蓉　　张　逸

Teacher's Book

高等教育出版社·北京

HIGHER EDUCATION PRESS　BEIJING

图书在版编目（CIP）数据

新编商务英语综合教程教学参考书.1/虞苏美,张春柏主编;张逸
分册主编.—2版.—北京:高等教育出版社,2011.8
ISBN 978-7-04-032980-3

Ⅰ.①新… Ⅱ.①虞…②张…③张… Ⅲ.①商务-英语-高等
职业教育-教学参考资料 Ⅳ.①H31

中国版本图书馆CIP数据核字(2011)第156930号

策划编辑 陈锡镖 王雪婷 责任编辑 王雪婷 封面设计 顾凌芝 责任印制 田 甜

出版发行	高等教育出版社		网　址	http://www.hep.edu.cn
社　址	北京市西城区德外大街4号			http://www.hep.com.cn
邮政编码	100120		网上订购	http://www.landraco.com
印　刷	北京宏伟双华印刷有限公司			http://www.landraco.com.cn
开　本	850mm×1168mm　1/16			
印　张	19.75		版　次	2005年6月第1版
字　数	506千字			2011年8月第2版
购书热线	010-58581118		印　次	2011年8月第1次印刷
咨询电话	400-810-0598		定　价	44.00元

本书如有缺页、倒页、脱页等质量问题,请到所购图书销售部门联系调换

版权所有　侵权必究
物 料 号　32980-00

第二版前言

《新编商务英语精读》出版后，承蒙广大师生厚爱，在全国多所大专院校使用。随着时代的发展和商务英语教学的深入，也暴露了一些缺陷，如部分材料陈旧，部分单元选题不当，缺少听力练习等。针对这些缺陷，此次对全书进行了一次全面修订，在《新编商务英语精读》基础上扩展为《新编商务英语综合教程》，教师用书也随之进行了修订，根据新的学生用书作了相应的修改和调整。

如何编写一本教师喜欢的教师用书？ 我们认为一本好的教师用书应在五方面给予教师指导：

1. 策略性指导。

2. 引导性指导。

3. 程序性指导。

4. 教学活动补充或拓展材料。

5. 参考答案。

策略性指导是对课堂教学的策略加以说明；引导性指导是为课堂教学提供一些引导性的参考资料；程序性指导是对课堂教学的过程有明确的指导；教学活动补充或拓展材料是对本单元的课堂教学提供补充或扩展活动的教学材料，以便进一步就本单元的教学内容展开深入的教学活动。参考答案是教师用书必不可少的，有助于减轻教师负担。本教程的策略性指导体现在本书的"用法说明"，对教材主要内容作了宏观指导，对教学法和教学模式进行了说明，这些策略性指导对全书的教学理念和方法作了概括性的提示，同时在全书中每单元的"教学目的"、扩展活动的部分注释以及部分教学提示也对教学策略给予了足够的指导；引导性指导体现在提供每单元的背景知识、语言点知识及丰富的例句。在学习语言和商务知识并重的主题单元教学大纲中，背景知识使教师能够为学生提供更多的输入，使学生在学习语言知识的同时，学习商务知识。语言知识的讲解是教学的重点，语言知识之于交际如同砖瓦之于建筑，没有语言知识，交际是一句空话。同时学生学习语言需要有语境，大量的例句既为教师减轻备课的负担，又为学生提供了大量的语境。因此教师用书在词语解释和语法运用方面下了很大功夫，提供了详尽的语言点知识和丰富的例句，教师还可利用这些例句编写课堂练习。程序性指导体现在导入和扩展活动的注释以及每单元的教学提示（Teaching Tips）。课堂教学是教材的活化，从这个意义上说，每一位教师都能创造性地运用教材，使之适应自己的学生。作为教材的编写者，对教材的使用有自己的看法，为此我们提供一些可操作的教学提示，供教师参考。这些提示是我们的教学心得，是从课堂实践中得来的，因此具有较强的可操作性。教学活动补充或拓展材料为课堂活动提供丰富的素材。在强调语言交际功能的今天，丰富多彩的课堂活动是语言教学的必须，教师往往苦于找不到合适的课堂活动素材，教师用书在这方面为教师准备了不少素材，供教师在开展课堂活动时选用。练习答案是教师用书必不可少的，本教程在原有的基础上进行了修订，增加了导入（Lead-in）部分的听力材料原文和练习答案，供教师参考。但由于语言的复杂性，书中的不少答案不是唯一正确的答案。又由于课堂活动的随机性，不可能有所谓的正确答案。因此教书用书中提供的答案有些只是一个参考答案。

修订后的教师用书第一册的每个单元设置六大板块：一、教学目的（Teaching Aim）列出本单元的重点；二、导入（Lead-in）增加了听力材料原文、练习答案，以及听写答案；三、背景知识（Background Information）为教师提供相关的背景材料；四、语言文化重点（Language and Culture Focus）为阅读I和II的课文提供详细的注释和词汇、语法方面的知识；为扩展性练习（Extended Activities）中的功能与结构（Function and Structure）提供文化和交际方面的注释；为专项用法（Special Use）提供详细的讲解和例句；为实用阅读（Practical Reading）提供阅读技能方面的注释；五、教学提示（Teaching Tips）提出一些教学的建议以及提供进一步开展课堂活动的素材；六、练习答案（Key）。

教师是教学成功与否的关键，教师用书只是一个工具，希望教师能各显神通，创造性地运用这个工具，在教学中取得成绩。同时也希望广大教师不吝赐教，对本书提出宝贵的意见。

编　者

2011年7月

于华东师范大学

第二版使用说明

本教材共分5册，每册有10个单元，每个单元都紧扣一个商务主题展开：

导入（Lead-in）部分安排了听力理解和听写填空两项任务。听力理解部分包含passage或dialogue一至两篇，设有若干练习，题型为多项选择（Multiple-choice Questions）、填空（Blank Filling）或配对（Matching），以考查学生对语篇主旨的把握和细节的辨析。在操作时建议教师先做练习1，然后将Difficult Words and Expressions讲解一遍，以扫除语言障碍；接着做练习2、3。听写练习(Spot Dictaion)的内容紧密围绕单元主题，旨在提高学生手、耳并用的能力，可以安排在Post-reading活动之前或Reading II之前进行，以检验学生对Reading I课文的掌握和作为Reading II的热身。

阅读I（Reading I）的读前准备活动（Pre-reading）设两项任务。Brainstorming部分，全班学生通过自由讨论的形式，复习与单元主题相关的内容。Pairwork部分，由学生双人结对，讨论与单元主题相关的若干问题，旨在引导学生进入单元主题，进一步激发学生学习课文（Text）的兴趣。教师可在学生讨论的基础上，作相应的点拨和总结；也可邀请部分学生对其讨论的结果作简短的陈述和介绍。读前准备活动的目的为：将单元主题的内容和学生以前获取的相关消息进行链接和沟通，为课文的学习做好心理准备。教师可视学生的实际情况对读前活动作适当的调整。

阅读I（Reading I）后配有丰富的练习题。练习I的目的为检查并加深学生对课文的理解。在处理练习I时，教师应注意引导学生用自己的话来回答问题，培养学生的分析、归纳和口头表达的能力，而不是生搬硬套原文。在校对练习II时，教师应要求学生援引课文内容，作一定的说明，提高学生对篇章的综合理解能力。练习III至V的目的为：加深学生对本课词汇的理解并提高学生对重点词汇的灵活运用能力。练习III要求学生在对课文理解和熟悉的基础上，用课文中所学的词汇完成句子。因此，不要把该练习当作单纯的词汇练习使用。练习IV针对课文的重点词组设计，教师要引导学生举一反三，掌握这些词组的正确使用方法，并对句中的个别难点予以解释。练习VI为词汇替换练习，进一步帮助学生巩固所学的词汇。原书中每课5个基本词汇学习的练习已放入光盘,教师可在课堂将基本词的不同词义,不同词性,不同用法,以及相关词和各种搭配予以介绍,引导学生举一反三,自己操练,连词成句,掌握这些词的用法。也可以让学生在练习中自己归纳领会这些词汇的不同用法,最后由教师总结归纳。

读后活动(Post-reading)系综合性的课堂交际活动,教师可视学生的实际语言运用能力和对单元主题的熟悉程度对活动要求进行适当的调整,合理安排活动的时间(如有些对专业知识的了解要求较高的活动,可安排在完成阅读 II后进行)。该项任务旨在使学生将课文中所学的内容和相关商务实践有机结合,融会贯通,灵活运用于各种交际活动。

阅读II(Reading II)系对阅读I的补充和强化,以帮助学生进一步了解与单元主题相关的知识并相应地提高其语言技能,对该部分的内容教师不必精讲,只需针对学生的理解难点作一些点拨即可。针对阅读II课文的理解,设有阅读理解(Comprehension)、讨论题(Discussion Questions)和词汇练习(Vocabulary)三项练习。教师可根据教学的具体情况,决定取舍,有些课文和练习可由学生自主学习或作为第二课堂的活动材料。

针对商务英语专业学生在以后工作实践中经常会运用到听写、翻译等技能,阅读II 部分还特别设计了其他几项练习:翻译练习(Translation)— 复习阅读I和阅读II中出现的重点词语,同时掌握一定的翻译技巧;完形填空(Cloze)的内容也与单元主题相关,该练习既能使学生对单元主题有更多的了解,也能训练其语言的运用能力。

扩展性练习(Extended Activitis)主要对课文的内容提供进一步的知识和语言练习。功能与结构(Function and Structure)系介绍一些日常生活或商务情景下常用的表达方式,并在充分的语言输入和操练基础上,辅之以灵活多样的交际任务,进一步提高学生的口语交际能力,在日后各种工作场景下均能轻松应对,教师可根据教学需求安排一些课堂教学活动开展交际任务;专项用法(Special Use)主要目的是帮助学生复习一些重要的语法和词汇用法知识,教师可根据学生的水平和教学需求进行讲解和操练;实用阅读(Practical Reading)采用商务往来中使用的真实语言材料,如数据、图表、案例、文函、广告等,实用性强,旨在帮助学生更好掌握语言基础知识并熟悉商务活动的真实场景;词汇扩展(Additional Vocabulary)进一步扩充学生对和主题相关的词汇的扩充,教师可鼓励学生在课外阅读中注意积累相关词汇,提高其学习的兴趣和自学的能力;商务世界(Business World)介绍商务和文化活动方面的小知识,旨在开阔眼学生的眼界,教师可鼓励学生多利用报刊、杂志、专业书籍和因特网等资源,发掘相关材料,互相交流,进一步拓展知识面,提高学习的主动性。

本书的教学建议以交际法为主,充分发挥结对学习和小组学习的作用,在任务和交际中学习英语。教师可根据教学实际,利用本教程提供的内容丰富、专业面广、趣味性强的商务材料开展灵活多样的英语课堂和课外活动,帮助学生掌握英语语言的基础知识,培养学生商务实践的基本技能。商务英语教学是一项艰巨的任务,在教学中一定要发挥学生的主动性,提高学生的学习兴趣,精讲多练,课堂内外相结合,定能使学习效果事半功倍。

编 者
2011年7月
于华东师范大学

CONTENTS

Unit 1
Essentials of Business

1. Cognitive Information（认知信息）: Basic Concept of Business
2. Language Focus（内容重点）

— **Key Words:** I. production, manufacture, service, merchandise, trade, land, labor, capital, entrepreneurship, distribute, accomplish, perform, go bankrupt, creditor, venture, profit; II. company, firm, a business, wholesaler, retailer, competitor, rival, compete, go into business, go out of business

— **Phrases:** I. relate ... to/with, be extracted ... from, to a certain extent, make ... of value, be responsible for, look for, decide on, up to, refer to, pay for, distribute ... to/among; II. in bulk, compete for, keep ahead of, have an advantage over, give an edge on

— **Useful Structures:** V+-ing as subj.   "where ..." relative clause
                               not ... unless ...   "whether ..." concessional clause

— **Grammar:** Countable and Uncountable Nouns

3. Communicative Skills（交际技能）

— **Expressions:** Expressions of "Meeting People"

— **Reading:** Timetables

Lead-in 导入

>>>>> **Listening Comprehension Tasks**

Difficult Words & Expressions

1. occupation: job; vocation 职业

2. be closely associated with: 同……紧密联系在一起

3. commerce: the buying and selling of goods and services, especially on a large scale 商业

4. an enormous range: 一个庞大的系列

5. household item: 家用产品

6. contribute to: 对……作出贡献

7. quality of life: 生活质量

8. donate: to give as a contribution 捐赠

9. rest house: 疗养院

10. terminally ill: 处于疾病晚期的

11. transform: to change 转变

Passage Script

The word business has many meanings. It can refer to a person's occupation, to a type of occupation, to a person's behavior, to a trade or commerce, or to a firm's activity, when he or she buys and sells. The modern word "business" comes from an old English word which meant "to do things". Nowadays business is about buying and selling. Business is the way that buyers buy and sellers sell goods and services. For buyers, business is about how they get what they want. For sellers, business is about how they do their selling and receive their money and income.

In our everyday life, we constantly come into contact with business. All businesses offer something to the community. No matter how big or small, businesses have an important role to play in society. Stores aim to meet the specific needs of certain groups. Department stores offer an enormous range of household items. Even though these stores represent a small part of the business environment, they play important roles within our society. They provide goods and services to meet the wants and needs of the community.

Businesses play a large social and economic role in our society. The social role can be seen when the actions of businesses contribute to the quality of life and happiness of members of our society. Businesses also play an enormous economic role by creating wealth, employment, and choice. Businesses provide employment and investment opportunities. Through the skill of business people, new ideas are transformed into products that enable us to enjoy a high standard of living.

Key

II. 1. c   2. a   3. d   4. a   5. c   6. d   7. d   8. d

III. 1. how   2. short   3. everyday   4. big   5. play   6. social   7. creating   8. opportunities
   9. economic   10. Without

➤➤➤➤➤ Spot Dictation

Business includes the <u>activities</u> of all commercial <u>producers</u> of goods and services. These producers <u>range</u> from small shops <u>owned</u> by one person to huge <u>organizations</u> owned by thousands of <u>stockholders</u> who have <u>shares</u> in the companies. The word *business* may <u>refer</u> to producers of the same product or <u>service</u>, such as the clothing business or the <u>insurance</u> business. An individual <u>enterprise</u> may also be called a business.

Background Information (背景知识)

1. Business

Business can mean buying or selling goods or services. That is, the activity of making money by producing or buying and selling goods, or providing services. When it is used in this meaning, it is uncountable. It can also be used to refer to an organization such as a company, shop, or factory that produces or sells goods or provides a service. When it is used in this meaning, it is countable.

2. Becoming a successful business

Becoming a successful business takes time, energy, motivation, and a bit of luck. Getting an idea, testing an idea, finding the right people and help, locating access to capital and credit, understanding and using technology, and planning ahead are just a few of the steps to the process. Throughout the various stages of the business lifecycle — starting, financing, expanding, training and counseling, management assistance, advocacy, and eventually closing a business — the right help at the right time can make all the difference between failure and success. Besides access to capital and credit, business owners need management and technical assistance, training and education, counseling and user-friendly access to information all along the way.

Language and Culture Focus (语言文化要点)

>>>>> Reading I

1. **civilization:** The word *civilization* comes from the Latin *civilis*, meaning *civil*, related to the Latin *civis*, meaning *citizen*. Civilization is an advanced state of human society, marked by progress in the arts and sciences, the extensive use of writing, and the appearance of complex political and social institutions. The level of advancement of a civilization is often measured by its progress in agriculture, long-distance trade, occupational specialization, and urbanism. Aside from these core elements, civilization is often marked by any combination of a number of secondary elements, including a developed transportation system, writing, standards of measurement (currency, etc.), contract and tort-based legal systems, characteristic art styles (which may pertain to specific cultures), monumental architecture, mathematics, science, politics, and astronomy. 文明；文明社会

【例句】the history of Western civilization 西方文明的全部历史

Chinese civilization is one of the oldest in the world.

2. **Making airplanes, building buildings, and constructing paper boxes...:** The *–ing* form of the verb can be used as the subject of a sentence.

【例句】Seeing is believing.

Taking good photos requires patience as well as keen eyes.

Watching television at spare time is a good entertainment.

3. **relate:** relate sth. to sth. else. 与……有关

【例句】The report seeks to relate the rise in crime to an increase in unemployment.

4. **辨析 capital & money:** **Capital** is the money or property that you use to start a business or to make more money. **Money** is what you earn by working and you use in order to buy things.

【例句】The recycling industry is making huge capital investments in equipment.

Do you have enough money to pay for the sandwiches?

Therefore, collocations related with **capital** are: capital intensive industries (资本密集产业); venture/risk capital (风险资本); intellectual capital (智识资本), etc.

Collocations related with **money**, on the other hand, are: money bags (有钱人); Money makes a mare go. (有钱能使鬼推磨); money worshiper (金钱至上主义者).

5. **Other forms of business include merchandising, which is the selling of products, and providing various services, such as accounting, distributing, and repairs.**

【译文】其他形式的商务包括销售,即出售产品、提供诸如会计、分销及修理等各种各样的服务。

merchandise: to try to sell goods or services using methods such as advertising; 买卖;推销

【例句】If this product is properly merchandised, it should sell very well.

这一产品如果促销得当,该是很畅销的。

We merchandise our furniture by advertising in newspapers.

我们在报上登广告推销家具。

distribute: to supply goods to shops and companies so that they can sell them 分发;分销;

synonym: give out

【例句】distribute sth. among/to sb.

Clothes and blankets have been distributed among the refugees.

Milk is distributed to the local shops by Herald's Dairies.

6. **entrepreneurship:** Entrepreneurship is a frequently used concept in English-speaking countries, but it is difficult to define and translate. It generally refers to a management concept characterized by development and renovation and the ability to implement this concept in marketing. (它指的是一种发展的、革新的经营观念,以及将这种观念贯彻在市场中的能力。) Successful entrepreneurs have an unshakable belief in themselves and in their ideas. They have drives, and can always bounce back after frustrations. That is, no matter what goes wrong, they can get up and try again. 企业家素质

7. **refer to:** 提到,涉及;指(的是)

1) refer to sb. or sth.

【例句】We agreed never to refer to the matter again.

Although she didn't mention any names, everyone knew who she was referring to.

2) refer to sb. or sth. as.

【例句】He likes to be referred to as "Doctor Khee".

8. **"where ..." relative clause:** "Where" can be used to introduce a relative clause.

【例句】The crisis has reached a point where the receiver (破产管理人) will have to be called in.

This is the hotel where we spent our honeymoon.

The place where he was going is dangerous.

"Where" functions as an adverbial in the relative clause. The other adverbs that can introduce relative clause are "when" and "why".

【例句】She remembered the day when Paula had first walked into her office.

This is the place where I hid the key.

In 1963 we moved to Boston, where my grandparents lived.

9. extract: extract something from sth. else. 拉出；提取

1) to remove an object from somewhere, especially with difficulty.

【例句】He extracted an envelope from his inside pocket.

2) to carefully remove a substance from something which contains it, using a machine, chemical process etc.

【例句】This substance is extracted from seaweed. 这种物质是从海藻中提取的。

Oils are extracted from the plants.

10. accomplish: succeed in doing sth.; successfully finish doing sth.; achieve. 完成；达到；实现

【例句】I don't think our visit really accomplished anything.

We have accomplished a great deal in the last few days.

"Accomplished" means "skilled", so a singer can be "accomplished", so can a writer or painter be. "Accomplished fact (既成事实)", however, is a legal term, which means something that is known to be true and cannot be doubted. "Accomplishment" is the noun form, which means "achievement" or "a skill".

【例句】Our 15% increase in sales last year was a major accomplishment.

Being able to play the piano well is one of his many accomplishments.

11. Therefore, to a certain extent the next factor, capital, can be used to replace labor or reduce the amount of physical and mental labor that humans have to use in order to conduct business.

【译文】因此，下一要素：资金，在某种程度上可用于替代劳动力或减少人们为开展业务而所化的体力与脑力的付出。

to a certain extent: indicating that sth. is partly true, but not entirely true; partly (= to some extent). 在某种程度上

【例句】We all to some extent /to a certain extent remember the good times and forget the bad.

I do agree with him to a certain extent.

replace: to remove someone from their job or sth. from its place, and put a new person or thing there. 代替

【例句】replace A with B 以 B 代替 A

They replaced the permanent staff with part-timers.

12. of value

1) worth a lot of money. 值钱的

【例句】The thieves took nothing of value.

2) useful. 有价值的

【例句】I hope this book will be of value to both teachers and students.

13. be responsible for: 为……负责；是造成……的原因

【例句】Police believe that the same man is responsible for three other murders in the area.

We are determined to bring the people responsible to justice.

14. not ... unless ...: 除非……，就不会……

Here "unless" is used to introduce a statement expressing a case in which an exception to a preceding statement may or will exist.

【例句】Do not leave the building unless you are instructed to do so.

Don't call me at the office unless it's absolutely necessary.

Sometimes "not" can be used with "unless" to indicate the only condition.

Then the phrase "not unless" means "only if".

【例句】— Will you go with her?

— Not unless she wants me to.

Nowhere to land, not unless you had a spaceship.

The old man had gone to bed with instructions not to be disturbed, not unless the plan failed.

In conditional clauses, "unless" is used to express that something will happen or be true if something else does not happen or is not true. So simply stated, it is a negative "if" clause "if ... not ...".

【例句】Unless some extra money is found, the theatre will close.

I think you should complain — unless, of course, you are happy with the way things are.

He won't go to sleep unless you tell him a story.

I can't leave her unless I know she's all right.

15. initiate: to arrange for sth. important to start, such as an official process or a new plan. 开始；发动

【例句】initiate a reform 开始改革

They have decided to initiate legal proceedings against the newspaper.

Intellectuals have initiated a debate on terrorism.

16. innovative: an innovative idea or way of doing sth. that is new, different, and better than those that existed before. 创新的；有新意的

【例句】an innovative approach to language teaching

innovative plans for recycling waste materials

17. look for: 寻找

synonym: search for

【例句】Could you help me look for my contact lens?

If you're looking for a bargain, try the local market.

18. decide on/upon sth.: to choose sth. or someone after thinking carefully. 对……作出决定

【例句】Have you decided on a date for the wedding?

19. "whether ..." concessional clause: "Whether" can be used to introduce a concessional clause (让步从句).

【例句】I will go, whether you come with me or stay at home.

It's not important whether he comes himself or sends a substitute.

Whether you like it or not it's going to happen.

Whether we do it now or later, it's got to be done.

20. bear: to bravely accept or deal with a painful, difficult, or upsetting situation. 负担, 忍受, 带给（past tense: *bore*; past participle: *borne*）

synonym: stand

【例句】She was afraid she wouldn't be able to bear the pain.

Make the water as hot as you can bear.

Experts were worried the financial system would not be able to bear the strain.

21. 辨析 pay & pay for

The most frequently used format is **pay (sb.) for (sth.).**

【例句】How soon can you pay me for the work?

Did you pay for that car?

Pay for may also mean "receive punishment or suffering for（为……而受惩罚；为……而吃亏/倒霉）".

【例句】These people must be made to pay for their crimes.

He paid dearly for his unfaithfulness to her.

I'll let him pay for ruining my chances.

We are paying for the fine summer with a wet winter.

今年夏季天气晴好, 而冬季却雨水不断。

On the other hand, **pay** means giving someone money for something you buy or for a service.

【例句】How much would you like to pay?

You'd get a discount for paying cash.

I paid him 5 to cut the grass.

After **pay** you can use the following words as object: bill, cash, cost, credit, debt, dollar, expenses, fee, fine, interest, loan, money, price, salary, rent, sum, tax, wage.

The other phrases using **pay** are: pay attention to, pay respect to sb., pay sb. a visit, or pay a visit to a place.

>>>>> Reading II

1. 辨析 a company, a firm, and a business

A company is an organization made up of people who work together for the purposes of making or selling goods or services in order to get money.

【例句】an insurance company 保险公司

a pharmaceutical company 医药公司

an automobile company 汽车公司

a private company 私人公司

a state-owned company 国营公司

A firm refers to a small business company that makes goods or provides services such as giving legal or financial advice.

【例句】a law firm 法律公司

an engineering firm 工程公司

A business is a shop, a factory or a company that sells goods or provides services, especially one that employs a small number of people or even only one person.

【例句】to start up a new business 新开一家商号

He runs a small business in the town. 他在镇上经营着一家小铺子。

【相关词】

corporation: a large company that employs a large number of people, such as IBM, Kodak, etc.

multinational: a very large company that has offices or factories in many different countries. 跨国公司

2. be said (据说): Followed by the infinitive "to do", this phrase can be used to introduce information or message. Besides "said", some other verbs can also be used, such as "assumed, believed, considered, estimated, expected, recognized, recommended, regarded, reported, supposed", etc.

【例句】He is said to be the richest man in the world.

The manager is supposed to be at his office now.

There is said to be plenty of gold in this area.

This structure can also be changed into "it is said that ...". "That" introduced a clause.

【例句】It is said that he is the richest man in the world.

It is supposed that the manager is at his office now.

It is said that there is plenty of gold in this area.

3. go into business: This phrase means "begin business, begin to make or sell goods or provide service for the purpose of making money". Its opposite is "go out of business". There are also some other verbs that can be used with "business".

【例句】set up a business   run/manage a business   expand business

4. stop doing and stop to do: Grammatically speaking, in the phrase "stop doing", "doing" is the object; while in "stop to do", "to do" functions as the adverbial of purpose. There they carry different meanings. "Stop doing" means "to give it up (停止做某事)". "Stop to do" means "to give up doing one thing and begin to do something else (停下来去做……)".

【例句】stop talking 停止说话

stop smoking 停止吸烟

stop to read 停下手头的事开始阅读

stop to have a rest 停下来休息

5. get (as a linking verb): When used as the linking verb, "get" can be followed by the adjective or the subject complement.

【例句】get angry   get big   get broken   get cold

get dark   get divorced   get dressed   get married

get old   get ready

6. expand: to increase sth. so that it covers a wider area or range of activities.

【例句】expand business   expand operation

expand market   expand knowledge

Shanghai is to further expand its hotel facilities for the coming of the World Expo.

Its noun form is "expansion", and the adjective is "expansive".

7. tonne: metric ton (公吨), measurement of weight, which is equal to 1, 000kg. It is also spelled as "ton". In the West, "pound (磅)" is also a frequently used measurement for weight. A pound is equal to 0.454 kilograms, that is, less than half a kilo gram.

8. increase production by 10%: Here the preposition "by" indicates the amount or degree of increase, and the Chinese for it is 增加了. Similarly, "to reduce ... by" means 减少了. If we use another preposition "to", it indicates the total amount including the part that has been increased. Therefore the Chinese for it is 增加到/减少到.

【例句】The price of oil fell by 2 a barrel.

Our car production has increased by 10 percent to 33, 000 a year.

9. in bulk: in large quantities.

【例句】buy/sell in bulk 整批或大批购买 / 出售

We always buy in bulk. It is so much more economical.

Since we got our freezer we always buy things in bulk.

Related to the verb phrase "buy in bulk", there is also a noun phrase "bulk buying", which means buying goods in large quantities.

【例句】Bulk buying has enabled the company to cut costs.

10. 辨析 wholesale & retail: Wholesale (批发) refers to the sale of goods in large quantities at a time, usually to storekeepers or others who will in turn sell them in small quantities to users. A wholesale merchant is called a wholesaler (批发商). **Retail** is the sale of goods in small quantities at a time, directly to the consumer. A retail dealer is called a retailer (零售商).

11. compete for: Used as the verb, "compete" means "to try to win something". The preposition "for" is used as the aim of the competition.

【例句】compete for attention 争着出风头

compete for the contract 为赢得合同而竞争

The phrase "to compete with/against" introduces rivals.

【例句】compete with/against each other 相互竞争

compete with a trading company for the contract

When Mr. and Mrs. Dell asked their son what he wanted to do, young Michael said, "To compete with IBM."

"Be in competition" carries the same meaning as the verb "compete".

【例句】be in competition with a trading company for the contract

A competitor (竞争者) is a person who tries hard to win or gain something wanted by others. "Competitive" is the adjective.

12. keep ahead of: be in a more successful position than ..., surpass. 胜过; 优于

【例句】Our company keeps ahead of its main rivals.

If she works hard, she will surely keep ahead of her colleagues.

13. have an advantage over: If you have the/an advantage over somebody, or something gives you the/an advantage over somebody else, you are in a better position than he is.(与……相比具有优势)

Here the preposition "over" introduces somebody or something being compared.

【例句】She has an advantage over other girls.

The company has an advantage over others.

Her beauty gives her an advantage over other girls.

Her teaching experience gave her a big advantage over the other applicants for the job.

His strength gives him the advantage over us.

14. **give/have an edge:** to have an advantage that makes sb. or sth. stronger or more likely to be successful.

【例句】Her wide relations give her an edge on the job market.

"Give sb./sth. an edge on ..." or "have an/the edge on ..." is used to mean "to be slightly better than or have a slight advantage over". The preposition "on" may be used to introduce somebody or something being compared.

【例句】Her wide relations will give her an edge on other applicants.

She has the edge on the other students because she spent a year in England.

>>>>> Extended Activities

A. Function and Structure: Meeting People

1. Using right vocabulary and phrases is important when you meet someone or introduce yourself in English. First impressions are important, so here's some guide to using the right expression in the right situation.

   Two friends' meeting:

   Friends often say "Hi" to each other. Then they often ask a general question, such as "How are you?" or "How are things?" or "How's life?" The reply to this question is normally positive. "Fine thanks, and you?" "Fine thanks, what about yourself?" "Not bad." or "Can't complain."

   Greeting people you don't know:

   You can say "Hello" to people you don't know. A more formal greeting is "Good morning/ afternoon/evening." The other person normally replies with the same greeting as you have used, and then makes some polite conversation, such as "How was your trip?" or "Did you find our office easily?"

2. Chinese like to greet each other by asking questions such as "Where are you going（去哪呀）?" "Have you had dinner yet（吃过了吗）?" or "Are you eating your lunch（吃饭呐）?" For Chinese, these questions are asked simply as sort of a greeting rather than a genuine request for information. But in English it is not appropriate to greet people in this way. Questions of this sort are usually interpreted as a lead-in to a suggestion or invitation; otherwise, it seems rather weird or rude to ask about something quite obvious or very personal.

3. Americans use "small talk" when they first meet another person. The most common topic of small talk is the weather; another very common topic is the speakers' current surroundings — the room or building they are in, the sidewalk where they are standing, etc. Later, Americans may talk about past experiences they have both had, such as watching a particular TV program, going to New York, or eating at a particular restaurant. Besides these very general topics of small talk, Americans talk about different things according to the life situation of people involved and the setting in which the conversation is taking place. Students are likely to talk about their teachers and classes; if they are of the same sex, they are likely to discuss their social lives. Adults may discuss their jobs, interests, houses, or family members. Men are likely to talk about sports or cars. Housewives are likely to talk about their children or about household matters or personal care (e.g., hairdos). Americans are taught not to discuss religion and politics unless they know the people they are talking to fairly well. Politics and religion are thought to be "controversial", and discussing a controversial topic can lead to an argument. There are other topics Americans generally avoid because they are "too personal". Financial matters is one. Inquiries about a person's earnings or about the amount someone paid for an item are usually not acceptable topics.

B. Special Use: Countable and Uncountable Nouns

1. 不可数名词

不可数名词通常指不能直接计数的名词(如 land, advice 等), 表示材料和成分的物质名词, 如 coal, oil, air, cloth 等, 和表示抽象概念的抽象名词, 如 music, love, equality, modernization, competition, trade, service, education 等。

2. 集合名词的单复数用法

集合名词指的是同一类人或物的集合体, 其中有的是复数含义。例如 police, cattle, clothes, people, goods 等; 但有的集合名词也是不可数名词, 如 furniture, equipment, merchandise, machinery 等。

3. 名词单复数的特殊变化

- 一些以 o 结尾的可数名词复数需要加 -es。例如: echoes, embargoes, heroes, Negroes, potatoes, tomatoes, vetoes, mosquito(e)s, buffalo(e)s 等。
- 一些以 f 或 fe 结尾的可数名词复数需要把 f 或 fe 变为 ves。例如 halves, knives, leaves, lives, loaves, selves, shelves, thieves, wives, wolves。
- 不规则变化:

foot — feet	tooth — teeth	woman — women	man — men
goose — geese	mouse — mice	child — children	ox — oxen

- 单复数形式相同的名词：

barracks（兵营）	deer（鹿）	fish（鱼）	headquarters（总部）
means（方法）	series（系列）	sheep（羊）	species（物种，种类）

但 fish 若指不同种类的鱼，复数为 fishes。

- 复合名词的复数变化：

passers-by	lookers-on	sisters-in-law
grown-ups	shoe-makers	step-mothers

如中心名词由 man 或 woman 修饰，man 或 woman 要随中心名词一起变为复数。例如：women doctors, men servants。

- 外来词的复数变化：

stimulus — stimuli	formula — formulae	bacterium — bacteria
curriculum — curricula	datum — data	analysis — analyses
basis — bases	crisis — crises	diagnosis — diagnoses
thesis — theses	criterion — criteria	
phenomenon — phenomena		

4. 可数名词和不可数名词的转化

- 不可数名词表示种类时，可以加不定冠词 a，也可以有复数形式。例如：

This is a famous French wine.

I work in all weathers.

Some foods are more nutritious than others.（几种食物）

- 当抽象名词表示抽象概念时，为不可数名词；但当抽象名词的意义具体化时，该名词为可数名词。例如：

She was a beauty in her youth.（美人）

She had much beauty in her youth.（美丽动人的气质）

There are two deaths in this area this month.（死亡事故）

The sense of sight may affect our judgement.（视觉）

There are many beautiful sights in Shanghai.（景点）

Knowledge is power.（力量）

China is now one of the five greatest powers in the world.（大国）

He is good at drawing.（画画的技能）

Are these drawings by Gogh?（一张张的画）

- 当物质名词纯粹表示物质时，为不可数名词；但当物质名词表示个体时，为可数名词。例如：

The bridge is made of stone.（石头）

He threw a stone at the bird. (一块石头)

- 不可数名词的复数形式有"广大"的意思。例如: waters 表示水域; seas 表示海域; snows 表示大片积雪。

- 动物的名称作个体解释时为可数名词; 作肉解释时为不可数名词。例如:

There are many chickens in the yard. (小鸡)

I like chicken. (鸡肉)

- iron 解释为"铁"时为不可数名词; 解释为"熨斗"时为可数名词。例如:

Iron is harder than aluminum. (铁)

We need an iron. (熨斗)

- experience 解释为"经验"时, 为不可数名词; 解释为"经历"时, 为可数名词。例如:

We share a common experience. (经历)

I have not much experience in teaching. (经验)

- hair 解释为"头发"时, 是不可数名词; 但若强调一根根头发或几缕头发, 则可数。例如:

These old men have long hair. (长头发)

Look! A hair is in my soup. (一根头发)

She has some grey hairs. (几根花白的头发)

- paper 解释为"纸张"时, 为不可数名词; 解释为"考卷"、"报纸"或"文件"时, 为可数名词。

- room 解释为"房间"时, 是可数名词; 解释为"空间"时, 是不可数名词。例如: make room for sb.。

- glass 表示"玻璃"时, 是不可数名词; 解释为"玻璃杯"时, 是可数名词; glasses 还可以解释为"眼镜", 是复数形式。

- space 表示"空间; 太空"时, 为不可数名词; 表示"空格"时, 为可数名词。

- word 表示"词语"时, 为可数名词; 表示"消息"时, 为不可数名词。例如:

How many words are there in this article? (单词)

Word came that the war had ended. (消息)

5. 一些名词与数量词的搭配

- cattle 为集合名词, 含有复数意义, 不与 a 连用。另外, cattle 也不能与 one, two, three 连用。但我们可以说: some cattle, many cattle, a lot of cattle, these cattle, those cattle。

- plenty of 既可以和可数名词连用, 也可以和不可数名词连用。例如: plenty of crops, plenty of rain。

- 同样, a large quantity of 既可以和可数名词连用, 也可以和不可数名词连用。

- this, that 既可以和可数名词连用, 也可以和不可数名词连用。例如: this job, this work, that job, that work。

- some 与可数名词单数连用表示"某一个"。例如: some book (某一本书)。

C. Practical Reading

时间表是一种实用文体，形式直观，阅读的关键是要注意通过纵横坐标确定要寻找的信息的位置。时间表往往涉及以下内容：事件及其发生的时间；事件的顺序，排位。

在考查这类文体的阅读效果时，往往是图表给出了一部分内容，要求学生根据文章填出其他部分或其他环节等。要完成这类任务，学生需要在准确把握文字内容的基础上，读懂图表，并能够利用图表解决有关问题。本题要求学生能通过文字部分完成列车时刻表，考查学生跳读（也叫寻读，即 scanning skill: glancing from point to point of, often hastily, casually, or in search of a particular item）的能力和推理的能力（inferring skill: deriving as a conclusion from facts or premises）。

根据原文前面 3 句话，我们可以将从 Stone 这个地方始发的时间，按照先后，一一列举出来。每个小时里的 15 和 50 分各有一班。

1. 50 分这一班中途不停，直达目的地 Keel，是快车，所用时间是 4 小时 20 分。利用这一线索，我们可以知道 6 点 50 分、7 点 50 分、8 点 50 分、9 点 50 分从 Stone 出发的列车，到达 Keel 的时间分别是 11 点 10 分，12 点 10 分，13 点 10 分和 14 点 10 分。

2. 15 分这一班在一小时和两小时 15 分后分别到达 Mont 和 Trent，这样我们就可以得到 6 点 15、7 点 15、8 点 15、9 点 15 从 Stone 始发的列车分别到达 Mont, Trent 以及终点站的时间。

3. 8 点 25 分和 9 点 25 分另有两趟慢车，到达三个站所需时间与 15 分始发车一样。

4. 注意：题目要求我们完成的只是时刻表的一部分。

5. 有了这个时刻表，要完成后面回答问题的练习，就一目了然了。

Notes

1. a stopping train: 每站停靠的列车，慢车。

2. a through train: 快车，直达列车。这里 through 的意思是 without stopping。

3. community college: In Canada and the United States, a community college, sometimes called a junior college, is an educational institution providing post-secondary education and lower-level tertiary education, granting certificates, diplomas, and associate's degrees. 美国、加拿大的社区大学，有点近似于我国培养大专生的地方性大学。

4. graduation ceremony: 毕业典礼

5. attend a conference: 参加会议

6. do a survey on: 做关于……的调查

7. marketing: 营销。注意营销不同于销售（sales）。营销是一个范围广泛、内容丰富的概念，是"人或组织进行的社会的、管理的过程，是通过创造并交换产品和价值来满足他们的基本需求和个性需求的过程"。（a social and managerial process by which individuals and groups obtain what they need and want through creating and exchanging products and value with others — Philip Kotler）

Teaching Tips（教学提示）

1. 本单元导入(Lead-in)部分安排了听力理解和听写填空两项任务。听力理解部分围绕关于 business意义的一个短篇共设有3项活动。第一项为预听活动（Warming-up Exercise），主要目的是让学生对所听语篇的主旨（Gist）有所了解，为接下来的听力活动做好词汇和背景知识的准备。完成预听后，建议教师将Difficult words and expressions 讲解一遍，以扫除语言障碍；第二项练习为多项选择题（Multiple-choice Questions），旨在考查学生对语篇主旨的把握和辨析细节的能力。第三项练习为完型填空（cloze），帮助学生掌握相关重点词汇和表达方式，解决在上两项练习中可能碰到的听音上的问题。教师可先不提供第二项练习的正确答案，让学生在完成第三项练习后，以pair work 或group work形式自行讨论并检查。听写填空(Spot Dictation) 是关于主题business 基本概念，可以作为导入活动安排在ReadingII课文讲解之前进行。

2. Reading I 的读前准备活动（Pre-reading）设两项任务。Brainstorming 部分，全班学生通过自由讨论的形式，复习与本单元主题（Essentials of Business）相关的已知词汇，列出英语中"从事商务活动的个人或组织"、"开展商务活动的地点"以及其他与商务活动相关联的单词和词组。教师可采取一定的奖惩措施，以提高学生参与的积极性。Pairwork部分，由学生双人结对，讨论与单元主题相关的若干问题，旨在引导学生进入单元主题，进一步激发学生学习课文（Text）的兴趣。教师可在学生讨论的基础上，作相应的点拨和总结；也可邀请部分学生对其讨论的结果作简短的陈述和介绍。读前准备活动的目的为：将单元主题的内容和学生以前获取的相关信息进行链接和沟通，为课文的学习做好心理准备。教师可视学生的实际情况对读前活动作适当的调整。

3. Reading I 的练习1至2题的目的为检查并加深学生对课文的理解。在处理练习1时，教师应注意引导学生用自己的话来回答问题，培养学生的分析、归纳和口头表达的能力，而不是生搬硬套原文。在做练习2时，教师应要求学生援引课文内容，作一定的说明，提高学生对篇章的综合理解能力。

4. 本单元ReadingI 的练习3至6的目的为：加深学生对本课词汇的理解并提高学生对重点词汇的灵活运用能力。练习3要求学生在对课文理解和熟悉的基础上，用课文中所学的词汇完成句子。因此，不要把该练习当作单纯的词汇练习使用。练习4教师可要求学生先复习本课新单词，然后再独立完成。做练习时不得参阅前面的词汇表，可在完成后对照词汇表检查完成情况。练习5针对课文的重点词组设计，教师要引导学生举一反三，掌握这些词组的正确使用方法，并对句中的个别难点予以解释。练习6为词汇替换练习，进一步帮助学生巩固所学的词汇。词汇学习（Word Study）是对五个基本词汇（risk, perform, replace, limit, share）的操练和扩展，要求学生对练习中给出的基本词举一反三，对其不同的词义，不同的词性，不同的用法，不同的派生词进行操练，掌握这些词的用法。教师可先对这些词汇的主要用法予以介绍，注意引导学生掌握不同的派生词, 然后要求学生在连词成句, 进行复习和巩固; 也可以让学生在练习中自己归纳领会这些词汇的不同用法, 最后由教师总结归纳。词汇学习的练习已一起移入书后, 教师可根据情况, 选择学生课堂练习或回家作业。

5. Post-reading系综合性的课堂交际活动, 教师可视学生的实际语言运用能力和对单元主题的熟悉程度对活动要求进行适当的调整, 合理安排活动的时间(如有些对专业知识的了解要求较高的活动, 可安排在完成阅读II后进行)。该项任务旨在使学生将课文中所学的内容和相关商务实践有机结合, 融会贯通, 灵活运用于各种交际活动。本单元Post-reading设计的是一个采访活动。学生双人结对, 分别扮演商界巨子和电视节目主持人。教材中提供了若干用于采访的问题供学生参考, 回答这些问题既是对课文I相关内容的复习和巩固, 又需要学生运用自己的想象力, 对平时所积累的商务知识予以延伸。教师可鼓励学生根据自己的兴趣和爱好设计、添加更多的采访问题。双人活动结束后, 教师可邀请部分学生或鼓励学生自荐在全班面前表演他们的采访活动。

6. Reading II 是对Reading I的补充和强化, 以帮助学生进一步了解与单元主题相关的知识并相应地提高其语言技能。针对Reading II 课文的理解, 设有阅读理解(Comprehension)、讨论题(Discussion Questions)和词汇练习(Vocabulary)三项练习。

7. 针对商务英语专业学生在以后工作实践中经常会运用到听写、翻译等技能, Reading II部分还特别设计了其他几项练习: 专项用法练习(Special Use): 主要目的是帮助学生复习一些重要的语法知识, 系统实用。本单元复习的是可数名词和不可数名词的一些特殊用法; 翻译练习(Translation): 复习Reading I 和Reading II 中出现的重点词语, 同时掌握一定的翻译技巧; 完形填空(Cloze)的内容也与单元主题相关, 该练习既能使学生对单元主题有更多的了解, 也能训练其语言的运用能力。

8. Additional Vocabulary

Fortune 500 Top 50 (《财富》杂志500强2003年排名前50位的公司):

排　名	公司名称	中文名称	总部所在地	主要业务
1	General Motors	通用汽车	美国	汽车
2	Wal-Mart Stores	沃尔玛商店	美国	零售
3	Exxon Mobil	埃克森美孚	美国	炼油
4	Ford Motor	福特汽车	美国	汽车
5	DaimlerChrysler	戴姆勒克莱斯勒	德国	汽车
6	Mitsui	三井物产	日本	贸易
7	Mitsubishi	三菱商事	日本	贸易
8	Toyota Motor	丰田汽车	日本	汽车
9	General Electric	通用电气	美国	电子电气
10	Itochu	伊藤忠商事	日本	贸易

（续　表）

排　名	公司名称	中文名称	总部所在地	主要业务
11	Royal Dutch/Shell Group	皇家荷兰壳牌集团	荷兰/英国	炼油
12	Sumitomo	住友商事	日本	贸易
13	Nippon Telegraph & Telephone	日本电报电话	日本	电讯
14	Marubeni	丸红商事	日本	贸易
15	AXA	安盛	法国	保险
16	Intl. Business Machines	国际商用机器	美国	计算机
17	BP Amoco	英国石油阿莫科	英国	炼油
18	Citigroup	花旗集团	美国	多种金融
19	Volkswagen	大众	德国	汽车
20	Nippon Life Insurance	日本生命	日本	保险
21	Siemens	西门子	德国	电子电气
22	Allianz	安联	德国	保险
23	Hitachi	日立	日本	电子电气
24	Matsushita Electric Industrial	松下电器	日本	电子电气
25	Nissho Iwai	日商岩井	日本	贸易
26	US Postal Service	美国邮政总局	美国	邮件包裹货运
27	Ing Group	荷兰国际集团	荷兰	保险
28	AT & T	美国电话电报	美国	电讯
29	Philip Morris	菲利普莫里斯	美国	烟草食品
30	Sony	索尼	日本	电子、娱乐
31	Deutsche Bank	德意志银行	德国	银行
32	Boeing	波音	美国	航空航天
33	Dai-ichi Mutual Life Insurance	第一生命	日本	保险
34	Honda Motor	本田汽车	日本	汽车
35	Assicurazioni Generali	忠利保险	意大利	保险
36	Nissan Motor	日产汽车	日本	汽车
37	E. ON (Veba and Viag)	（费巴、维尔格合并）	德国	贸易
38	Toshiba	东芝	日本	电子电气
39	Bank of America Corp.	美洲银行公司	美国	银行
40	Fiat	菲亚特	意大利	汽车
41	Nestlé	雀巢	瑞士	食品

（续　表）

排　名	公司名称	中文名称	总部所在地	主要业务
42	SBC Communications	西南贝尔电信	美国	电讯
43	Credit Suisse	瑞士信贷	瑞士	银行
44	Hewlett-Packard	惠普	美国	计算机
45	Fujitsu	富士通	日本	计算机
46	Metro	麦德龙	德国	零售
47	Sumitomo Life Insurance	住友生命	日本	保险
48	Tokyo Electric Power	东京电力	日本	电力供应
49	Kroger	克罗格	美国	零售
50	Total Fina Elf	道达尔菲纳埃尔夫	法国	炼油

Key（练习答案）

>>>>> Reading I

Pre-reading

I.

People or Organizations Engaged in Business	Places to Conduct Business Activities	Other Terms Frequently Used in Business Operation
company	market	sell
salesman	department store	goods
businessman	supermarket	buy
joint-venture	stock exchange	order
manager	hotel	profit
enterprise	restaurant	invoice
merchant	bank	customer

II. 4. These points are often thought to be key to business success: good management; adequate planning; sufficient financial resources; healthy cash flow; controlled spending and the ability to collect money owing; effective marketing; a good product and service.

Exercises

II. 1. d   2. c   3. b   4. d   5. d

III. 1. Business ... services   2. Land   3. Labor ... goods   4. Capital

      5. Entrepreneurship   6. loss   7. bankrupt ... debts   8. innovative

      9. initiates ... business

IV. 1. distribute   2. accomplish   3. manufacture   4. conduct

      5. bankrupt   6. secure   7. purchase   8. capital

      9. finance   10. profit   11. initiate   12. share

      13. data   14. extract   15. process

V. 1. look for   2. up to   3. pay for   4.extracted from

      5. responsible for   6. going bankrupt   7. related to   8. to a certain extent

      9. referred to   10. to decide on

VI. 1. Some raw materials may be extracted from the air.

      2. To conduct business successfully involves a lot of factors

      3. The entrepreneur should bear all the risks of the business.

      4. This letter relates to the sale of the house

      5. If the company goes bankrupt, many people will lose their jobs

      6. He failed to secure the top job with the bank.

Post-reading

Top 10 Checklist for Start-ups

☐ *Are you ready to start a business?* Know what you want and understand what will be involved, including the personal sacrifices. Be willing to devote long hours to your endeavor.

☐ *Have you done your homework?* Conduct research to ensure there is a need for your product or service. Be sure market conditions can support your business. Talk with friends, family, and advisers to obtain business information. Government agencies, trade associations and other organizations offer services and programs to help get businesses started.

☐ *How will you utilize your skills and compensate for your weaknesses?* Evaluate your personal qualities and skills. Use your talents and recognize the areas you need help with.

☐ *What form will your business take?* Decide on a structure — incorporation, partnership or sole proprietorship.

☐ *How will you promote and market your business?* Just how are you going to distinguish yourself from the competition?

☐ *What is your pricing strategy?* What does the price say about your product (and its quality versus the competition)? Think about what you will charge people for your product/service. Estimate your break-even point and revenues.

☐ *Have you prepared a detailed business plan?* It is imperative.

☐ *What funding sources will fuel your enterprise?* Secure sufficient financial resources for start-up and operations.

☐ *Where will you locate?* Pick a business location that makes sense for you and your customers.

☐ *How will your business operate on a daily basis?* How will you deliver your product or service and manage your business? Figure out what you will need for the day-to-day smooth functioning of your business.

>>>>> Reading II

Exercises

I. 1. F   2. T   3. T   4. F   5. T   6. F   7. F   8. T   9. NM   10. T

III. 1. a   2. d   3. a   4. a   5. c   6. b   7. a   8. d

IV. 1. The crew of an airliner should be responsible for the safety of all the passengers.

2. Please distribute these English newspapers and magazines to every subscriber as soon as possible.

3. The college has decided on a lecture series and Business English majors must be present.

4. For additional explanation, please refer to page 58 of the teacher's reference book.

5. Most people will be interested in what relates to themselves.

6. Recently, more and more people have gone into business.

7. A businessman who sells goods in bulk is called a wholesaler.

8. It's reported that nowadays wages are, to a certain extent, still one step ahead of prices.

V. 1. a   2. c   3. a   4. d   5. b   6. d   7. b   8. c   9. c   10. b

11. b   12. c   13. d   14. b   15. d

>>>>> Extended Activities

A. Function and Structure

I. Greeting People

1. Tim: Hi!

   Dan: <u>Hi, Tim!</u>

   Tim: How are you?

   Dan: <u>Not bad.</u>

2. (*John sees a friend on the bus.*)

   John: <u>Hi, Jane!</u>

   Jane: Hi, John.

   John: <u>What's happening?</u>

   Jane: Nothing much.

3. (*Two classmates greet each other on the school campus.*)

   Rita: <u>Hi, Mark! How are you doing?</u>

   Mark: Not so good. I' ve got a bad cold.

   Rita: <u>Yeah, a lot of people have colds. It's this crazy weather — cold one minute and hot the next.</u>

4. (*in an office*)

   Secretary: <u>Good morning, Mr. Edwards.</u>

   Mr. Edwards: Good morning, Mary. <u>How are you?</u>

   Secretary: Fine, thank you.

II. Saying Good-bye

1. (*Two classmates have just met for the first time and are ending their conversation.*)

   Bob: Well I've got to go. I have a class at nine. Nice to meet you.

   Ted: <u>You, too. See you later.</u>

   Bob: Yeah. See you around.

2. (*Two roommates are getting ready to leave the house in the morning.*)

   Jeff: It's already nine. I've got to hurry.

   Brad: <u>Me, too. See you tonight.</u>

   Jeff: So long.

3. (*A student is talking to his academic advisor.*)

   David: I really should leave for class now. Thank you very much for your help.

Ms. Williams: <u>You're welcome, David. Have a good time. Good-bye.</u>

David: The same to you. Good-bye.

4. (*A student meets one of her former teachers in a bookstore. After they chat a while, they say good-bye.*)

Rebecca: It was so good to see you again, Mrs. White.

Mrs. White: <u>I hope so, too. Have a good day.</u>

Rebecca: The same to you. Good-bye.

Mrs. White: <u>Bye.</u>

B. Special Use

1. equipment	2. an assistant manager	3. land	4. data	5. capital
6. trade	7. wealth	8. competition	9. service	10. activities
11. quality ... quantity	12. materials	13. production	14. education	15. Memos
16. a space	17. experience	18. advice	19. lives	20. varieties

C. Practical Reading

I.

Stone Dep.	Mount Dep.	Trent Dep.	Keel Arr.
06 : 15	07 : 15	09 : 30	10 : 55
06 : 50	—	—	11 : 10
07 : 15	08 : 15	10 : 30	11 : 55
07 : 50	—	—	12 : 10
08 : 15	**09 : 15**	11 : 30	12 : 55
08 : 25	09 : 25	**11 : 40**	13 : 05
08 : 50	—	—	13 : 10
09 : 15	10 : 15	12 : 30	13 : 55
09 : 25	10 : 25	12 : 40	14 : 05
09 : 50	—	—	**14 : 10**

II. 1. 12 : 55.

2. 1 hour 25 minutes.

3. The 12 : 30 train from Trent.

4. 7 : 15, 10 : 15.

D. Additional Vocabulary

1-1;　　　2-7;　　　3-2;　　　4-12;　　　5-11;　　　6-6;　　　7-18;　　　8-3;　　　9-4;　　　10-5;

11-14;　　12-17;　　13-8;　　14-20;　　15-15;　　16-13;　　17-9;　　18-16;　　19-10;　　20-19

Unit 2
Marketing

Teaching Aim （教学目的）

1. Cognitive Information（认知信息）: Basic Concept of Marketing

2. Language Focus（内容重点）

— **Key Words:** I. market potential, feasibility, feasible/viable, assess, stand (*n.*), trade fair, exhibit, sample, prospective customer, publicity, representative, brochure, booklet, catalogue, press conference, promote, range, model, display, campaign, launch, order, delivery, replacement, spare part, after-sales service, component, service (*v.*), machinery, client; II. purchase, supply, conversely, equilibrium price, shortage, surplus, maximize profits

— **Phrases:** I. in other words, hand out, make up, for short, know as; II. in ... terms, in large/small quantities, agree on, in the end

— **Useful Structures:** to see if/what

as many ... as possible

"Whether ... or not" noun clause as subject and object

"assuming ..." adverbial phrase

choose + to inf.

far more + *adj.*

— **Grammar:** Numerical Expressions (1)

3. Communicative Skills（交际技能）

— **Expressions:** Expressions of "Introducing People"

— **Reading:** Price List

Lead-in 导入

>>>>> Listening Comprehension Tasks

Difficult Words & Expressions

1. make a deal with: 与……做交易

2. value (v.): to regard highly 重视

3. focus: a center of interest or activity 中心

4. process: a series of actions, changes, or functions bringing about a result 过程

5. identify: to recognize 识别

6. anticipate: to feel or realize beforehand 预期

7. fair: free of bias; impartial 公平的

8. solution: the method of solving a problem 解决方案

9. arouse: to stir up 激起；唤起

10. Volkswagen's Polo Sporty: 大众波罗的运动型轿车

11. fantastic: wonderful 美妙的

12. guarantee: to assume responsibility for; to undertake to do sth. 承诺；担保

13. credit the original price: 原价收购

14. depreciation: a decrease or loss in value as because of age, wear or market conditions 折旧

15. detail: particulars considered individually and in relation to a whole 细节

Passage Script 1

Marketing probably started with one cave man finding that he had too much meat, but no fresh vegetable. So he made a deal with another cave man who had vegetables, but no meat. A simple exchange. Both cave men were happy because they had exchanged something they valued for something of equal value. Meanwhile, an old woman helped a man with his cooking in exchange for having her garden dug. Both exchanged services rather than goods.

Simple exchanges soon became impossible. So people invented money. Each item can have a separate value, and a price can be fixed for everything. All goods or services can be sold for cash, and the cash used to buy what is needed. Life is about exchanging one value for another. We use money to help us buy and sell quickly and easily.

Marketing is a central focus for this exchange process. It is the management process responsible for identifying, anticipating and satisfying customer requirements profitably. Marketers make their living by finding out what people value and then by providing a fair exchange. It takes knowledge and skill to plan and manage a fair exchange. Marketing's job is to:

· discover what people need and what they will value,

· create a solution to the identified needs and a product that people will value,

· arouse a desire in people to buy the product,

· and satisfy the needs that were first discovered and provide the value that people want.

Passage Script 2

Man: Interested in a Volkswagen?

Woman: Mm.

Man: Group 1 Automotive has a fantastic deal for you on the Polo Sporty range.

Woman: Oh, I like the Polo Sporty.

Man: When you buy a Polo Sporty from Group 1 Automotive, not only will you get a great price for you old car, but — would you believe it — they guarantee to exchange it within 12 months and credit the original price you paid.

Woman: No depreciation?

Man: No.

Woman: Oh, I'll take it.

Man: For details, get onto www.group1auto.com or ring Group 1 Automotive, Houston, on 647 5700.

Woman:	Sorry, www.group1...?
Man:	www.group1auto.com
Woman:	And the phone number?
Man:	647 5700.
Woman:	Thanks.

Key

II. 1. d　　2. b　　3. c　　4. b　　5. b　　6. d

7.

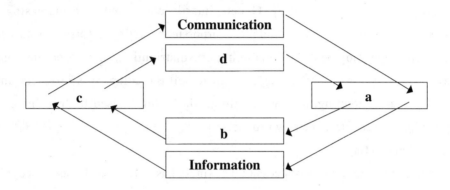

8. d

III. 1. Volkswagen's Polo Sporty.

2. Group 1 Automotive.

3. The woman will not only get a great price for her old car, but be guaranteed to exchange the Polo Sporty within 12 months and credit the original price without depreciation.

4. www.group1auto.com, 647 5700

5. In Houston.

>>>> Spot Dictation

　　We have 3, 600 employees worldwide and sales of $ 3, 716 million. We manufacture nearly 20, 000 cars, 3, 500 trucks, 888 buses, and thousands of industrial engines. Our position as a major international group in 24 European countries and 15 Asian countries is the result of quality, safety and caring for people and the environment.

Background Information（背景知识）

1. Marketing

The average consumer would probably define marketing as a combination of advertising and selling. It actually includes a good deal more. Modern marketing is most simply defined as activities that direct the flow of goods and services from producers to consumers. It encompasses, however, a broad range of activities including product planning, new-product development, organizing the channels... In advanced industrial economies, marketing considerations play a major role in determining corporate policy. Once primarily concerned with increasing sales through advertising and other promotional techniques, corporate marketing departments now focus on credit policies, product development, customer support, distribution, and corporate communications. Marketers may look for outlets through which to sell the company's products, including retail stores, direct mail marketing, and wholesaling. Marketing is used both to increase sales of an existing product and to introduce new products.

2. The role of marketing

The role of marketing in the success of a business has only recently been recognized. In earlier years, marketing was viewed as not much different from selling. The major emphasis of marketing was on maximizing profitability by generating sales volume through advertising and personal selling. Many companies believed that with enough effort and expense, almost any product could be sold by high-powered selling and aggressive advertising. As time went by, a number of firms had gradually become aware that good sales techniques could no longer compensate for the mistakes of producing wrong products, and that the satisfaction of particular customer needs was essential

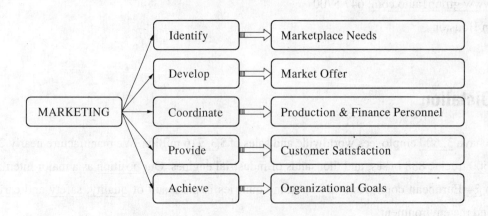

for success. Essentially, the marketing concept focuses all the activities of the organization on satisfying customer needs by integrating these activities with marketing to accomplish the organization's long-range objectives.

3. Market

The word market has different meanings. In commerce, it can mean a place or event at which people gather in order to buy and sell things (市场, 集市). It can also mean the people who might want to buy something, or a part of the world where something is sold (市场, 销路). In economy, it refers to an organized group of buyers and sellers of a particular economic good who are sufficiently in touch with each other personally of by telephone for all to know the current conditions of demand and supply, so that there is only one price, market price, for the good.

Language and Culture Focus (语言文化要点)

>>>>>Reading I

1. **market potential:** Potential means the possibility that something will develop in a particular way, or have a particular effect. Market potential means the possibility that certain goods will be developed and sold successfully in the market. 市场潜力

2. **feasible:** be able to be made, done or achieved; possible or reasonable. 可行的

   【例句】a feasible solution

   　　　Now that we have the extra resources, the scheme seems politically/financially/technically feasible.

   　　　It's quite feasible (=possible) (that) we'll get the money.

   Feasibility (可行性) is the noun form of feasible.

3. **to see if/what:** to find out information or a fact. 发现; 认定

   1) to see what/how/when, etc.

   【例句】I'll call him and see how the job interview went.

   　　　She went outside to see what was happening.

   2) see if/whether.

   【例句】I've just come to see if you want to go out for a drink.

4. **in other words:** to put it in another way; that is to say. 换言之; 那就是说

【例句】Your performance in the exam did not reach the required demand, in other words, you failed.

5. viable: be able to succeed in operation. 切实可行的　　**synonym: feasible**

【例句】The scheme is not economically viable.

"Viability" is the noun form of viable and it means feasibility.

【例句】commercial viability 商业上的可行性

the long-term financial viability of the company 公司的长期财政活力

6. One way to assess the market potential is to take a stand at a trade fair where companies can exhibit samples of their products and see what response they get from prospective customers.

【译文】评估市场潜力的一种方法是在交易会上设摊，公司可在此展出他们产品的样品，来观察潜在顾客的反应。

assess

1) to judge the importance, worth, or value of. 评定; 评价 **synonym: evaluate**

【例句】He's so lazy that it's difficult to assess his ability.

It's too early to assess the effects of the new law.

2) to calculate or decide the value of. 估价; 估计

【例句】They assess the value of the house at 60, 000.

7. stand: a booth, stall, or counter for the display of goods for sale. 售货的亭子、摊位或者柜台

【例句】a hotdog stand

an exhibition stand

8. trade fair: a large commercial and industrial exhibition where buyers and sellers meet to do business. 贸易展销会; 商品交易会

Fair can also mean a gathering held at a specified time and place for the buying and selling of goods; a market or an exhibition, as of farm products or manufactured goods, usually accompanied by various competitions and entertainments. (博览会, 通常带有竞争性和娱乐性。)

【例句】a state fair 国家博览会

9. exhibit: to present in a public exhibition or contest. 展览

【例句】Her paintings were exhibited at a galery.

10. sample: an example usually given free of an article or commodity being offered for sale, so that possible buyers can examine and test it. 样品

【例句】samples of a new shampoo

11. prospective customer: someone who may buy in the future. 潜在的客户

12. publicity: the act, process, or occupation of disseminating information to gain public interest. 宣传

【例句】We have planned an exciting publicity campaign with our advertisers.

The pop group's arrival by hot-air balloon was just a publicity stunt (=an unusual way of attracting the public's attention).

辨析publicity & propaganda

Publicity (宣传; 宣扬) means the business of bringing someone or something to the attention of the public. **Propaganda** (贬义词, 尤指政府为了影响民意而进行的宣传), on the other hand, is usually a derogative word meaning information that is spread in planned or official way, esp. by a government, in order to influence public opinion.

【例句】We will hold a big publicity campaign to highlight the dangers of smoking.

Their speeches have been exposed as pure propaganda.

Therefore, the Chinese expression 宣传部 should not be translated into "Propaganda Department", instead, a proper translation should be "Publicity Department".

13. representative: one that serves as a delegate or an agent for another. (公司)代理人

【例句】The role of the sales representative is extremely important in the organization's overall sales effort.

14. hand out: to give (sth.) to each member of a group of people. 分发; 散发 **synonym: distribute**

【例句】Hand out the books to everyone in the classroom.

He's very good at handing out advice!

"Handout" is the noun form, which means information given out, usu. in the form of printed sheet. （发给出席讲座等的听众的印刷品; 讲义）

15. 辨析brochure, booklet & catalogue

A brochure is a small booklet or pamphlet, often containing promotional material or product information. 小册子, 常包括推销材料或产品信息

【例句】a travel brochure

A booklet is a very thin book with a small number of pages and a paper cover, often giving information about something. 小册子

【例句】We bought a booklet about the castle from the tourist office.

A catalogue (商品目录) is a complete list of things that you can look at, buy, or use, for example, in a library or at an art show.

【例句】a mail order catalogue

an online catalogue

16. press conference: meeting where reporters from newspapers are invited to hear news of a new product. (产品的)新闻发布会

17. promote *vt.*

1) to give a higher position or rank. 提升

【例句】My daughter's just been promoted.

The young army officer was promoted to the rank of captain.

They promoted him captain.

2) to bring (goods) to public notice in order to encourage people to buy. 推销(货物)

【例句】They staged a big advertising campaign to promote their new product.

3) to help in the growth or development of. 促进; 增进; 推动

【例句】Milk promotes health.

We must make new efforts to promote human peace and development.

【相关词】

promotion

18. **model:** a style or design of an item. 产品型号或款式

【例句】a luxury/new model

the latest model

19. **make up**

1) to form as a whole. 形成; 组成; 构成　　**synonym: constitute**

【例句】Farming and mining make up most of the country's industry.

2) to invent, often in order to deceive. 虚构; 捏造; 编造

【例句】He made up an excuse for his being late.

3) to use special paint or powder on so as to change or improve the appearance. 化装; 化妆

【例句】She never goes out without making herself up first.

They made him up as an old man for the last act of the play.

"Make-up" (化妆; 化妆品) is the noun form, which means the powder, paint, etc. worn on the face, either by actors or for improving one's appearance. Therefore, we have the following phrases: eye make-up (眼影); stage make-up (舞台化妆)

20. **display:** to present or hold up to view. 呈现; 展示

【例句】Why don't you display your ad on the notice board where everyone can see it?

The permit should be clearly displayed in the front window.

21. **for short:** as a shorter way of saying it. 简略为; 简称

【例句】My name is David, or Dave for short.

A similar phrase containing "short" is "in short" (简而言之), which means "to put it into as few words as possible".

【例句】This is our most disastrous and embarrassing defeat ever; in short, a fiasco (惨败).

22. **campaign:** an operation or series of operations energetically pursued to accomplish a purpose. 以达到某一目的而采取的一项/系列活动

【例句】an advertising campaign for a new product

23. "on" in "an advertisement campaign on a new product"

Here "on" means "affecting/relating to" (关于).

【例句】a book on China

new evidence on the matter

a tax on cigarettes

his influence on young people

There will be new restrictions on the sale of weapons.

What effect will these changes have on the tourist industry?

When used in this sense, "on" is always compared with "about". They are basically the same, but "a book on rabbit" is more formal and scientific than "a book about rabbits" which might, for example, be a children's story.

The preposition "on" can also be used in the following ways:

1) touching or supported by a particular surface. 在……上

【例句】a lamp on the table

a ring on your finger

When used in this sense, it is always compared with "over" and "above". "Over" means "directly above; higher than, but not touching", while "above" means "higher than, but not touching".

【例句】The doctor leaned over the sick child.

The lamp hung over the table.

We flew above the clouds.

This city is 500 meters above sea level.

However, "above" and "over" can often be used in the same way.

【例句】Let's hand the painting over/above the fireplace.

But if there is an idea of movement, "over" is used. (如果有表示动作的意思, 就用over。)

【例句】The birds flew over the lake.

The sheep jumped over the wall.

2) supported by, hanging from, or connected to. 由……支持; 自……垂下; 与……连接

【例句】to stand on one foot

a ball on a string

the wheels on my car

We're not on the phone.

24. (be) known as/to be: 以……而闻名   **synonym: be reputed as/to be**

【例句】Hangzhou and Suzhou are known as paradise on earth.

America has long been known as a melting pot.

China is known to be a populous country.

25. 辨析customer & client

A customer is a person who buys goods or a service.

【例句】Mrs. Low can't come to the phone — she's serving a customer.

Mrs. Wilson is one of our regular customers.

There were two assistants to serve the customers.

A client is a person who receives services; so if you are paying for services, for example, from a lawyer or a bank, you are a client.

【例句】Mr. Black has been a client of this firm for many years.

We always aim to give our clients personal attention.

26. order: a request to make, supply or deliver food or goods. 订单

【例句】Can I take your order now or would you like to have a drink first?

I would like to place (=make) an order for a large pine table.

"Order" can also be used as a verb, meaning to ask for (something) to be made, supplied or delivered, esp. in a restaurant or shop. (订货, 下订单)

【例句】Are you ready to order, or would you like to look at the menu for a little longer?

The customer says she ordered the books six weeks ago and she still hasn't received them.

27. as ... as possible: This phrase can be used to make up a lot of useful phrases and sentences.

【例句】as soon as possible

as many as possible

as simple as possible

as early as possible

28. However, before a client places an order, he wants to know many things — how long delivery takes, whether the company can supply replacements and spare parts, what the after-sales service is like, etc.

【译文】然而, 在客户下订单前, 他想知道许多事情, 例如: 送货时间长短, 公司是否会提供配件及备用件, 售后服务如何等。

29. delivery (of goods): transport of goods to a customer's address. 交货

30. replacement: sth. that replaces another thing. 代替者, 替换物

【例句】We are out of stock and waiting for replacements. 我们现无存货, 正等待进新货。

31. spare parts: small pieces of machinery used to replace part of a machine which is broken. 备件

32. component: one of several parts that together make up a whole machine, system, etc. 元件, 部件

synonym: constituent

【例句】These companies make electronic components for computer products.

33. service: If someone services a machine or vehicle, they examine it and do what is needed to keep it working well. 维修, 保养

【例句】I'm having the car serviced next week.

34. machinery: machines in general and is thus uncountable. (总称)机器

【例句】New machinery is being installed in the factory.

35. 辨析affect & effect

First, **affect** is a verb, meaning "to have an influence on" (影响), while **effect** is usually a noun, "the result of a particular influence" (结果).

【例句】The divorce affected every aspect of her life.

　　　The team's performance was affected by the rain.

　　　I think all the worry has affected my brain!

　　　The disease only affects cattle.

　　　I was deeply affected by the film (=It caused strong feelings in me).

　　　The radiation leak has had a disastrous effect on/upon the environment. ［C］

　　　I tried taking tablets for the headache but they didn't have any effect. ［U］

　　　That drink has had quite an effect on me — I feel light-headed! ［C］

　　　Government policy will not affect us/will not have any effect on us.

Second, when **effect** is used as a verb, it means "to bring about, usually according to one's wishes" (产生, 引起).

【例句】He was able to effect certain changes in government policy.

36. "Whether ... or not" noun clause as subject and object: "Whether ... or not" can be used as the subject or object of a sentence.

【例句】Whether you will go with me or not is not decided yet.

　　　Whether a company can provide good after-sales service or not may directly affect the sales of its products.

　　　I wonder whether or not we should tell her.

When "if" and "whether" clauses are used as objects, they are interchangeable in the sense of "if ... or not (是否)".

【例句】He asked me whether/if she was coming.

　　　It was uncertain whether/if she would recover.

But we must use "whether" instead of "if" (1) before infinitives (不定式); (2) after prepositions (介词); (3) in sentences containing "or not".

【例句】The question is whether to go or stay.

　　　It depends on whether he's ready or not.

I asked him whether or not he was coming.

>>>>>Reading II

1. supply

1) *n.* an amount of something that is available to be used. 供应量; 供给量

【例句】bring a large supply of food with you

There was a plentiful supply of cheap labour.

The nation's fuel is in short supply (供应不足).

To protect the food supply, the government ordered the slaughter of affected cattle.

2) *vt.* to provide (sth. that is needed), or to provide something that is needed to (someone). 供应

【例句】Electrical power is supplied by underground cables.

The tourist office can supply information about accommodation and activities in the area.

① supply sth. to sb.

【例句】The government supplies free books to schools.

I'm afraid I can't supply the answer to your question.

② supply sb. with sth.

【例句】The firm that used to supply us with legal consultation has moved to another street.

Our allies kept us supplied with weapons.

2. In economic terms, a market is not a specific place, like a supermarket, but an exchange process between buyers and sellers.

【译文】在经济学领域, 市场并不是一个类似超市的场所, 而是指买卖双方进行交易的过程。

in economic terms: "in ... terms/in terms of ..." means "with regard to ..., from the point of view of ...".

【例句】in business terms 从生意角度来看

in political terms 从政治方面来说

in terms of sales 从销售情况来看

3. specific: We use "specific" to refer to a particular fixed area, subject, or something else.

【例句】a specific area　　a specific tool　　a specific age group

4. How much of what product a company offers for sales and who buys it depends on the laws of demand and supply.

【译文】一家公司销售什么产品, 销售多少, 以及谁来购买, 这些都是由供求法则来决定的。

the laws of demand and supply: the laws that balance the amount of goods for sale and the amount that people actually want to buy. The laws of demand and supply influences prices, as is stated in the text.

5. simply stated: This phrase means "simply speaking, to put it simply". When used in this way, "state" should be in the form of past participle.

【例句】briefly stated

roughly stated

6. as its price drops: The conjunction "as" can be used to introduce an adverbial clause of time.

【例句】She wept bitterly as she told the story.

He witnessed the accident as he was crossing the street.

7. assuming you like corn chips: Here "assuming" is the equivalent of "if", which introduces an adverbial clause of condition.

【例句】Assuming agreement can be reached on working conditions, what about the promotion system?

"Assume" is the verb form; "assumption" is the noun.

【例句】Let us assume that everything goes according to plan.

His suggestions are based on an assumption that the prison system is out of date.

8. at a price of: The preposition "at" is usually used with "price/cost/speed".

【例句】at a lower price

at any cost

at the speed of

9. in large quantities: in bulk.

【例句】to manufacture expensive cars in large/small quantities

10. conversely: on the other hand; taking the opposite point of view.

We can use "conversely" to introduce a statement about a situation that is the opposite of the situation that we have just described.

【例句】$1 will buy 100 *yen* worth of Japanese goods. Conversely, 100 *yen* will buy $1 worth of American goods.

This newspaper story could damage their reputation; conversely, it will give them a lot of free publicity.

11. In the market for any product, the laws of demand and supply interact to set a market or equilibrium price and quantity on which buyers and sellers agree.

【译文】在商品市场中，供求法则交互作用从而产生了市场价格或平衡价格以及买卖双方达成一致的交易额度。

interact: When people interact with each other, they communicate or work together in a situation; when one thing interacts with another, the two things react together in the same situation, so that they affect each other's development or condition.

【例句】Some bacteria's genes interact with those of many plants.

The two ideas interact.

12. **equilibrium price:** "equilibrium"(平衡，均衡) is a balance existing between several different influences or aspects of a situation so that none is more important or powerful than another.

【例句】equilibrium of supply and demand 供求均衡

We must try to keep all economic forces in equilibrium.

"Equilibrium price" (均衡价格) refers to the balanced price made between the buyer and the seller.

13. **agree on:** If people agree on something, they reach a joint decision on it.

【例句】Both parties agreed on a price for the new car.

14. **intersection:** An intersection (交叉点) is a place where roads or other lines meet or cross. In this text, it refers to the point where the demand line and the supply line meet.

15. **the demand and supply curves:** smooth and bending lines that indicate the change and development between demand and supply. 供求曲线

16. **choose to do:** Here, "choose to do" means "decide to do".

【例句】They chose to ignore her warning.

He chose not to go home until later.

17. **inefficient:** A person, organization or system that is inefficient is badly organized and does not use resources, equipment, or time in the best possible way.

【例句】an inefficient secretary

inefficient farming

She says this school is inefficient and operates at a very low standard.

【相关词】

inefficiently (*adv.*); inefficiency (*n.*)

If a person, organization or system is well organized and uses resources, equipment to the full, we say he/it is "efficient".

18. **sell sth. for:** The phrase "sell sth. for ..." is usually followed by the price.

【例句】I hope to sell the house for 30, 000 pounds.

He sold the painting for 5, 000 dollars.

19. **a surplus of:** A surplus is a quantity of something that is extra or more than is needed.

【例句】a surplus of crude oil　　labor surplus

20. **maximize its profits:** If we maximize something, we make it as great in amount or importance as we can. "Maximize its profits" means to increase profits to the greatest possible amount.

【例句】The company's main objective is to maximize profits.

We need a strategy that will maximize the use of the country's existing airports.

21. **involve:** If a situation or activity involves someone or something, it includes them as a necessary part or it concerns and affects them.

　　【例句】This business seems to involve an enormous amount of sales.

　　　　　　The accident involved a bus and a truck.

22. **far more complex:** Some adverbs such as "even, far, many, much, still, rather, slightly, a bit, a few, a little, a lot, some, two, twice, three times" can be used with the comparative degree of the adjective and the adverb. "Very, much" can not be used in this way.

　　【例句】much better; far worse; a bit earlier; even redder; rather more difficult; two degrees hotter; some more books; a few more chances

23. **in the end:** "In the end" means "finally", and often as a result of the previous situation.

　　【例句】They kept on raising the price and in the end he got thirty thousand for it.

▷▷▷▷▷ Extended Activities

A. Function and Structure: Introducing People

1. Like all interactions, introductions vary in degrees of formality. Some situations call for formal introductions; some need informal ones. Some people seem to favor formal introductions to persons of importance. Different situations require different expressions for greeting and introducing. In introductory conversations, "How do you do?" suggests non-acquaintanceship and formality, while "Hello." or "Hi." is the least formal greeting used between young people, friends or colleagues.

2. When one is with a friend or an acquaintance, and bumps into someone he knows, it is always polite to introduce them to each other. This introduction should include names, titles where appropriate, and a very brief description of the relationship to him so that the two people have a basis to start a conversation if they wish to.

3. When people are being introduced in very formal situations, you may have noticed that rank is the most important consideration followed by age and then gender. Therefore, people of a lower rank should be introduced to people of a higher rank first; younger people should be introduced to older people first; and men should be introduced to women first.

4. Most conversations, however, are not carried on in formal speech situations, and forms of address are another important decision to make. A social acquaintance of a newly hired colleague of approximately the same age and rank is usually introduced on a first-name basis. It is polite and common to shake hands when people are introduced to each other in China. But in the United States

or some other countries, people don't always do so. However, in a formal or business situation, people almost always shake hands whatever their nationalities are.

5. **Mr., Mrs., Miss and Ms.:** Mr. is the title placed before a man's last name, e.g. Mr. Johnson. Mrs. and Miss are also titles. Mrs. is placed before a married woman's last name and Miss before the last name of an unmarried woman or a girl. Nowadays, the title Ms. is also used to address both married women and single women. Notice these titles are used only before last names. They are not used with first names only, e.g. you can say: Mr. Baker, or Mr. Henry Baker, but you shouldn't say Mr. Henry.

B. Special Use: Numerical Expressions (I)

英语中的数词主要分为三类：基数词(cardinal numbers)，序数词(ordinal numbers)和倍数词 (multiplicative numbers)。基数词表示数目，如 one, two, three 等；序数词表示顺序，如 first, second, third 等；倍数词表示的是倍数，如 twice, double, treble, half 等。

1. 基数词和序数词的写法

英语中的基数词除了用个位、十位和百位计数外，还有三个基本的单位，即千(thousand)、百万 (million)和10亿(billion)。用英语书写两位数的数字要在十位和个位间加连字符；用阿拉伯数字 表示四位或四位以上的数字要用逗号三位三位地隔开。例如：

twenty-three	fifty-nine	eighty-two
1, 258	365, 310, 715	1, 003, 597

英语中的序数词有缩写形式，即阿拉伯数字加上最后两位字母。例如：

1st	2nd	3rd	4th	5th

但在朗读的时候，我们仍读：

first	second	third	fourth	fifth

2. 数词的读法

1) 多位数的读法

- 三位或三位以上的数字要在十位数前加 and。例如：

5, 804	five thousand, eight hundred and four
4, 697	four thousand, six hundred and ninety-seven

- and 也可连接以千、百万为单位的各部分。例如：

350, 480	three hundred and fifty thousand, four hundred and eighty
306, 000, 000	three hundred and six million
151, 432, 638	one hundred and fifty-one million, four hundred and thirty-two thousand, six hundred and thirty-eight

- 如果结尾是整百时，一般不用and。例如：

| 6, 500 | six thousand, five hundred |

2) 年份的读法

- 年份通常是两位两位地读。例如：

1990	nineteen ninety
1789	seventeen eighty-nine
2010	twenty ten

- 如果年份恰逢整百或整千，则直接用hundred或thousand读。例如：

| 1900 | nineteen hundred |
| 2000 | two thousand |

- 如果是公元前，我们在年份后加B.C.; 如果是公元后，我们可以在年份前加A.D., 当然A.D.也可以省略。例如：

| 500 B.C. | A.D. 1300 |

- in the 1980s/1980's 表示在20世纪80年代；in the 60s/60's 表示在60年代；in my twenties 表示在我20多岁时；in his fifties 表示在他50多岁时。

3) 日期的读法

- 英语中的日期有多种写法。如4月3日可以写成：

| April 3rd | April 3 | 3rd April | 3 April |

- 但读的时候，我们只能读April the third或the third of April。千万不能读成three。

4) 钟点的读法

- 如果时间是整点，我们直接在数字后加o'clock或hundred。例如：

| 9 : 00 | nine o'clock/nine hundred |
| 14 : 00 | fourteen o'clock/fourteen hundred |

- 如果时间不是整点，我们要使用介词past或to。当然，我们也可以直接读出数字。例如：

5 : 30	half past five/five thirty
10 : 30	half past ten/ten thirty
12 : 10	ten past twelve/twelve ten
4 : 55	five to five/four fifty-five

- 另外，15分钟也可以用a quarter表示。例如：

| 3 : 15 | a quarter past three |
| 5 : 45 | a quarter to six |

5) 分数的读法

- 读分数时，分子用基数词，分母用序数词。例如：

| 1/3 | one third |

| 1/5 | one fifth |
| 1/2 | one half/a half |

- 若分子大于一，分母用复数。例如：

| 2/3 | two thirds |
| 3/7 | three sevenths |

- 我们也可以用in或out of表示分数。例如：

1/10	one in ten
9/10	nine out of ten
2/3	two out of three

6) 小数的读法

- 小数点读作point。小数部分的数字依次直接读出。例如：

| 10.34 | ten point three four |

- 但读货币时，小数点应略去不读。例如：

| 7.15 | seven dollars and fifteen cents/seven fifteen |

7) 零的读法

- 在算术中，零通常读作字母O, zero或nought。例如：

603.05	six O three point O five
8.04	eight point nought/O/zero four
0.05	point nought/O five

- 在温度中，零读作zero。例如：

| 0.03摄氏度 | point zero three degrees centigrade |
| 零下5摄氏度 | five degrees centigrade below zero |

- 在电话号码中，零读作字母O。例如：

Dial six two five O seven O five O, and ask for extension two four O one. 拨62507050, 再转2401分机。

- 在体育比赛中，零比分通常读作nil, nothing。例如：

The result of the football match was 4 : 0. (读作four nil/four to nil/four to nothing)

- 在网球、乒乓球和羽毛球比赛中，零比分读作love。例如：

Russia leads by 30 : 0 in the first game of the second set. (读作thirty love)

Five love, your service. 五比零，你发球。

3. 数词的单复数形式

- 当hundred, thousand, million, dozen和score与确切的数字连用时，不以复数形式出现。例如：

| six hundred | ten thousand | two dozen eggs |

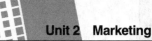

• 然而, 当它们与模糊数字或of连用, 它们多以复数形式出现。例如:

hundreds of people　　　　　thousands of books

dozens of eggs　　　　　　　scores of ships

of的这种用法通常不与确切的数词连用。我们不能说: six thousands of books。

C. Practical Reading

练习I: 本练习的要求是比较简单的口头练习, 只需要读懂表格中缺少什么项目, 就可以向partner提问以获得答案了。

练习II: 本练习考查学生利用表格解决问题的能力。4个问题的答案都比较容易得到, 这里的技巧是scanning, 即带着问题快速查阅答案。第4题只需要简单的计算; 第5题只要排除非PVC产品即可。

Notes

Code No.: 也叫article number, 即货号。

Description: 规格, 这里包括颜色、尺寸以及质地。

Price in $: 价格, 本商品价格以美元计算。

Delivery: 交货期。其中, Immediate Delivery指即期交货; To order only指凭指示交货。

Teaching Tips （教学提示）

1. 在安排学生进行Lead-in 听力训练之前, 教师可先结合背景知识1部分的内容, 让学生谈谈他们对marketing一词的理解; 背景知识2可在Pre-reading活动之后, 讲解Reading I课文之前予以介绍; 背景知识3建议安排在Reading II课文前讲解, 讲解前可先让学生讨论market一词的含义。

2. 本单元导入(Lead-in)部分安排了听力理解和听写填空两项任务。听力理解部分包含passage和conversation各一篇, 共3项听力任务。听力理解部分的第一段是围绕关于Marketing概念的一个片段, 主要目的是让学生对所听语篇的主旨(gist)有所了解, 初步把握听音和理解上的难点所在, 为接下来的听力活动做好词汇和背景知识方面的准备, 可要求学生作一些笔记。完成预听后, 建议教师将Difficult Words and Expressions讲解一遍, 以扫除语言障碍; 第二项练习为多项选择题(Multiple-choice Questions), 旨在考查学生对语篇主旨的把握和辨析细节的能力, 其中第七题是一个信息转换（information transfer）的图表填空题，要求学生把听到的信息填入图表，训练学生把文字信息转换成图表信息的能力。第三项练习是一段对话，设计了 5 道简答题，要求学生掌握对话的人物、地点、内容等细节，对话中涉及了诸如 "credit the original price 原价收购" 和 "depreciation 折旧" 等较为专业的词汇，教师应予以一定的解释。在听对话前，教师可询问学生对大众公司 Polo Sporty 是否有所了解。建议教师在课前准备一些 Polo Sporty 这款车型的图片资料，在课堂上展示给学生看。教师可先不提供练习的正确答案，让学生以 pair work 或 group work 形式自行讨论并检查。本单元听写填空（Spot Dictation）重点是听数字，主要帮助学生掌握数字的表达方式，提高听写数字的能力，可以作为导入活动安排在 Reading II 课文讲解之前进行。

3. 背景知识 1 和 2 可在 Pre-reading 后，Reading I 课文前讲解；背景知识 3 可在 Reading II 课文前讲解，讲解前可先让学生讨论 market 一词的含义。

4. Reading I 中的 Brainstorming，全班学生通过自由讨论的形式，列出他们作为顾客在购物时可能会考虑的各种因素，常见的如价格、品牌、款式、性能等。教师也可通过向学生询问下列问题来进一步引导学生：不同年龄层次的顾客或不同性别的顾客在购物时首先会考虑什么；顾客在购买不同的商品（如 mobile phone, automobile, beauty and health products, computer, clothes 等）时会分别考虑什么。

5. Reading I 中的 Pairwork，由学生双人结对，讨论与本单元主题 Marketing 相关的 5 个问题。众所周知，在当今商务领域，形形色色的营销和促销活动已遍及我们日常生活的方方面面，教师可鼓励学生结合他们的生活实际，讨论一些熟悉的 marketing 和 promotion 方面的个案或现象，以激发他们学习课文（Text）的兴趣。

6. Reading I 中的练习 II，Question 2 中 campaign 一词可指军事上的战役、政治活动，竞选运动或商业性的活动，本文取其最后一个解释。Question 5, option a 中 the company profile 指公司的简介，也经常会出现在产品目录上，但课文中并未提及，故不选。

7. Reading I 中的练习 IV，Question 2 中 selling point 是 "卖点" 的意思，指的是在广告宣传或市场营销中特别强调的某一产品或服务的一个方面，如产品特色、服务特色等。Question 8 中 feasibility study 指可行性研究。

8. Reading I 中的 Post-reading，要求学生以小组为单位设计一个简单的产品营销方案，使学生熟悉营销活动的一些基本概念和步骤：1) 确认顾客需求；2) 设计能满足顾客需求的产品或服务项目；3) 如何将新产品或新服务项目的信息传递给预期的客户群；4) 为产品确定一个能反映其成本、市场竞争状况以及顾客购买能力的价格；5) 提供相应的售后服务以确保顾客购买后的满意度。为激发学生参与活动的积极性，教师还可指定一产品，由各小组在课外独立设计各自的营销方案，然后再评选出最佳的方案，予以一定的奖励。

9. Reading II 中 Cloze 的 Question 3, create 指 "有目的地把原材料制成新产品"，也指 "创造出原来不存在或与众不同的事物"，如：We've created a beautiful new building out of an old barn.

discover指 "通过观察或研究来获得知识"，也指 "第一个找到或观察到本来就存在的东西"，如：Columbus discovered America in 1492. invent指 "通过想像、研究、劳动，创造出前所未有的东西"，尤指 "科技上的发明创造"，如：Edison invented the light bulb. form指 "塑造或浇铸成一特殊形状"，也指 "通过训导形成、训练或发展"，如：Children are taught to form good habits. 所以此处选c，意为 "Dr. John Styth Pemberton发明了一种新型的饮料"。

Question 7, register指 "正式或官方的注册，登记"，如：to register the birth of the child。 enroll指 "在花名册、名单上登记记录使成为成员，如入伍、入会、入学等"，如：to enroll the child in kindergarten; We enrolled in the army. 所以此处选a，指 "注册过的商标"。Question 8, recent指 "最近的，属于或发生于现时之前很短一段时间里的"，如：a recent visit to the city; recent news。 present指 "现在，目前"，如：the present government; at the present time。 所以此处选b, present day 意指 "现今"。

Question 9, soft drink 软性饮料，指不含酒精的、调味的碳酸饮料，通常进行商业化生产并且以瓶装或听装出售。

Question 10, 1900's 指20世纪，也可写成1900s; 如：1970's 或1970s即指20世纪70年代。

Key（练习答案）

>>>>>Reading I

Pre-reading

I.

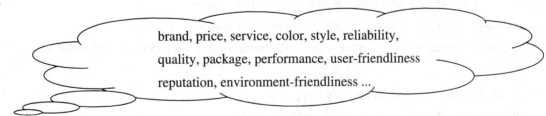

brand, price, service, color, style, reliability,
quality, package, performance, user-friendliness
reputation, environment-friendliness ...

Exercises

II. 1. a　　　　2. b　　　　3. a　　　　4. b　　　　5. c

III. 1. client   2. promote   3. catalogue   4. delivery   5. market

     6. launch   7. company   8. range   9. after-sales service   10. campaign

IV. 1. in other words   2. publicity   3. is known as   4. for short   5. potential

     6. hand (it) out   7. viable   8. feasibility   9. is made up   10. prospective

     11. campaign   12. assessing

V. 1. The United States of America is called the USA for short.

2. Peace and honor could not be assessed in dollars.

3. Do you think the plan for the new product is viable?

4. The purpose for taking a stand at a trade fair is to see the response from prospective customers.

5. The firm placed an order for a new fax machine last week.

6. Your performance in the exam did not reach the required standard — in other words, you failed.

>>>>>Reading II

Exercises

I. 1. F   2. F   3. F   4. T   5. F   6. T   7. F   8. T   9. NM   10. T

III. 1. market   2. demand   3. supply   4. law of demand   5. law of supply

     6. equilibrium   7. profit   8. consumer   9. surplus   10. shortage

IV. 1. The general manager handed out the important documents to the department managers.

2. Cheating customers and evading taxes made up their business policy in those days.

3. Mathematics can be called maths or math for short in English.

4. This city is known as leading the economic cooperative zone.

5. Although the couple agreed on the price of the furniture they wanted to buy, they disagreed about the style.

6. I bought a laptop last month but only at a price.

7. The parents work hard to pay for their children's tuition.

8. Your dishonesty was the reason why I had to break off our relationship in the end.

9. His uncle chose to settle in the countryside rather than in the city.

10. The manager handed out the project plan on the press conference, but most of the people doubted the feasibility of the project.

V. 1. d　　2. a　　3. c　　4. a　　5. d　　6. a　　7. a　　8. b　　9. a

　　10. d　　11. b　　12. a　　13. a　　14. a　　15. c

>>>>>Extended Activities

A. Function and Structure

I. 1. Susan:　　Mary, <u>this is my brother Joe.</u>

　　　Mary:　　I'm very glad to meet you, Joe.

　　　Joe:　　<u>It's a pleasure to meet you.</u>

　　2. Betty:　　Oh, Susan, I'd <u>like you to meet</u> my colleague Wendy.

　　　Wendy:　　Hi.

　　　Susan:　　<u>Nice to meet you.</u>

　　3. Miss Green:　　Mrs. Blake, <u>I'd like to introduce a friend of mine</u>, Shellie Rhoda.

　　　Mrs. Blake:　　Nice to meet you.

　　　Shellie:　　<u>Hello.</u>

　　4. Helen:　　<u>Hello. I'm Helen.</u> I'm your next door neighbor.

　　　Linda:　　Hi. I'm Linda. <u>Nice to meet you.</u>

　　　Helen:　　<u>Nice to meet you</u>, too. By the way, what's your major?

　　　Linda:　　Business English. And how about you?

　　　Helen:　　I'm in Accounting Department.

　　5. Mr. Smith:　　Mr. King, <u>have you met</u> Mr. Thatcher before?

　　　Mr. King:　　I don't think I had the honor.

　　　Mr. Smith:　　Well, let me introduce you to him. Mr. Thatcher, <u>I'd like you to meet Mr. King</u>, head of our department. And <u>this is Mr. Thatcher</u>, Assistant Manager of AT&T.

　　　Mr. Thatcher:　　<u>I'm glad to meet you.</u>

　　　Mr. King:　　I'm glad to meet you too.

B. Special Use

1. a　2. c　3. d　4. a　5. c　6. a　7. b　8. d　9. a　10. c

C. Practical Reading

I.

Code No.	Description	Price in $	Delivery
0048	Green 58 × 72cm PVC	33.85	3 weeks
0049	Pink 44 × 72cm PVC	28.00	Immediate
0050	Red 88 × 88cm PVC	79.75	10 days
0057	Green 44.5 × 25cm nylon	15.00	7 days
0057B	White 44.5 × 25cm nylon	14.00	14 days
0059	Clear 78 × 95cm PVC	89.50	To order only

II. 1. 0057B.　　2. 0049.　　3. On Oct.16.　　4. 115.5 *yuan* (RMB)

　　5. Four types:

0048	33.85
0049	28.00
0050	79.75
0059	89.50

D. Additional Vocabulary

1-15;　　2-13;　　3-17;　　4-20;　　5-19;　　6-18;　　7-16;　　8-14;　　9-12;　　10-11;

11-6;　　12-7;　　13-3;　　14-1;　　15-5;　　16-8;　　17-2;　　18-4;　　19-10;　　20-9

Unit 3

Career Development

1. Cognitive Information（认知信息）: Career Development
2. Language Focus（内容重点）
   — **Key Words:** I. career, contentment, conscious, extent, well-being, craftsman, carpenter, brick, admire, misled, complaint, capacity, conquer, tough, mark, personality, demonstrate, limb, measure, command, aspect, emotional, jealousy, behavioral, disclose, regular, predictable, intense, pressure, beyond, derive, collectively, status, self-confidence, assume, envy, competent, average, association, prestigious, institution; II. tirelessly, accountancy, statutory, financial, publication, involvement, integral, challenge, banking, crucial, audit, community, comment, reliable, statement, aftermath, anticipate, regulate, underline, sector, profile, perspective, professionals, standards, boundary, melt, conclude
   — **Phrases:** I. be conscious of, long for, regard... as, after all, in significant measure, at work, tend to, on the whole, adjust to, work off; II. devote... to, lead to, not so... as... , melting pot
   — **Useful Structures:** This is not to say...   whether it be...

                                       think of... as...   Given... , main clause
   — **Vocabulary & Grammar:** Describing One's Appearance

3. Communicative Skills（交际技能）

— **Expressions:** Expressing and Responding to "Thanks"

— **Reading:** Business Cards

Lead-in 导入

>>>>>Listening Comprehension Tasks

Difficult Words & Expressions

1. option: choice 选择

2. ongoing: currently taking place 进行中的；正在发生的

3. foundation: base 基础

4. personality: the pattern of collective character, behavioral, temperamental, emotional and mental traits of a person 个性；性格

5. unique: without an equal or equivalent 独特的

6. strength: a quality of particular worth or utility 长处；优点

7. limitation: a shortcoming or defect 弱点

8. counselor: a person who gives advice 顾问

9. passion/passionate: boundless enthusiasm/ardent 热情/充满热情的

10. inspire: to encourage; motivate 激励

11. regardless of: 不管；不顾

12. take the time: 从容不迫，慢慢来

Passage Script 1

Career planning is a process of understanding oneself, exploring career options, making wise decisions and moving forward. What is difficult is that people, careers and organizations are always changing. Therefore, career planning is not something done one time early in your career. Rather, it's an ongoing process throughout your life. It doesn't matter what's your profession, your industry or your place of employment. The reality is that your career will change with the change of lives, professions, industries and organizations.

The foundation of career planning, today and for the future, is based on a very clear understanding of who you are as an individual and as a professional person. The greater the match between who you are — your skills, values, interests and personality — and your career choices, the greater personal career satisfaction.

Since everyone has a unique mix of skills, strengths and limitations that change over time, the first step in career planning is to look at who you are and what your career is all about. Also, knowing yourself clearly will help you make better decisions in the future when opportunities come.

Here are some simple questions to start you on this journey:

· What do I see as my personal strengths?

· What are some of my personal limitations?

· What are my abilities — things I'm good at and enjoy doing?

Passage Script 2

The following is a conversation between Tony Foster, a professional counsellor, and Catherine Lee, an office lady.

Catherine: I find my job increasingly meaningless, but I have to do it. What shall I do?

Tony: It's all about passion. One of the most important elements of personal happiness is being passionate about your career and your job. You do not want to be one of those people who live for the weekends and dread Sunday evenings, do you?

Catherine: Will you love your work and your career as much as your passion for other things and people?

Tony: Why not? It is completely possible to not only find the career a perfect match of your skills and interests, but also one that inspires you to work harder.

Catherine: Do you think I'm too old in my current career?

Tony: Regardless of where you are in your career, there is always time to discover — or rediscover — what you're truly passionate about and turn that passion into a new career.

Catherine: So I need to take up a new career?

Tony: Finding a career that you have a passion for is all about what you need to do. Some of the jobs may also not be the highest-paying jobs in the world, but career passion is not about the money. It's about how the job makes you feel inside. So, take the time to find your career passion.

Key

II. 1. d 2. c, b, a and d 3. c 4. c 5. d 6. b 7. d 8. d
III. 1. b 2. f 3. c 4. d 5. a

>>>>> Spot Dictation

Career planning is a <u>popular</u> topic, <u>since</u> everyone needs personal <u>development</u>. However, <u>chance</u> always <u>waits</u> for those <u>who</u> are ready for it. So it's <u>important</u> to make a <u>plan</u> of career for <u>oneself</u> ahead. There are too many different <u>options</u>. Career planning <u>helps</u> you know your <u>goals</u> clearly and <u>how</u> to develop your life <u>in</u> the right <u>way</u>. Life is a <u>competition</u>, in which only the <u>fittest</u> can <u>survive</u>. If you can't <u>fit</u> the <u>requirements</u> of society, you may <u>get out of</u> the game. Therefore, the career planning is <u>like</u> a blueprint. With this plan in your <u>mind</u>, you can <u>match</u> your <u>personality</u> with your career <u>goals</u>, and <u>grasp</u> every <u>opportunity</u> the society has given you. <u>Try</u> your <u>best</u> and career planning will <u>make</u> your <u>future</u> more <u>successful</u>.

Background Information（背景知识）

1. Choosing your career

Your career choice determines the course that your life will take — it determines how successful you are, how happy you are and whether you live a good, bad or indifferent life. You have to think through what you want to achieve with your life in important areas such as your career, your family, artistic or sporting goals and public service. A crucial part of this is setting priorities in these different areas. No one has the time to excel in all areas — if the major focus of your life is to spend a lot of time with your family and contribute to voluntary organizations, then you must recognize that this will limit the time and effort you can dedicate to your career. If you want to focus exclusively on your career, then you must understand and manage the consequences. Bear in mind that your priorities will probably change over time — many people focus completely on their careers in their twenties as they make a place for themselves in the world. In their thirties, they may take more of a family focus, and other things may become important later on — this is a normal part of life.

2. Planning your career

In order to choose an appropriate career which suits your abilities, skills, ambitions and ideals, you have to plan your career very carefully. Here are the steps you can follow:

1) Develop a career plan. Think about what you want to do and find out more about the kind of training, education, and skills you will need to achieve your career goal.

2) Assess your skills and interests. Think hard about what you enjoy, what you are good at, what kind of personality you are, and the values you hold.

3) Research occupations. Find out more about the nature of the jobs that interest you, such as educational requirements, salary, working conditions, future outlook, and anything else that can help you narrow your focus.

4) Compare your skills and interests with the occupations you've selected. The career that matches your skills, interests, and personality the closest may be the career for you.

5) Choose your career goal. Once you've decided what occupation matches up best with you, then you can begin developing a plan to reach your career goal.

Language and Culture Focus (语言文化要点)

>>>> Reading I

1. 辨析career & profession

Career is a job or profession for which one is trained and which one intends to follow for part or the whole of one's life. (需要特别训练的并终身或长期从事的)职业; 一生的事业

【例句】 choice of career　　a career in banking　　a change of career

　　　　He realized that his acting career was over.

Career can also be an adjective, which means professional.

【例句】 career soldier 职业军人　　career diplomat 职业外交家

career woman/girl 职业女性

However, **careerist** is always found in negative use, since it refers to someone who puts success in their profession before all other things, such as friends or family, and may be willing to act unfairly to gain advancement. 名利心特别重的人；野心家

Profession is a form of employment, esp. one that is possible only for an educated person and after training (such as law, medicine, or teaching) and that is respected in society as honorable. (尤指受过教育和专门训练的法律、医学、教育等脑力劳动方面的)专业、职业

【例句】He is a lawyer **by profession**.

The teaching profession claim(s) to be badly paid.

He was well respected in the medical profession.

Professional is the adjective form.

【例句】professional standard 专业标准　　a professional photographer 职业摄影师

professional foul (体育运动中的)故意犯规　　He is a footballer who **turned professional**.

Professional can also be a noun, which refers to a person who has great experience and high professional standards. 专业人士；专家；内行

【例句】He's a real professional.

2. **contentment:** a feeling of quiet happiness and satisfaction. 满足；满意

3. **be conscious of/that:** to be aware of and responding to one's surroundings. 意识到的，自觉的；感到的

【例句】I was not conscious of having made a mistake.　　They were conscious that he disapproved.

4. **extent:** area or length; amount 范围；程度to... extent: 在……程度上（参看本书Unit 1 Reading I Note 11）

【例句】Considering the extent of his injuries, he's lucky to be alive.

Discontent had grown to such an extent that the government had to withdraw the new tax.

They examined the extent to which (=how much) age affected language-learning ability.

To what extent (=how much) did she influence his decision?

The community is, to a very large extent, a closed one.

Its success will depend to a large extent on local attitudes.

5. **psychological wellbeing:** a term referring to a healthy mental state with happiness, health and prosper.

well-being: the state of being comfortable, healthy, or happy. 康乐、安乐，安康

【例句】an improvement in the patient's well-being

6. **long for:** to want sth. very much (+n.) 渴望；long for someone to do sth. (+to v.) 渴望 (别人做某事)

【例句】They longed for green trees and open spaces.

　　　　This was the excitement that she had secretly longed for.

　　　　She was exhausted and longing for them to go.

7. see sb./sth. do sth.: to notice sb./sth. do sth.

【例句】I saw you put the key in your pocket.

　　　　I saw her face go pale. 我看见她的脸变苍白了。

注意:此结构表示看到的动作已完成或经常发生,see后面的动词不加to。

【例句】I saw him leave a few minutes ago. 　 I see him cross this street every day.

辨析: see sb./sth. doing sth. 结构往往表示看到的动作正在发生。

【例句】The suspect was seen entering the building.

8. mislead: (past and past participle *misled*) to cause someone to have a wrong idea or impression. 误导

【例句】I was misled by his innocent expression.

　　　　Don't be misled by appearances, he's a good worker.

　　　　Don't be misled into thinking that scientific research is easy.

9. capacity *n.*

　　1) the power or ability to do or understand sth. 能力,资格,力量

【例句】a capacity to learn languages

　　　　This book is beyond the capacity of young readers. 这本书非少年读者所能理解。

　　2) the maximum amount that sth. can contain/produce. 容量,容积; 生产力

【例句】The stadium has a seating capacity of 18, 000.

　　　　The hotel has a large capacity.

10. conquer: to overcome and take control of (a place or people) by military force. 攻取,攻克,征服

【例句】conquer a city

　　　　conquer an enemy

11. tough: difficult; strong enough to withstand adverse conditions or rough handling; not easily broken or weakened or defeated not easily broken or weakened. 困难的,艰苦的; 坚固的,牢固的

【例句】a tough problem

　　　　have a tough time

　　　　Some plastics are as tough as metal.

　　　　These toys are made from tough plastic.

　　　　Children's shoes need to be tough.

　　　　These plants are not tough enough to survive outside in winter.

　　　　You have to be tough to be successful in career.

12. mark: a line, figure, or symbol made as an indication or record of sth. 符号,标记; a small area on a surface having a different color from its surroundings. 痕迹，污点

【例句】 I've put a mark on the map where I think we should go for a picnic.

What do those marks in the middle of the road mean?

His fingers had left marks on the table's polished surface.

I'm afraid the acid will leave a permanent/indelible mark on your car.

13. **personality:** the combination of characteristics or qualities that form an individual's distinctive character. 人格；个性

【例句】 the formation of personality

The environment shapes personality.

That boy may be smart, but he has no personality.

14. **regard... as:** to think about someone or sth. in a particular way; to consider or have an opinion about.

【例句】 His work is regarded as very good by art experts.

Her parents always regarded her as the cleverest of their children.

辨析 **regard or consider**

These two words have the same meaning, but they are used in different patterns and structures.

Consider must be used with a complement or clause: you can **consider sb./sth. to be sth.** or **consider sb./sth. as sth.,** although very often the **to be** or **as** is left out.

【例句】 He considers himself an expert.

They are considered a high-risk group.

Regard is used in a narrower range of structures. The most frequent structure is **regard sb./sth. as sth.**; the *as* cannot be left out. You cannot regard sb./sth. to be sth.

15. **after all:** in spite of any indication or expectations to the contrary. 毕竟，终究；究竟

【例句】 I rang and told her I couldn't come after all.

16. **the ability of your mind to control your limbs and hands and words:** the capability of performing or behaving skillfully.

demonstrate: to show clearly；prove；clearly show the existence or truth of (sth.) by giving proof or evidence. 显示；证明

【例句】 demonstrate a philosophical principle

The lawyer demonstrated that the witness was lying.

17. **in... measure:** to... extent. 在一定程度上；一部分；有几分

短语 in large measure/in some measure

【例句】 In a measure John answered my question.

It is in some measure true to say that we don't work hard enough.

His success was in some measure due to his being in the right place at the right time.

The improvements are due in large measure to his leadership.

18. **command:** to have control or authority over. 控制；指挥；(to give someone) an order. 命令

【例句】In Britain, the party that commands a majority of seats in Parliament forms the government.

The general commanded his men to attack the city.

The officer commanded his men to shoot.

He commanded that they should come early.

19. **aspect:** a particular part or feature of sth. 方面

【例句】We must consider a problem in all its aspects.

20. **at work:** in action. 在工作；在运转

【例句】Researchers were convinced that one infectious agent was at work.

21. **tend to:** to regularly or frequently behave in a particular way or have a certain characteristic. 易于，往往会

【例句】Plants tend to die in hot weather if you don't water them.

Does he tend to lose?

22. **emotional:** arousing or characterized by intense feeling. 感情的；情绪的

【例句】in a state of emotional stress

an emotional debate

【相关词】

emotionless 感情冷漠的

23. **out in the world:** in relation with other people.

24. **This is not to say there aren't arguments and jealousies, but, on the whole, behavioral research discloses that human relations at work are just easier, perhaps because they are more regular and predictable and thus simpler to adjust to than the more intense and less regular relationships in the community.**

【译文】这并非说工作中没有争执与妒忌，但行为学研究揭示，工作中的人际关系总体来说比较容易相处，可能因为它们更有规律及可预测，所以比社区中更激烈且不规则的人际关系更易适应。

behavioral research: the study of behavior of human beings or other animals on the basis of behaviorism. 基于行为主义的行为学研究

behavioral: involving, relating to, or emphasizing behavior. 行为的，行为方面的

【例句】a behavioral trait

a behavioral approach to children's language

behaviorism: Behaviorism is a theory which emphasizes watching human actions and behavior to discover facts esp. about the human brain, rather than looking at private conscious experience or mental events. 行为主义; 行为学派

25. That is (not) to say... , but... : The pattern is used to introduce or follow an explanation or further clarification of preceding word or words. 不是说……而是……

【例句】 She is a talented student. This is not to say she has no weakness, but she can perform well in different situations.

He's a local government administrator, that is to say a civil servant.

26. jealousy: the state or feeling of being jealous. 嫉妒; 妒羡

【例句】 burn with jealousy

show jealousy of sb.'s success

feel a natural jealousy toward the winner

27. on the whole: taking everything into account; in general. 总的看来; 大体上

【例句】 I think, on the whole, we had better stay at home.

28. disclose: to make (secret or new information) known. 揭露; 泄露, 透露; 使公开

【例句】 They disclosed her name to the press.

disclose information to sb.

disclose one's views about sth.

29. regular: arranged in or constituting a constant or definite pattern; recurring at short uniform intervals. 定时的, 正常的; 规则的

【例句】 regular flight from Shanghai to Beijing

regular heartbeats

It's long past his regular bedtime.

30. predictable: able to be predicted. 可预言的; 可预料的, 可预报的

【例句】 The result is predictable.

The market is never predictable.

31. adjust to: to alter or move (sth.) slightly in order to achieve the desired fit appearance, or result; adapt or become used to a new situation. 改变……; 以适应; 适应

【例句】 adjust a seat to the height of a person

adjust expenses to income

adjust to energy shortages

He adjusted well to Washington.

32. intense: of extreme force, degree, or strength. 强烈的, 剧烈的

【例句】 the job demands intense concentration

an intense blue

33. pressure: to attempt to persuade or coerce (someone) into doing sth. 对……施加压力（或影响）；迫使；说服

【例句】She pressured her son to accept a job offer from the bank.

　　　　It might be possible to pressure him into resigning.

34. rough edge: If a person has rough edges, they do not always behave well and politely.

【例句】I knew him before he was successful, and he had a lot of rough edges back then.

35. work off: to gradually overcome unpleasant or embarrassing feelings. （通过工作、活动等）消除，去除

【例句】work off one's shame 洗刷耻辱

　　　　　work off excess weight 减轻过重的体重

　　　　work off one's anger 发泄怒气

　　　　work off a debt 抵偿债务

36. beyond: happening or continuing after (a specified time, stage, or event). 远于，越出（范围）

【例句】What these children go through is far beyond what most adults endure in a lifetime.

　　　　The landscape has changed beyond recognition.

37. whether it be... : it is not important if; used to show that sth. is true in either of two cases. 此结构可看作一种带有疑问词的让步状语从句，可译为"不管……"。后面的系动词可用虚拟语气或陈述语气。

【例句】whether it is (or be) true or not, the rumor will be believed.

　　　　(Whether your be) rich or poor, we remain close friends.

　　　　Well, I'm going to go, whether it be risky or not.

　　　　Someone's got to tell her, whether it's (it be) you or me.

　　whether... 结构可引导 "it be... " 以外的让步从句，可参见本书Unit 1 Reading I Note 19。

38. derive: to obtain sth. from (a specified source), arise from or originate in. 取得；形成；起源

【例句】The river derives its name from an Indian chief.

　　　　This movie is derived from a novel English word "chauffeur" (汽车司机) is derived from French.

39. collectivity: the quality or condition of being collective；the people as a whole；the practice or principle of giving a group priority over each individual in it. 集体性；集体

【例句】This shows that relationship between the nation and the collectivity are more systematic and normal, but not closer.

　　　　它标志着，国家与基层集体组织的关系更加制度化和规范化，但这并不说明，国家与基层社会之间的关系越来越紧密了。

　　　　This new education system can fully stimulate initiative and develop creative spirit, and thus promote collectivity qualities. 新的教学系统能充分调动学生学习的积极性，培养学生的创新精神，因此能提高全体学生的素质。

The collectivity innovation capability is the uppermost competitive capability of a modern enterprise. 集体创新能力是现代企业最主要的竞争能力。

40. think of: to consider that someone or sth. is a particular thing or has a particular quality. 认为；考虑

常用句型为: think of sb./sth. as sth. 把……看作

【例句】Peter had always thought of Kate as someone to be avoided.

I want you to think of this as your home.

What do you think about/of (= what is your opinion of) my new dress.

I'm thinking about/of (= considering) buying a new car.

41. status: relative social or professional position. 地位，身份

【例句】an improvement in the status of women

The award enhanced the musician's status.

42. self-confidence: a feeling of trust in one's abilities, qualities, and judgment. 自信

【例句】He began to lose his self-confidence.

43. envy: to desire to have a quality, possession, or other desirable thing belonging to (someone else). 妒忌，羡慕

【例句】He was filled with envy of me at my success.

do sth. out of envy

She envied John for his success.

44. competent: having the necessary ability, knowledge, or skill to do sth. successfully. 有能力的，能胜任

【例句】a competent teacher

be competent in (for) one's work

a highly competent surgeon

45. average: of the usual or ordinary amount, standard, level, or rate. 平均的；中等的；平常的

【例句】an average growth of 2 per cent

What was the average temperature yesterday?

46. association: a mental connection between things. 联想

【例句】Her hometown has happy associations for her.

47. prestigious: inspiring respect and admiration; having high status. 有威信的，有声望的，受尊敬的

【例句】The most prestigious school in this country.

cheap quarters in less prestigious parts of a town

48. They assume, usually with good reason, that others regard them more highly, even envy them, and that they are more competent than the average because of this association with a "winner," a prestigious institution.

【译文】他们总是有充分的理由认为别人更重视他们，甚至羡慕他们，并认为他们自己比普通

人更能干,因为他们与"胜利者",即有声望的机构联系在一起。

49. **institution:** an organization founded for a religious, educational, professional or social purposes. 社会公共机构

【例句】an educational institution

powerful institutions such as world banks

A church, school, university, hospital, or prison is an institution.

the Government and other political institutions

>>>>>Reading II

1. **ACCA:** Association of Chartered Certified Accountants. 特许公认会计师公会

2. **the Czech Republic:** a landlocked country in Central Europe with Prague（布拉格）as its capital. Its area covers 78, 866 km^2 and its people amounts to 10, 674, 947. 捷克共和国

3. **devote... to... :** to use time, energy, or effort for a particular purpose.

【例句】He has devoted all his life to the banking business.

I don't think we need to devote so much time to the question.

4. **accountancy:** the theory or practice of keeping or inspecting the money accounts of businesses or people. 会计工作

accountant: a person whose job is to control and examine the money accounts of businesses or people. 会计师

5. **finance:** the management of money, loans, credits or grants by governments, companies, or large organizations. 财政, 金融

【例句】finance and trade 金融贸易

the Ministry of Finance 财政部长

public finance 公共财政

financial: connected with finance. 财政的, 金融的

【例句】financial difficulty 财政困难

financial year 财政年

6. **statutory audit:** 法定审计

statutory: fixed or controlled by law. 法定的

【例句】statutory employment rights 法定的就业权利

She's below the statutory age for school attendance. 她还不到法定的上学年龄。

audit: *n.* official examination of the accounts of a business or organization 审计

v. to make an official examination of (the accounts of a business). 审计

【例句】 yearly audit 年度审计

The fund is audited annually by an accountant.

auditor: *n.* 审计员, 稽核员

【例句】 statutory auditor 法定审计师

7. publication: sth. published as a book or magazine, etc. 出版物

【例句】 a long list of publications

8. involvement: someone's involvement in/with sth. means someone's taking part in it.

【例句】 involvement in public affairs

the active involvement of thousands of people in the election

9. integral: essential or necessary to the completeness of the whole. 不可或缺的

【例句】 an integral part of the whole system

10. challenge: sth. difficult that requires great effort or determination if one is going to succeed. 挑战

【例句】 The long-term challenge facing the present government is how to keep prices stable and create more opportunities for employment.

当前政府面临的长期挑战就是如何保持物价稳定并创造更多的就业机会。

11. banking: the business of a bank or a banker. 银行业

【例句】 the banking system 银行业体系

12. lead to: to result in. 导致

【例句】 The new system will lead to more troubles in the future.

Overuse of the medicine will lead to serious heart problems.

13. appoint: to choose or ask sb. for a particular job or position. 任命, 委任

【例句】 She has been appointed as sales director to the new department.

The president has appointed a committee to investigate the scandal.

14. crucial: extremely important.

【例句】 a crucial moment in the negotiation 谈判的关键时刻

He believes that work is the crucial for the welfare of the family.

15. community: a group of people united by shared interests, religion, etc.

【例句】 the academic community 学术界

the business community 商界

16. comment: to say sth. and give one's opinion. 评论

【例句】 The minister refused to comment on the rumour of his resignation.

17. reliable: that can be trusted; dependable.

【例句】 a reliable person

a reliable source of information 可靠消息来源

18. financial statement: 财务报表

19. reporting season: a period when companies declare their dividends. 业绩宣布期

20. not so... as... : (used in comparisons) not to the same degree. 不像……那样……（后面可以接名词或从句）

【例句】 He was not so quick a learner as his brother.

The bed was not so comfortable as his own.

It wasn't so good as last time.

It's not so easy as you'd think.

21. aftermath: the result or period following an event or situation. 后果,余波

【例句】 the aftermath of the war

the danger of disease in the aftermath of the earthquake

22. anticipate: to realize beforehand; to expect and foresee. 预期; 期望

【例句】 You'd better anticipate every possible trouble before you open the new factory.

Why do you still keep the machine since you don't anticipate using it?

23. regulate: to control especially by means of rules or laws.

【例句】 a well-regulated family 管理有方的家庭

His life is too well regulated to be affected by such disturbances.

The volume of economic activities is regulated by the supply of money.

经济活动的总量是由资金供给总量控制的。

24. enhance: to increase in value or amount. 提高; 增加; 加强; 增进

【例句】 enhance friendship between to parties

This campaign will greatly enhance your reputation.

The growth of a city often enhances the value of land close to it.

城市的发展常常会提高其附近的地价。

25. underline: to give force to an idea or feeling; to emphasize. 强调

【例句】 An article in the newspaper underlined the same problem.

The letter of invitation underlined the private nature of the meeting.

26. sector: a part or division of economy, business, trade, etc. 部门

【例句】 employment in the public and private sectors 国营和私营部门的就业情况

the banking sector 银行界

the manufacturing sector 制造业

27. be noted for: to be famous because of a special quality or ability. 因……而闻名

【例句】 This small town is noted for its cheese.

He is noted for his generosity.

The city is noted for its picturesque scenery.

28. **profile:** a short description of someone containing all the most important or interesting facts about them. 对一个人的能力、个性的简要描述; 简况; 人物简介

　　【例句】 Some journalist had written a profile about him in which some of the facts were untrue.

　　　　　　The newspaper publishes a profile of a leading sportsman every week.

　　　　　　该报每周刊登一篇关于一名优秀运动员的简介。

29. **adopt a global perspective:** to accept an understanding of the interdependency of nations and peoples and the political, economic, ecological, and social concepts and values that affect lives within and across national boundaries (采取全球化的视角). Adopting a global perspective involves seeking to understand worldwide business and communication, as well as the links between our own lives and those of people throughout the world.

If you adopt a particular attitude, plan, or course of action, you begin to have it or to carry it out.

　　【例句】 After the war, they adopted a more open policy towards the West.

　　perspective: a particular way of thinking about something, especially one that is influenced by your beliefs or experiences. 视角

　　【例句】 He always argues from a strange perspective.

　　　　　　The company's achievements should be looked at in the proper perspective.

　　global: concerning the whole world. 全球的

　　【例句】 global climatic change

　　　　　　global energy output

30. **There is hardly a better example of the globalisation of financial markets than what is happening now:** 从来没有一个比现在情形更好的全球化金融市场。

31. **standard:** a level or degree that is considered proper or acceptable. 标准

　　【例句】 the standard of living 生活水平

　　　　　　the safety standards 安全标准

　　　　　　gold standard 金本位制

32. **boundary:** the dividing line between two areas of land. 分界线

　　national boundary: the dividing line between two countries. 国界线

34. **melting pot:** a place where people of different races and nationalities mix together. 大熔炉

35. **conclude:** to finish what one is supposed to say. 得出结论; 断定

　　【例句】 He concluded, "That's why we are still so poor."

　　　　　　Perhaps I should conclude with some more light-hearted questions.

36. **Given... :** *prep.* knowing about, considering. 考虑到

【例句】Given the circumstances, you've done really well.

Given the time available to us, we'll have to submit the report in draft form.

Given (the fact) that the patients have some disabilities, we still try to enable them to be as independent as possible.

37. **ACCA Achievement Award:** The award is given annually by the Association of Chartered Certified Accountants (ACCA) to outstanding figures who have significantly contributed to the development of the accountancy and finance profession on an international scale.

38. **recognition:** favorable public attention or appreciation that is given to someone because of his outstanding achievements or abilities; the state of being accepted as valuable. 认可, 承认

【例句】He is a young writer struggling for public recognition.

他是一位为得到公众认可而努力奋斗的青年作家。

He was awarded a knighthood in recognition of his truly great contribution to the nation. 为了表彰他对国家的卓越贡献,他被授予骑士勋章。

>>>> Extended Activities

A. Function and Structure: Expressing and Responding to Thanks

1. It is important to learn how to say thanks and how to show your appreciation the proper way. Here are some tips:

At a Party — Take your cue from the host. If he went to the trouble to mail an invitation, send him a note in return.

Receiving a *Gift* — If you thank a person profusely (极多地) after receiving a gift, it's not necessary to send a note — so it makes you look extra-classy when you do.

A *Business Function* — If you've been at a formal business meeting and want to thank potential clients or business partners, type a paper note. If the event is a lunch or social function, write it by hand.

2. In business, it is customary to express appreciation to people who help your company succeed. In fact, the absence of a "thank you" may be misunderstood to mean the effort was not appreciated. Thanking customers has always been very effective for building royalty, demonstrating corporate commitment to service, generating referral business and differentiating a business from the rest. There are a variety of ways to express gratitude. The way in which you thank your customers does not have to cost a lot of money and nothing says "you are important" like a handwritten note. A short handwritten note has

the power of personal engagement and high impact. It's a small gesture but keeps customers coming back. Inside a business, when a boss wants to motivate his or her employees, a simple "thank you" also works best. A smart employer knows it well that frequent recognition of accomplishments is the best way to encourage employees.

B. Special Use: Describing People's Appearance

1. 整体描写和局部描写

在描写人物时,我们通常会使用一些形容词描述人的身体各部分: 体形、脸形、面颊、鼻子、眼睛、嘴巴、下巴、牙齿、头发的颜色和发型以及肤色等。有些形容词属于整体描写,例如: cool(酷)、fashionable(时髦的), healthy, strong, tall, meager, smart, kind等; 有些形容词属于局部描写,需要与某些身体器官搭配使用,例如: round face, deep-set eyes(深陷的双眼), red cheeks(红色的面颊), crooked nose(鹰钩鼻子), pointed chin(尖下巴), big mouth, even teeth(平整的牙齿), blonde hair(金发), curly hair(卷发), sunburned skin(晒黑的皮肤)等。

2. 生理特征的描写和人格特征的描写

以上与人体器官搭配的形容词都属于生理特征描写。但除了生理描写外,我们也可以描写人的性格特征,例如: generous(慷慨的), modest(谦虚的), honest, serious, obstinate(固执的), self-conceited(自负的), kind-hearted(善良的)等。

3. 单个形容词和复合形容词

有些形容词由单个词构成,例如: tall, short, fat, thin, slim; 有些形容词有两、三个词共同构成,成为复合形容词,例如: snow-white(雪白的), sun-tanned(黝黑的), ordinary-looking(相貌平平的), warm-hearted(热心的)等。

4. 常用于人物描写的语法结构

• 系动词+形容词

【例句】My brother is tall and handsome.　　He is tall and sturdy (强壮).

The boy is extremely bright.　　My mother is thrifty with money.

As a child, he is meager (瘦的) and weak.　　The old man looks thin.

He looks old and his hair is all white.

The girl tends to be jealous of those who make greater progress.

• 系动词+of+名词

【例句】She is of medium build.

• 形容词+名词

【例句】a serious-looking face　　　　　a grey-haired woman

a wrinkled face　　　　　　　　a pretty girl

- 动词＋形容词＋名词

He has a bushy beard and a double chin.　　The girl has wavy hair and watery eyes.

Tom has a strong body and high intelligence.　　He is a heavy-built man.

She is a slim woman.

- 介词＋名词

When we entered the room we saw a face with a big forehead.

She greets us with smiles.　　He is a man with a bad temper.

She dressed in red.

5. 描写人物的委婉语

对人物的描写常会涉及一些令人不快的现象,如直接描写往往会令人难堪,出于礼貌,这时应尽量避免直接使用令人难堪的词语,而用委婉语来代替这些词语。例如:

用delicate纤细的, slender苗条的, slim 苗条的, 代替thin瘦的, skinny皮包骨头;

用plump丰满的, 代替fat 肥胖, obese非常胖的;

用ordinary 平常的, plain相貌平平的, 代替ugly难看的, awful丑陋的。

6. 描写人物的基本原则

- 描写要具体,避免笼统化,应注重细节描写,体现人物的音容笑貌。

在实践中,学习者要避免一些泛泛而谈的词,例如: awful, bad, beautiful, fine, good, great, interesting, lovely, nice, pretty, wonderful等。好的描写需要注意具体的细节,所以用词要具体化。

【例句】He was thin, short, and dark. His hair was like a bundle of straw. His dirty clothes and tired look were clearly signs of a long travel. His clothes were made of cheap cloth. The coat was too short and the trousers too loose. And he wore a pair of rubber shoes, which were very unfashionable. He did not look smart at all.

- 生理特征描写应与人物的性格、思想和要表达的情感相结合,并通过具体的事例得以体现,表现出人物的特性和特征。

【例句】Most Jewish women of her age were sickly, weak, broken in body. But this washwoman, small and thin as she was, possessed a strength that came from generations of peasant ancestors.

His gaunt, expressive face was dominated by piercing eyes, conveying a mixture of intensity and repose, of wariness and calm self-confidence. He wore an immaculately tailored gray coat, at once simple and elegant. He moved gracefully and with dignity, filling a room not by his physical dominance but by his air of controlled tension, steely discipline, and self-control. As if he were a coiled spring. He conveyed an easy casualness, which, however, did not deceive the careful observer. The quick smile, the comprehending expression that made clear he understood English even without translation, the palpable alertness, were clearly the features of a man who had had burned into him by a searing half-century the vital importance of self-possession.

C. Practical Reading

1. 商务名片一般由四部分组成: 1) 公司 / 企业名称(name of organization)；2) 姓名(name)；3) 头衔 / 职位(title / occupation)；4) 联系方式(contact)，包括地址、电话、传真、电子邮箱、网址等。

2. 第1题问会议室要装潢需要找谁。比较而言，当然是找艺术设计总监（art director），而不会去找出口销售部经理或国际销售部经理。

3. 第2题问购买"专用小型交换机"应该联系谁。从公司的名字我们可以知道该公司的业务范围，从带有Tele字样的Telecon一词，我们可以推理，该公司属于做电信业务的公司，因此，应该找TELECON公司。

4. 第3题问购买tool boxes即工具箱，应该联系谁。因为这属于硬件产品，我们从公司的名字中带有Hardware字样可以判断应该联系Brian Conroy。

5. 第4题涉及信息服务问题，从卡片中的INFO字样，可以确定应该找Michael Martin。

6. 第5题和第6题也比较容易定位，关键信息分别是Software和COSMETICS。

7. Abbreviations:

   Plc: public limited company: a company whose shares can be bought and sold by the public and whose debts are limited if it fails financially. 股份有限责任公司

   Inc.: incorporated: used in the names of US companies that are legally established 公司（美国）

   INFO: information

   TEC.: technology

   IL: the abbreviation of Illinois, US 美国伊利诺斯州的缩写

Teaching Tips （教学提示）

1. Lead-in: 本单元导入部分安排了听力理解和听写填空两项任务。听力理解部分包含passage和dialogue各一篇，共设有3个练习，题型为多项选择（Multiple-choice Questions）和配对（Matching），以考查学生对语篇主旨的把握和细节的辨析。建议教师先做练习1，然后将Difficult words and expressions 讲解一遍，以扫除语言障碍；然后做练习2。练习3可选择放在阅读II之前进行。听写填空的主题为职业规划（Career Planning），可以安排在Reading I的Post-reading活动之前进行。

2. Reading I: Brainstorming，全班学生通过自由讨论的形式，列出他们认为最有趣的、最乏味的、最有前途的和最有压力的职业。教师也可另外列出一些关于职业的词汇或让学生参见扩展性活

动部分中Additional Vocabulary给出的词汇，请学生从中挑选他们最感兴趣的或最讨厌的职业，并用英语简单地陈述各自的理由。

3. Reading I: Pairwork 在学生结束第一和第二题的讨论后，教师还可随意挑选一些学生进行"采访"，请他们谈谈将如何选择和规划自己未来的职业，父母的态度会对他们择业取向产生怎样的影响。讨论题3 What are reasons for people to work other than for money or survival alone? 旨在导入Reading I的课文Why People Work，激发学生对课文学习的兴趣。 教师可在学生双人结对讨论完毕后，在黑板上写下Why do people work? 这个问题，邀请学生把他们的答案列在黑板上。

4. Reading I: Post-reading，设有两项任务。教师可事先将下面提供的卡片复印若干套供课上使用。第一项任务通过调查问卷的形式，由学生对自己的兴趣、能力、爱好、个性进行简单的评估。进行这项活动前，教师先向学生简单介绍6种类型的人(The test measures how similar you are to six basic types of people: realistic type, investigative type, artistic type, social type, enterprising type and conventional type. Occupations can also be grouped according to these six types. Generally, you will be happiest in a job that matches your personality type. Now, let's have a look at the questionnaire in your textbook and find out what type of person you are exactly.)。在学生完成问卷后，教师可请学生估测一下自己属于哪一个类型。然后把学生分成若干个小组，并将事先复印好的卡片分发给每个小组，请学生讨论、比较他们各自的答案，确定自己属于哪一类型的人，最适合哪一类的职业。第二项任务由学生分别扮演求职者和职业咨询服务人员的角色，进一步了解职业咨询和职业规划的重要性。

The Realistic Personality Type

· likes to work with animals, tools, or machines;

· generally avoids social activities like teaching, counseling, nursing, and informing others;

· has good skills in working with tools, mechanical drawings, machines or animals;

· values practical things you can see and touch — like plants and animals you can grow, or things you can build or make better;

· sees self as practical, mechanical, and realistic.

In the Realistic group, for example, there are jobs like animal caretaker, farmer, firefighter, guard, police detective, architect, engineer, surveyor, inspector, cost estimator, aircraft pilot, upholsterer, plumber, carpenter, mason, mechanic, sailor, production manager, driver, operator, clerk, librarian, chef, jeweler, welder, computer programmer, optician, appliance repairer, landscape architect, electrician, etc.

The Investigative Personality Type

· likes to study and solve math or science problems;

· generally avoids leading, selling, or persuading people;

· has good skills at understanding and solving science and math problems;

· values science, and sees self as precise, scientific, and intellectual.

In the Investigative group, for example, there are jobs like scientist, astronomer, chemist, geologist, meteorologist, physicist, urban planner, sociologist, marketing researcher, historian, economist, dentist, surgeon, biomedical engineer, information system manager, computer software engineer, network administrator, statistician, computer support specialist, curator, actuary, lab technician, etc.

The Artistic Personality Type

· likes to do creative activities like art, drama, crafts, dance, music, or creative writing;

· generally avoids highly ordered or repetitive activities;

· has good artistic abilities — in creative writing, drama, crafts, music, or art;

· values the creative arts — like drama, music, art, or the works of creative writers;

· sees self as expressive, original, and independent.

In the Artistic group, for example, there are jobs like biographer, editor, writer, poet, architect, cartoonist, commercial/graphic/industrial/interior designer, painter, sculptor, photographer, actor/actress, dancer, director, disk jockey, producer, radio and TV announcer, composer, musician, orchestra conductor, singer, etc.

The Social Personality Type

· likes to do things to help people — like teaching, counseling, nursing, or giving information;

· generally avoids using machines, tools, or animals to achieve a goal;

· has good skills at teaching, counseling, nursing, or giving information;

· values helping people and solving social problems;

· sees self as helpful, friendly, and trustworthy.

In the Social group, for example, there are jobs like coach, umpire, recreation and fitness worker, schoolteacher, special education teacher, instructional coordinator, librarian, childcare worker, personal and home care aide, dietitian, clergy or religious worker, employment counselor, probation officer, social worker, registered nurse, etc.

The Enterprising Personality Type

· likes to lead and persuade people, and to sell things and ideas; generally avoids activities that require careful observation and scientific, analytical thinking;

· is good at leading people and selling things or ideas;

· values success in politics, leadership, or business;

· sees self as energetic, ambitious, and sociable.

In the Enterprising group, for example, there are jobs like counter/rental clerk, sales agent, sales representative, travel agent, hair stylist, bartender, flight attendant, reservation or ticket agent, waiter/waitress, lawyer, judge, business manager, management consultant, top executive, school superintendent, public relations specialist, reporter, news analyst, desktop publisher, customs inspector, occupational safety and health specialist, etc.

The Conventional Personality Type

· likes to work with numbers, records, or machines in a set, orderly way;   generally avoids ambiguous, unstructured activities;

· is good at working with written records and numbers in a systematic, orderly way;

· values success in business;

· sees self as orderly, and good at following a set plan.

In the Conventional group, for example, there are jobs like computer operator, data entry keyer, file clerk, mail carrier, office clerk, measurer/checker, typist, bank teller, cashier, dispatcher, receptionist, switchboard operator, loan officer, secretary, administrative assistant, accounting clerk, billing clerk, book-keeper, stock clerk & order filler, claim examiner, hotel/motel desk clerk, etc.

5. Reading II Cloze

Question 2　take over 接管；接手；接任

take away 拿走；减去；剥夺

take off 拿掉；取消；脱衣；起飞

take down 拿下；记下；拆卸；病倒

此处选a，意思是"我 15 岁的时候，就已在家中接下了为父母的晚宴烹调菜肴的任务。"

Question 5　for fun　固定搭配，指"开玩笑，不是认真的"。

【例句】He's learning English just for fun.

Question 7　put up 举起；提供；建造；提名；推举

put out 伸出；生产；消除；打扰

put on 穿上；把……放在上；假装；增加

put off　推迟；拖延

此处选d，意思是"我是那么地喜欢烹调，我确信我再也不能拖延了，我得马上告诉我的父母。"

Question 8　Firstly 意为"in the first place, to begin with; used to refer to the first thing in the list, 第一；首先"。

【例句】There are two very good reasons why we can't do it. Firstly, we don't have enough money, and secondly, we don't have enough time.

First 作为副词可解释为"before anything else 首先"，作此意解时同firstly。

【例句】First(ly), let me deal with the most important issue.

也可解释为"for the first time 第一次"。

【例句】When we first met...

At first 意为"in or at the beginning, 开始"。

【例句】At first I thought he was joking but then I realized he meant it.

First of all 意为"before anything else, 首先"，也可写作first。

【例句】First (of all) (UK also First off), let me say something about our plan.

此处选c，意思是"起先是一片沉寂，然后我的父亲问我为什么。"

Question 10　此处选c，writing和painting a picture并列作为like的宾语，要求保持结构平衡。

Key（练习答案）

>>>>> Reading I

Pre-reading

I. Here are some words about occupations. Teacher can use these words to help students to decide which one is the most interesting, promising, boring, or stressful. Ask students to give their reasons. There is no definite answer for this brainstorming task.

teacher	waiter/waitress	businessman	typist
driver	engineer	shop assistant	accountant
pilot	tailor	journalist	writer
doctor	secretary	technician	worker

II. 3. Reasons to work:

To support yourself and your family; to be challenged; to help people in need; for the pleasure/calling of doing the work; for the impact your work makes on the world; for the reputation you build in the community; to be part of a group and to experience the mission; to be appreciated; for the respect and admiration your work brings you; for personal fulfillment and satisfaction; to make a difference in someone else's life...

Exercises

II. 1. a　　2. c　　3. a　　4. c　　5. d

III. 1. personality　2. institution　3. contentment　4. complaint　5. demonstrate
6. conscious　7. aspect　8. association　9. mark　10. admire
11. status　12. capacity　13. assume　14. carpenter　15. derive

IV. 1. longed for　　　　2. in significant measure　　3. adjust to
4. to some extent　　5. worked off　　　　　6. are conscious of
7. On the whole　　　8. at work　　　　　　9. after all
10. tend to　　　　　11. regarded as　　　　12. demonstrate

V. 1. They became conscious of a peculiar smell in the room.

2. Computer virus can damage computer files. This is not to say that we should refuse to use computers, but we should take proper measures to protect our files against computer virus.

3. Whether it be successful or not, we can be sure that we did our best.

4. The day, after all, turned out fine.

5. It is true, in some measure, that we don't work hard enough.

6. I regard him as someone who will always help me.

7. He tends to do something wrong.

8. On the whole, he doesn't take medicine, but sometimes he does.

9. He worked off the objections to the original plan.

10. Can you adjust your way of thinking to the new life style?

>>>>>Reading II

Exercises

I. 1. T   2. F   3. T   4. F   5. F

6. T   7. T   8. T   9. F   10. NM

III. 1. b   2. a   3. d   4. c   5. a

6. d   7. b   8. a   9. c   10. d

IV. 1. I was conscious that he had changed his way/approach.

2. To a large extent/ In a significant measure, his warnings have proved correct.

3. Many people believe that personality is inborn/innate, but in my opinion, the environment shapes personality.

4. It should be recognized that he was, after all, a schoolboy.

5. Given the limited investment, the movie, on the whole, is worth watching.

6. You should not be always complaining, as the university you're studying in is one of the most prestigious in the district.

7. Whether you are a carpenter or a brick layer, you need to try your best to demonstrate your capacity.

8. No one has been so admired as them for discipline.

9. They always thought of me as emotionless and tough.

10. The new regulation will lead to the improvement in the city's water supply.

11. Since we haven't devoted sufficient time and effort to this research project, up till now we have made no progress.

12. He was presented with a gold watch in recognition of his thirty-year service to the company.

V. 1. c   2. a   3. d   4. a   5. a

6. c   7. d   8. c   9. a   10. c

11. b   12. b   13. d   14. a   15. b

>>>>>Extended Activities

A. Function and Structure

I. 1. Tim：I think it's about time we got going. <u>Thank you very much</u> for a wonderful evening.

John: <u>It's a pleasure</u>. I'm very glad you enjoyed it.

2. Cathy: <u>I can never thank you enough for</u> what you've done for me, Tom.

Tom: <u>It's nothing</u>. Glad to be of help.

3. Mary: Hi, Susan. I've got two tickets for tonight's rock'n'roll concert. Would you like to come with me?

Susan: Wonderful! <u>Much appreciated</u>.

Mary: <u>Don't mention it</u>. I know it's your favorite.

4. Mr. White: I have to leave a bit early today. My wife calls to say my little daughter isn't feeling well.

Miss Gray: Oh, no! Is it serious?

Mr. White: I don't know. My wife says she has a stomachache, and she's crying all day. I'll have to go home now.

Miss Gray: Oh, I'm so sorry to hear that. I'll type all these letters for you. Don't worry about them.

Mr. White: <u>I'm much obliged to you</u>.

Miss Gray: Forget it. I'm sure <u>you would have done the same in my</u> position.

C. Practical Reading

1. Sandy Vincent.

Because he is an art director.

By phone at 081-743-5892 or by fax at 081-743-6351.

Phoning is more convenient, for it can reach the very person you want immediately and more directly.

2. TELECON.

23 via Roma, Torino, Italy.

Fax: 11 657 2943.

3. Brian Conroy.

His surname is Conroy and his first name is Brian.

He's working in the International Sales Department.

Hardware.

He's American.

4. I'd advise him to contact Michael Martin. Because he works for INFO TEC, which will provide him with useful information.

Chief Information Official.

Office: (513) 529-6672; Home: (513) 529-2417.

5. I'll contact SHINICHI SUZUKI.

He is a software engineer.

IMPEX IMP. & EXP. LTD.

6. John Halley.

Salesman.

By sending an E-mail to him.

D. Additional Vocabulary

1-15; 2-1; 3-21; 4-13; 5-9; 6-6; 7-26; 8-3; 9-4; 10-5;

11-8; 12-18; 13-30; 14-11; 15-23; 16-2; 17-10; 18-25; 19-29; 20-22;

21-12; 22-19; 23-16; 24-7; 25-17; 26-27; 27-14; 28-28; 29-24; 30-20

F. Humor Time

1. Cook   2. Teacher   3. Officer   4. Editor

Unit 4
Job-hunting

Teaching Aim（教学目的）

1. Cognitive Information（认知信息）: Jobs and Occupations
2. Language Focus（内容重点）
   — **Key Words:** I. influence, trait, initiative, outgoing, realm, inherit, bestow, disloyal, quit, loyalty, recipient, patron, lifelong job security, family honor, job hopping, mobility, qualify, root, personnel, opportunity, newcomer, salary, seniority, bounce; II. transition, academic, depressing, recession, flight slot, redundancy, leave, participate, job sharing scheme, crisis, volunteer, recruit
   — **Phrases:** I. expertise, candidate, competency, initial, teamwork, recruiters, self-awareness, confidence, interpersonal, daunt, CV, relevant, criteria, applicants, specification, match, outcomes, concise, present, achievement, responsibility, voluntary
   — **Useful Structures:** keep doing sth.

      as if

      the best of sth.

      It is not uncommon to ...

      It is not enough to do sth.
   — **Vocabulary:** Words of Job Application

> 3. Communicative Skills（交际技能）
> — **Expressions:** Describing One's Occupation
> — **Reading:** Job Advertisements

Lead-in 导入

>>>>>Listening Comprehension Tasks

Difficult Words & Expressions

1. job-hunting: 求职

2. efficient: acting or producing effectively 高效的

3. focused: of or toward a central point 聚焦的

4. go after: 追求

5. consistently: in a way of being coherent and uniform 一贯地

6. isolation: the condition of being solitary 孤独

7. coach: a trainer or tutor 教练, 辅导员

8. option: sth. chosen or available as a choice 选项

9. location: site 地点

10. directory: a book containing an alphabetical or classified listing of names, addresses and other data 人名地址录, 电话号码簿

11. resume (*n.*): curriculum vitae 履历, 简历

12. version: a particular form or variation of the original type 版本

13. access: a means of approaching, entering, or making use of 通路, 入口, 使用途径

14. recruiter: someone engaging in the solicitation of individuals to fill jobs or positions within a corporation 招聘人员

15. voicemail: a centralized system of stored telephone messages that can be retrieved later 语音信箱

16. legally: in a way of conformity with law 合法地

17. monitor (*v.*): to check the content of 监测

18. trace (*v.*): to locate or discover by searching; to follow the course of 查出; 跟踪

19. available: ready for use; obtainable 可用的, 可获得的

20. identity: the set of behavioral or personal characteristics by which an individual is recognizable as a member of a group 个人身份

21. spam: unsolicited commercial e-mail 垃圾邮件

Passage Script 1

Today's lecture on job-hunting is about a 7-step process that lays the foundation for an efficient and successful job search online.

First, get comfortable with your computer and being online.

Step 1. Decide What You Want to Do

It's nearly impossible to find a job if you don't know what you want to do. "What am I looking for?" is the first question you will be asked when you say that you are job hunting. You will have a more focused — and a more successful — job search when you know what you want, and go after it. Not knowing what you want to do is the number one mistake job seekers make!

Step 2. Get Support for Your Job Search

More "heads" are definitely better than one — the old saying is absolutely true, so don't do your job search in isolation. Friends, your school or college's career center, career counsellors, and/or a job search coach can help you enormously. They will help you find resources and contacts, keep your spirits up, give you ideas, and help you explore your options.

Step 3. Collect Information

Identify the jobs, employers, and locations that interest you, and then find out what you can do about them. The web is a treasure of useful information with links to "how-to" articles, directories of employer websites, lists of employers, and more to help you find potential employer. The information you have gathered will help you prepare an attention-getting cover letter and impress interviewers with your knowledge of them and their organization.

Step 4. Pull Together Your Resume

Once you know the job you want and have collected information, you need to create your resume, actually, two or three versions — for print, for e-mail, and for completing online forms.

Passage Script 2

Step 5. Get a Personal E-mail Account

If you don't already have an e-mail account, establish one now. Particularly, if you are employed, use a personal account that your employer can't read and enables potential employers and other job search contacts to stay in touch with you easily and safely. Don't use your current employer's e-mail. In case you lose your job, you will no longer have access to the work e-mail address. Then how would a potential employer find you?

Step 6. Get a Personal Cell Phone

A personal cell phone enables potential employers and other job search contacts to stay in touch with you easily and safely. Should a recruiter or a potential employer wish to contact you during the work day, you don't want them to call you at work using your current employer's telephone. If someone leaves a message, or even a voicemail, for you regarding your job hunting, you could lose your job. Employers can and do legally monitor their telephone and voicemail systems. You can put your personal cell phone number on your resume in place of a phone number which could be traced to your home. Recruiters or potential employers will be able to call you on your personal cell phone without risk to your job or life.

Step 7. Protect Your Privacy

Your complete work history, education and contact information on some job sites are available to anyone who can pay the access fee — employers and recruiters, hopefully, but also sales people, identity thieves, etc. What are the risks of not protecting your privacy? If you have a job and your employer finds your resume online, you could be fired. Someone could steal your identity. You may be buried with "spam" as well as direct marketing to your home or business. Someone interested in harming you can find you easily with your complete contact and employment information.

Key

II. 1. c 2. d 3. a 4. b 5. d 6. d 7. a 8. b

IV. 1. Answer: Statements (C, E, L)

2. Answer: Statements (B, C, G, J)

3. Answer: Statements (A, F, H, I, K)

V. 1. There are 7 steps in job-hunting online. They are Step 1. Decide What You Want to Do, Step 2. Get Support for Your Job Search, Step 3. Collect Information, Step 4. Pull Together Your Resume, Step 5. Get a Personal Email Account, Step 6. Get a Personal Cell Phone, and Step 7. Protect Your Privacy

2. This is an open-ended question. Generally speaking, they should be Step 1 Decide What You Want to Do and Step 7 Protect Your Privacy.

>>>>>Spot Dictation

I get up <u>at five</u> and start the day <u>with</u> a cup of tea, but I <u>rarely</u> have breakfast. I just don't <u>feel</u> <u>hungry</u> in the morning. I usually <u>get to</u> the office at about <u>half past seven</u>. <u>During</u> the day I <u>speak to</u> many people <u>on the telephone</u> and meet them <u>as well</u>.

I always <u>have lunch</u> with <u>colleagues</u>, but we don't just <u>talk about</u> work. On a <u>normal</u> day I work <u>until</u> about 7 pm. Then I go home to <u>have dinner</u>. In an <u>average week</u> I have <u>two or three</u> business <u>dinner</u> <u>appointments</u> with <u>clients</u>, <u>staff</u> and <u>managers</u>. I go to bed at <u>eleven or twelve o'clock</u> and so I get five or <u>six hours of</u> sleep.

Background Information（背景知识）

1. Words related to jobs and occupations: please refer to the notes for *Special Use: Words of Job Application* in this unit.

2. Job-hunting techniques

It's easy to talk about all the nice things you desire in a job offer, but it's far from easy to land yourself on a job which is not very desirable, especially for a young man without much work experience and social connections. The following tips may be helpful for young jobseekers:

- Chances of getting a job are better with smaller companies than with large ones.
- Do homework on yourself. Identify your skills in great detail, and in priority.
- Research your potential employer. Find out all you can about the organization.
- Be persistent. Keep at the job hunt — make return visits.
- Investigate many different organizations or businesses for job openings. Don't limit yourself to

one type of organization.

- Don't "put all of your eggs in one basket" — such as relying only on relatives, just sending out resumes, or just applying to your first employer choice.
- Determine what makes you better at the job you are after than other people.
- Get as many other people helping you look for a job as possible: friends, relatives, coworkers, professionals, and so on.
- Look as sharp as possible. Be clean, well-dressed and alert.
- No one "owes" you a job. It's up to you to "win" a job by showing a potential employer you have the right attitude and skill.

3. Looking for job vacancies

Before beginning a search for a job, you will need to think about the types of vacancies you are hoping to find. If you think in terms of broad job areas, rather than specific job titles this will give you wider opportunities and more possible vacancies as employers often use different titles for similar jobs. You should consider temporary and part-time work as this could give you experience, is good for your CV, and will provide the chance to make contacts that may know about other jobs. Some temporary jobs may also become permanent. If you are looking for a vacancy, you may try:

1) *Careers center*: Employers may advertise their vacancies here for young people. For some jobs, careers officers may be able to telephone on your behalf to arrange interviews. Careers officers also offer a counseling and advice service for young people and help in finding training places or jobs.

2) *Local/national newspaper/radio/TV advertisements*

3) *Internet*: There are many job search websites. Some have search facilities allowing you to search on geographical area, by wage/salary and so on. Recruitment agencies also advertise on websites and some allow jobseekers to register on there as well.

4) *Journals/trade magazines*: Specialist journals published by professional bodies or trade organizations may advertise jobs. These may come out monthly or quarterly and feature adverts on a national basis.

5) *On their own premises*: Some employers advertise their vacancies outside their premises on notice boards or signs.

6) *Private employment agencies/ recruitment agencies*: These match job seekers with employers' vacancies. Agencies display adverts in their shop windows and/or display boards for public access. They will also contact people registered with them when vacancies arise. Many vacancies are never advertised. Tapping into this pool of vacancies involves making speculative approaches. This means contacting employers just in case they have a suitable vacancy or a vacancy coming up. It is likely that you will suffer a number of setbacks and disappointments with this method, as

many of your approaches will be rejected. It is still worthwhile investing your time even if there are rejections and you should consider these types of speculative approaches:

- Going to the employers' premises in person to ask if there are any vacancies. Take copies of your CV with you to leave if there are no current vacancies.
- Ringing up to ask whether there are any vacancies with speculative telephone calls.
- Sending your CV with a covering letter introducing yourself and what you have to offer.

4. Job-hopping

Not all employers will interpret a resume filled with many jobs the same way. How well or badly your job-hopping is taken depends on a number of factors. Think about these factors before your next interview.

- What market are you in? In some high-powered cities, having a series of jobs of less than two years is not necessarily seen as a bad thing — it is seen as a mark of an ambitious person who is constantly moving forward. In addition, some industries, like politics and consulting, are prone to frequent job movement.
- Are you moving up? Job-hopping is fine if there is a clear pattern of increasing responsibility. Employers tend to be sympathetic to a quest for greater responsibility. A lateral move can also be explained as exploring other careers or gaining relevant experience that would have been unavailable otherwise.
- How old are you? Most employers expect a certain amount of career exploration from recent grads. But the higher you go in your profession, and the more investment the company has to make in you, the less likely they are to want to invest in someone who they think will leave in a year.

Language and Culture Focus (语言文化要点)

>>>>>Reading I

1. **get ahead:** to do well; succeed. 取得进步, 获得成功

   【例句】In many parts of the world, personal influence is almost essential in getting ahead.

2. **on that basis alone:** only because of that. This is from the phrase "on the basis of".

   on the basis of: 在······的基础上

   【例句】The government prohibits discrimination on the basis of race, color, or national origin.

   　　We will work hard to build a new international order on the basis of the Five Principles of

Peaceful Coexistence.

3. Here traits which lead to success are generally considered to be the willingness to work hard (at any kind of job), scholarship or skill, initiative, an agreeable and outgoing personality.

【译文】这里，走向成功的品质通常被认为是努力工作(任何工作)的意愿、学识或技能、主动性以及随和外向的性格。

lead to: to result in. 导致(无被动形式)

【例句】This will lead to trouble in the future.

This scandal led to him/his resigning.

4. personality: the totality of qualities and traits, as of character or behavior, that are peculiar to a specific person. 人品，人格(品质和性格的总称。包括个性或行为，特别是指确定的人。)

【例句】Despite their different personalities, they became best friends.

A disease may cause changes in behavior and personality.

5. realm: an area of interest or activity. 界；领域，范围　　**synonyms: field, sphere**

【例句】The change in people's attitudes will slowly move from the realm of theory into the sphere of practice.

6. by and large: on the whole. 大体上；总的说来

【例句】By and large, your plan is a good one.

By and large, the principles and practices suggested here also will be of interest to any adults.

7. bestow: (formal) to give someone sth. of great value or importance. 给予

【例句】bestow sth. on/upon sb.

Honors were bestowed on him by the Queen.

8. disloyal: lacking loyalty. 不忠实的；不忠诚的

【例句】Two newspapers have been criticized for disloyal reporting of the war.

9. quit

1) to give up. 放弃；抛弃

【例句】quit a job

2) to abandon or put aside. 放弃；抛弃

【例句】I advised them to quit their dissipated (放荡的) ways.

10. 辨析 recipient, sponsor & patron

Sponsor is a business which pays for a show, broadcast, sports event, etc., usu. in return for advertising. 出资用表演、广播、运动比赛等做广告的节目赞助人

【例句】The opera house could not survive without commercial sponsors.

Sponsor also means a person who agrees to pay someone money, usu. for charity, if they complete (part of) an activity. 出于慈善目的而支持某人完成某行动的赞助人

Patron refers to a person or group that supports and gives money to an organization or activity that is regarded as valuable and deserving support. 赞助者；资助人

【例句】a patron of the arts

Many artists were dependent on wealthy patrons.

Patron also refers to a person who uses a particular shop, hotel, etc., esp. regularly. 老顾客/主顾

【例句】a special offer for our regular patrons

Recipient is someone who receives something. 接受者，领（承）受人

【例句】They are welfare recipients.

11. **security:** things that are done to keep a person, building, or country safe from danger or crime.

【例句】Workers want greater job security (=not being in danger of losing one's job).

This insurance plan offers your family financial security in the event of your death.

12. **mobility:** the movement of people, as from one social group, class, or level to another. 人的流动（如从一个社会集团、阶级或阶层移向另一社会集团、阶级或阶层）

【例句】There was downward mobility for Americans as a whole during the Great Depression.

在大萧条时期，美国人总的来说向下层社会阶层流动。

13. **better oneself:** to educate oneself. 自求上进；充实自己

【例句】People considered leisure time to be an opportunity to better oneself through learning, not merely to indulge in fun and games.

To function as a successful part of the team, a new director must fit the company's profile for personality, skills, and goals to better oneself.

14. **move upward(s)/up:** to get a better job in a company, or change to a more advanced group, higher rank, or higher level. 升职；上涨

【例句】To move up, you'll need the right training.

Share prices moved up this month.

The possibility for individuals to move upward in status is based on wealth, occupation, education, or some other social variables.

It's sure the price will move upward and may touch the price of 35 *yuan*.

Costs are moving upwards.

15. **qualify:** If something qualifies you to do something, you have the necessary skills, knowledge, ability, etc. to do it. 具有资格

It is usually used in this pattern: **qualify sb. for sth.**

【例句】Fluency in three languages qualifies her for work in the European Parliament.

16. **keep (on) doing sth.:** to continue doing sth. or to do the same thing many times; continue in an activity. 继续做下去

【例句】I keep thinking about Joe, all alone in that place.

I keep telling you, but you won't listen!

She pretended not to hear, and kept on walking back and forth.

I wish you wouldn't keep interrupting.

Keep going till you reach the traffic lights.

17. 辨析 personnel & personal

Personal is an adjective, which means "private; concerning, belonging to, or for the use of a particular person (私人的；个人的)".

【例句】the president's personal bodyguard

personal letter/matter/opinion/computer

Personnel refers to "all the people employed by a company, in the armed forces, or working in any organization (全体人员；员工；全体职员)".

【例句】army personnel

shortage of skilled personnel

She is studying personnel management.

Personnel may also mean "a department in an organization that deals with the complaints or difficulties of the people (人事部门)".

【例句】She works in personnel.

Personnel has/have lost my tax forms.

Speak to the personnel office about this.

18. somebody's roots: your relation to a place because you were born there, or your family used to live there. 根，根源

【例句】immigrants keeping in touch with their cultural roots

Alex Haley's story about his search for his roots became a bestseller.

19. as if ...: in a way that makes it seem that sth. is true or that sth. is happening. 仿佛；就好像

As if/though is usually used together with the subjunctive construction if it indicates this was actually not the situation.

【例句】I couldn't move my legs. It was as if they were stuck to the floor.

Why doesn't she buy us a drink? It isn't as if she had no money.

He spoke to me as if/though I were deaf.

He behaves as though he were better than us.

We've missed the bus. It looks as if we'll have to walk.

20. deal with:

1) to take action about; to tackle. 对付；应付；处理

【例句】Effective measures have been taken to deal with drug smuggling.

All complaints will be dealt with by the manager.

2) to do business/trade with. 与······做生意/交易

【例句】I've dealt with this store/person/company for 20 years.

21. They do not understand that a great many Americans like to move about.: "About" in this sentence means "here and there; in all directions or places (到处)".

【例句】They always go about together.

Papers are lying about on the floor.

There are a lot of colds about at the moment.

22. challenge: sth. that tests strength, skill, or ability, especially in a way that is interesting. 挑战

【例句】The company is ready to meet the challenges of the next few years.

23. be content with: to be happy and satisfied with. 满足于

【例句】We'll be content with a respectable result in tomorrow's match.

24. had the best of the man's thinking: got the best ideas from the man.

the best of sth.: a person or thing that is best.　最好的人；最佳之物

【例句】Even the best of us sometimes forgets things.

They're all good players, but he is the best of the bunch.

She's the best of the new young writers.

25. bring in

1) to cause to come in; introduce. 引进

【例句】They brought experienced people in to help.

Civic Association pledges to bring in money for school.

The policeman brought in (=to the police station) two boys he had caught stealing.

2）to produce as profit or income; earn. 获利；赚钱

【例句】The sale brought in over 200.

She is bringing in 250 a week.

26. start at a lower salary: In this phrase, "at" shows a price, rate, level, age, speed, etc. 表示价格、比率、水准、年龄、速度等以······；在······

【例句】sold at a price of ten cents each

stop working at 60

The temperature stood at 40 degrees.

The horse set off at a gallop.

I saw it at a distance.

Gas is selling at about \$1.35 a gallon.

You should have more sense at your age.

27. **Hopping is so readily accepted here, in fact, that a good man may bounce back and forth among two or three corporations, being welcomd back to his original company more than once through his career, each time at a different level.**

【译文】事实上，跳槽是件平常事，一个能人可能在2、3家公司间频繁跳槽，在他的职业生涯中不止一次地被欢迎回到原来公司，而每次回归层次都不同。

good: skilful; able to do sth. well

【例句】You can't keep a good man down. 优秀的人是抹杀不了的。

Bad times make a good man. 艰难困苦出能人。

28. **bounce:** to move up and down, especially because you are hitting a surface that is made of rubber, has springs, etc. 弹起

【例句】The kids were bouncing on the sofa.

29. **back and forth:** going in one direction and then in the opposite direction, and repeating this several times. 来回地，来来去去地

【例句】We travel back and forth all the time between Canada and England.

He was pacing back and forth across the room.

>>>>>Reading II

1. **Many positions are open to graduates of any discipline as employers are often interested in your potential rather than your existing knowledge.:** Many positions are available for graduates with different academic backgrounds because the bosses are more interested in those factors that will promote your further development instead of what you have learned in the past years.

【译文】有些职位并不讲究专业对口，不同学科和专业的毕业生都可以申请，因为雇主们感兴趣的是你的发展潜能，而不是你已掌握的知识。

be open to: If a job **is open to** someone, it means the job is available for someone to apply for.

【例句】I am afraid the vacancy is not open to those who have no working experience.

If someone is open to ideas or suggestions, it means he or she is willing or ready to accept them.

discipline: a branch of learning studied at a university. 大学的学科

2. **expertise:** special skill or knowledge in a particular field. 专门的技能和知识

【例句】professional expertise 职业技能

Her business expertise will be of great help to me.

She demonstrated considerable expertise in oil painting.

3. candidate: a person who wants to be chosen for a job.

【例句】We are prepared to take candidates from any academic discipline.

They are interviewing candidates for the position of sales manager.

A **candidate** can also be a person who wants to be chosen in an election (候选人) or a person who is prepared to take an examination (考生).

4. demonstrate motivation and skills: If you demonstrate a particular skill or something else, you show to other people that you have it.

demonstrate: to show or display (展示).

【例句】She has not demonstrated much generosity.

I will demonstrate how to operate the machine.

motivation: the state of being encouraged or inspired (动机, 动力).

【例句】The stronger the motivation, the more quickly one will learn a foreign language.

As his father is a millionaire, he has no motivation to get a job.

5. procedure: the right way or order of doing sth. 手续

【例句】the procedure for opening a savings account 存折开户手续

the procedure for tax refund service 退税手续

the proper procedure to be followed in decision making

6. have become explicitly focused on motivation and competency: to have clearly given more attention to motivation and competency.

explicitly: clearly. If something is explicit, it's clearly and fully expressed so that there is no doubt about what is meant.

【例句】This was explicitly admitted by the Prime Minister.

focused on: to direct one's attention to sth.; to look at sth. or think about sth. carefully; to concentrate on. 关注, 集中注意力

【例句】Focus your attention on your work.

Today we are supposed to focus on the issue of unemployment.

competency: the ability to do sth. well or effectively. 能力

7. It is not uncommon to find ...: It is quite common and natural to find ...

It is not uncommon for sb. to do sth.: It is usual for sb. to do sth ... 并不少见

【例句】It is not uncommon for students to have bank loans.

It is not uncommon that a sunny morning will turn out to be a cloudy day at this time of the year. 一个晴朗的早晨变成阴天, 每年这个时候都并不少见。

注意: 否定词＋uncommon 表示经常发生的现象

【例句】Violent crimes against the elderly are not uncommon in this district.

Such attitudes were not at all uncommon thirty years ago. 这些看法在 30 年前很常见。

8. **teamwork:** the ability of a group of people to work together effectively. 团队协作

9. **be popular with:** to be liked by many people.

　【例句】The teacher is very popular with the students.

　　　　　Swimming is very popular with people of all ages.

10. **recruiter:** a person who hires or finds new members for a company or organization.

11. **via electronic means:** by using electronic equipment.

　via: through; by means of

12. **appropriate:** suitable for a particular occasion.

　【例句】This is an appropriate moment to raise this issue. 此时此刻提出这个问题非常合适。

13. **constructive:** useful; helping to improve or develop sth. 建设性的

14. **take on:** to accept (tasks); agree to do some work or be responsible for sth. 接受或承担（任务）

　【例句】Don't take on too much work — the extra cash isn't worth it.

　　　　　The doctor advised me not to take on any more work.

15. **contribute to:** to help make sth. successful. 有助于；促成

　【例句】The advertising campaign has greatly contributed to the success of the new car.

　　　　　Smoking is a major factor contributing to cancer. 吸烟是致癌的一个重要因素。

16. **take the lead (in doing sth.):** to start to act ; to be the first to start doing sth. or be most active in doing sth. 占主要地位, 率先, 带头

　【例句】The US took the lead in declaring war on terrorism

　　　　　He always takes the lead in group discussions.

　　　　　China has taken the lead in car production. 中国在汽车生产中居首位。

　　　　　They took the lead in conducting the experiments. 他们带头做试验。

17. **logical:** having or showing clear reasoning.

　【例句】It is logical that people who earn money should pay more taxes.

18. **self-awareness:** the ability to perceive one's own existence, including one's own traits, feelings and behaviors. Self-awareness is a personal understanding of the very core of one's own identity. 自我意识

19. **put ... across:** to describe or explain sth. to someone successfully. 解释清楚；说明

　【例句】You need the skill to put your ideas across.

　　　　　It's very difficult to put across the fact.

20. **interpersonal:** concerning the relationship between people. 人与人之间的, 人际关系的

　【例句】interpersonal relationship

　　　　　interpersonal communication skills

21. **daunt:** to make someone lose courage or determination. 使气馁, 使胆怯

【例句】He was daunted by the high quality of work they expected.

He was not daunted by the difficulties facing him.

dauntless: not easily discouraged; fearless. 无畏的

【例句】dauntless fighter

22. **It is not enough to mention that you are a good communicator:** If you just mention that you are good at communicating with people, it's not enough. You need to do something more than that.

It is not enough to do sth.: 仅仅做某事是不够的

【例句】It is not enough for a student to attend the class. Moreover she/he should preview the lesson ahead.

It's not enough for an employee to save some money. She/he should buy comprehensive insurance.

23. **CV:** curriculum vitae. 简历

24. **you need to qualify it with a description of relevant experience:** you need to add a more detailed description of your relevant experience so that it may become more specific.

If you qualify a description or statement, you add more details to it so that it becomes more specific.

【例句】You will have to qualify your statement with more details.

relevant: connected with what is being talked or written about.

【例句】You'd better offer some information that is relevant to this issue.

25. **set criteria:** fixed standards or principles on which a judgement or decision is based. 固定的标准

26. **applicant:** a person who makes a request for a job.

【例句】a long waiting list of applicants for jobs

We have 200 applicants for the job.

27. **These may be laid out clearly in the person specification or be identifiable from the job description, advertisement or the organization's web pages.**

【译文】这些标准可能清楚地写在了用人要求中，或者也可以从岗位介绍、招聘广告或该机构的网页上找到。

lay out: to express or present ideas and information.

【例句】The article has laid out all the advantages of exploring overseas market.

person specification: an extension of the job description. It is a profile of the type of person needed to do a job.

identifiable: easy to be discovered or recognized.

28. **match:** If one thing matches something else, they are the same as one another, or they have similar qualities.

【例句】We have developed a throw-away mentality to match the throw-away products.

29. **outcome:** result.

【例句】to predict the outcome of the general election

A series of coincidences have led to an unexpected outcome.

30. **concise:** short and clear; expressing effectively without any unnecessary words. 简明的，简洁的

   【例句】a concise explanation

   a concise speech

31. **Employers cannot simply take your word for it:** Employers will not simply believe what you have talked or written about. 老板不会只相信你所说的话。

   take ... for: to consider them in a particular way. 以为，把……看作

   【例句】Of course I won't tell anyone! What do you take me for? (=what sort of person do you think I am?)

   I take it (=I assume) you've heard that Rick's resigned

32. **focus on presenting evidence:** to give full attention to the provision of evidence. 关注证据的提供

   focus on: direct one's attention to something and think about it carefully.

   【例句】focus on the issue of homeless people

   present: *v.* to offer or show sth.

   【例句】present a new image

   present figures in different ways

   present my point of view

33. **academic projects and achievements:** 学业任务和成就

   Academic is frequently used to describe work done in schools, colleges and universities, especially work that involves studying and reasoning rather than practical or technical skills. 学术的，学业的

   【例句】academic standards 学术标准

   academic studies 学术研究

   academic qualifications 学术资格

   academic year 学年

34. **voluntary activities:** actions that one chooses to do without being paid for it. 志愿者活动

   voluntary: acting willingly, without being forced or paid.

   【例句】voluntary society 志愿者团体

>>>>>> Extended Activities

A. Function and Structure: Describing One's Occupation

1. Expressions presented in this part can be used to describe one's job and job-related experiences, but

don't forget that it's often considered to be very impolite or even rude to inquire about a person's income directly. In some corporate cultures, employees are not allowed to compare and exchange information about salaries, rewards, bonuses, or other benefits they receive respectively. A probe into the details of one's work responsibilities is also prohibitive in most cases. But for most young job starters, to learn something about the job they are going to take is essential for them to avoid job-hopping later: Is this job at the right level for you? Are you going to be proud of what you are doing? Are you earning less than others in the same position? You may approach friends, relatives or career advisors for such information. It's also a good idea to explore further into a certain job position at the interview. To discuss things like what you are expected to do exactly at work and what you can obtain from the job will impress the interviewers that you are rather serious about the job offer.

2. What's your line: Line here refers to one's trade, occupation, or field of interest. Your line of business or work is the kind of work that you do.

【例句】The best job you can get in our line is in a nationalized industry.

3. Words and expressions relating to income:

- **salary:** fixed compensation for services, paid to a person on a regular basis 薪水, 薪金, 付给一个人的固定劳动补偿, 尤指公职人员、职员等拿的按年、按月或按周计算的年薪、月薪或周薪。

- **wages:** payment for labor or services to a worker, especially remuneration on an hourly, daily, or weekly basis or by the piece 尤指按小时、天数或周给或按工作量给的工资。

- **pay:** money given in return for work done 酬金, 包括工资, 薪金。
  overtime pay: payment for additional work done outside of regular working hours 加班费, 对在正常工作时间之外做的额外工作所付的报酬。

- **bonus:** a sum of money or the equivalent given to an employee in addition to the employee's usual compensation 奖金, 给雇员工资以外的一笔钱或相应的东西。

- **income:** the amount of money or its equivalent received during a period of time in exchange for labor or services, from the sale of goods or property, or as profit from financial investments 收入

- **allowance:** something, such as money, given at regular intervals or for a specific purpose 津贴, 补贴

- **fringe benefits:** an additional benefit provided to an employee, for example, a company car or health insurance 额外福利

4. shift: It can mean "a group of workers who work for a period of time during the day or night, and are then replaced by another group who continue the same work". （轮班的工人）

【例句】Despite double shifts in some of its car assembly plants, the company failed to meet the targets.

It also can mean "the period of time during which one of these groups of people is at work". （轮班的时间）

【例句】In order to look after her baby, Mary chose the midnight to 8 shift. Peter is on the day shift and I am on the night shift.

go on shift 上班

go off shift 下班

to work in three shifts 三班制

5. **punch out**: to leave work, or record the time of departure from work by inserting a personalized card into a time clock. 打卡下班或离岗

knock off: to finish work at the end of the day, or to stop working or doing something in order to take a break. 收工

B. Special Use: Words of Job Application

英语中有许多表达与工作和求职有关。在这一部分，我们将围绕 job 一词，学习一些相关的词和词组。

1. the type of work that someone does:

- **profession:** a type of work such as teaching, medicine, or law, for which you need special training and have to pass special examinations and which people usually regard with respect.

  【例句】the teaching/medical/legal profession

- **occupation:** a word used especially in an official context meaning someone's usual full-time job.

  【例句】Men in manual occupations tend to be less prone to stress-related illnesses.

- **business:** the general area of work that you are involved in such as buying and selling a particular type of thing.

  【例句】In our business the first rule is that the customer is always right.

- **trade:** a type of job which you use your hands to do skillful work such as building houses, making furniture, or repairing cars. 手艺

  【例句】Most of the men had worked in skilled trades such as carpentry or printing.

- **career:** the type of work that you do or wish to do for most of your working life.

  【例句】Like his father, Tommy chose a career in the army.

- **vocation:** a job such as being a nurse, a priest or a teacher, which you do because you have a strong feeling that you want to do it, especially in order to help other people, and not because you want to get a lot of money.

  【例句】Nursing is hard work and often low paid, but for many people it is a vocation.

2. a job that you have in addition to your main job:

- **sideline:** a job that you do in addition to your main job, especially because it is something that you enjoy or are interested in.

  【例句】She's a lawyer, but she sells her own paintings as a sideline.

- **on the side:** if you do a job on the side, you do it secretly or unofficially, in addition to your main job.

  【例句】It is difficult to estimate the number of people doing part-time jobs on the side.

3. a job in a company or organization, esp. one that involves responsibility:

- **post:** a word meaning a job in an organization, especially a permanent and fairly important position.

  【例句】She has been offered the post of director.

  　　　　When he took up his teaching post he was only 23.

- **position:** a word meaning a job at a particular level in a company or organization, used especially when advertising a job.

  【例句】We have decided to offer you the position of sales assistant starting next Monday.

  　　　　What position did you hold at your previous company?

  　　　　The position has already been filled.

4. to have a job:

- **fill a vacancy:**

  【例句】In times of recession, employers have no trouble filling vacancies.

- **have/get/keep a job:**

  【例句】George had a well-paid job in a computer company.

- **be in work:**

  【例句】She was the only one in the family to be in work.

- **hold down a job:** keep a job even though it is difficult to do.

  【例句】It's difficult taking care of three children and holding down a full-time job in a busy office.

5. not to have a job:

- **not have a job:**

  【例句】I don't have a job yet, but I'm going for an interview tomorrow.

- **be without a job:**

  【例句】She has been without a job for three months.

- **be out of / lose work:**

  【例句】At the age of 40, he suddenly found himself out of work.

- **unemployed:**

【例句】The accused man was an unemployed clerk from South London.

- **jobless:**

  【例句】Because of the recession, many workers find themselves not only jobless but also homeless.

- **be on the dole:**

  【例句】I'm fed up with being on the dole. I want a job.

6. to give someone a job:

- **employ:**

  【例句】I was employed as a night-watchman by the local hospital.

- **hire:**

  【例句】Some politicians hire experts to write speeches for them.

- **appoint:**

  【例句】I can't understand why they decided to appoint Wilson as managing director.

- **recruit:**

  【例句】Corporations are being encouraged to recruit more black and women workers.

- **sign up:**

  【例句】The famous soccer star was signed up by an Italian club.

- **take on:**

  【例句】We are not taking on any more staff at the moment.

- **make:**

  【例句】No one thought they would make him manager.

7. other useful expressions:

resign from/quit a job	辞职
job satisfaction	对工作的满足感
job security	对工作的安全感
job-hopping	跳槽
job-hopper	经常跳槽的人
lay off	解雇；下岗
career development	职业发展
career advancement/progress	工作升迁
career prospect	工作前途
a rise/raise in salary	加薪
close down	破产；关闭
challenging job	具有挑战性的工作
self-realization	自我实现

steady	稳定的
expertise	专业技术
seniority	资历
promotion	晋升
adjust oneself	自我调整
head hunting	猎头

C. Practical Reading

这是一道图表题。这类题目其实比较简单，关键是要读懂图表中各个项目之间的关系，抓住其中的关键词（通常都是实词），逐项填妥即可。请注意以下内容：

1. PR: Public Relations 公关

2. to do ten things at once: 字面上是"同时做10件事"，相当于说"办事高效"

3. leading: 领先的

4. a superb opportunity: 口语化说法，意思是"绝佳的机会"

5. a *Fortune* 500 US manufacturer: 一家名列《财富》杂志500强的美国制造商

6. has ... open: 有……职位空缺

7. Associate Bachelor Degree: 大专文凭

8. equivalent: 同等水平

9. secretarial skills: 文书工作

10. power point documents: 电子幻灯演示文档

11. files: 档案资料

12. corporate culture: 企业文化

13. competitive compensation & benefit package: 有竞争力的补助和福利套餐

14. Human Resources Department: 人力资源部

Teaching Tips （教学提示）

1. Lead-in 本单元导入部分含听力理解和听写填空两项任务。听力理解部分围绕单元主题job hunting安排了一篇关于网络求职的讲座类材料。在进行听力活动前，教师可以先请学生谈谈求职者一般可以采取哪些方式来寻找就业机会，这些求职方法各自的优缺点，以及他们对网络求职的看法。语篇篇幅较长，被分为两个部分，共设有五项听力练习。第一和第二项练习针对语篇的上半部分，第二和第三项练习针对语篇的下半部分，第五项练习则为针对全篇的综合性练习。第一和第三项练习均为预听活动，主要目的是让学生对所听语篇的主旨（Gist）有所了解，初步把握听音和理解上的难点所在，为接下来的听力活动做好心理和词汇上的准备。第二和第四项练习属于在预听基础上进行的精听活动，旨在考查学生对语篇主旨的把握以及细节的辨析能力。第二项练习系最常见的多项选择题（Multiple-choice Questions）题型；第三项练习要求学生从给出的 12 个短句（Short Statements）中选择正确的答案来回答问题。教师在听音前应提醒学生，该题系多选题型，每个问题不止一个答案，学生必须借助适当的笔记，对所听到的信息点快速地进行甄别和归类。第五项练习为简答题。第一题要求学生列出网络求职具体的 7 大步骤，相当于作一个大纲式（outline）的笔记，列出各部分的标题 (heading)。第二题其实是一个开放式的问题，教师可以安排学生以 pair work 或 group work 的形式，结合讲座中所提到的内容，做一个简短的口头陈述来说明自己的观点。听写填空（Spot Dictation）主要检验学生对介词用法、时间表达和日常活动词语的掌握，可以作为导入活动安排在 Reading II 课文的讲解之前进行。

2. Reading I Brainstorming: 全班学生通过自由讨论的形式，列出他们在求职时可能会考虑的一些因素，描绘他们心目中最理想的职业。有些因素人人都会考虑，有些则是因人而异。教师可以用 What does an ideal job mean to you? Good pay? High status? What is your first consideration in choosing your job? 之类的话导入对该问题的思考。教师也可给出一些情境进一步激发学生的思考，如：Suppose you are a mother with a young baby to look after/Suppose you are allergic to cigarette smoking/Suppose you like traveling very much/Suppose you are a very ambitious young man/Suppose you want to have more free time for your hobbies ... what will you consider first in choosing jobs?

3. Reading I Pairwork: 由学生双人结对，讨论与本单元主题 jobs and occupations 相关的问题。这些问题其实是 Brainstorming 活动的延伸和扩展。在处理 Question 1 时，教师可让学生按 priority 来排列在 Brainstorming 活动中列出的各项内容，和同伴互相对照，并说出各自的理由。在讨论 Question 2 时，学生可能会只局限于 a well-paid job 或是 a poorly paid job 两种选择，为活跃课堂气氛，提高学生学习兴趣，教师也可根据不同的课堂反应，给出一个学生意想不到的回答，如 I will choose a well-paid job first, no matter I like it or not. And I will work hard and try to accumulate as much wealth as I can. Then I will quit my well-paid job to do whatever I really enjoy, no matter it pays well or not. Question 3 中最后关于学生对 job-hopping 的看法旨在导入对本单元课文的学习。

4. 关于职业和收入的词汇，可参考 Special Use: Words of Job Application 和 Notes for Function and Structure。

5. Reading I 练习 IV: Question 7 中 merit 指的是 demonstrated ability or achievement, 能力或功绩。本句的意思是"应根据功绩而不是资历来提拔或是奖赏一个人"。Question 10 中 white collar 白领，指非体力劳动者，脑力劳动者。类似的说法还有 blue collar 蓝领，上层体力劳动者。pink collar 粉领，指主要由妇女从事的工作，如秘书、护士、职员等。

6. Reading I Post-reading: 由三项活动组成。第一项活动要求学生列出人们job-hopping的各种原因，教师可建议学生参照Brainstorming的讨论结果。第二项活动由学生分组讨论job-hopping的正负面。对job-hopping这一现象，仁者见仁，智者见智，意见不一。课文对job-hopping的正面涉及颇多，可要求学生仔细阅读课文，予以归纳总结。job-hopping的负面可参见下文：

Disadvantages in Job-hopping

Changing jobs frequently can do your career more harm than good. If you have been in more than three jobs over the last five years, you may need to seriously assess your job-hopping habit.

Potential employers are often cautious about employing job-hoppers and they would want to know why you have not stayed long in any particular job.

Changing jobs frequently reflects badly on your resilience and loyalty as an employee. You could be seen as someone who lacks self-motivation, is directionless or prone to feeling restless at the workplace. In addition, recruiters may not be convinced that you have gained enough experiences and on-the-job skills since you have not stayed in any particular company for very long. They are also worried that you may leave them shortly after they have hired you, forcing them to start the recruiting process all over again! Certain workers may feel that job-hopping provides them with a wide exposure to different work environments. By changing jobs frequently, they have found that their network of business contacts is wider and in some cases, switching jobs has meant a faster way of getting a salary raise. However, these workers need to weigh such advantages against the negative perception that potential employers would have about their constant job-changing habits.

Workers with a set career plan would see that the short-term benefits (for example, a quicker salary jump) will not make up for the depth of experience that they stand to gain from staying on a job. Under what circumstances will it be considered acceptable to job-hop? During the initial stage of your career, you may find that you are not sure of which direction to take, or which job and industry will suit you best.

During this uncertain period, it would be common to see young workers staying on a job for one or two years. Potential employers might find this acceptable and understand the need for young people to try out a few jobs before finding their "niche".

However, if you are already at executive or management level, job-hopping would be frowned upon. A minimum stay of three or four years is required to give a worker good grounding. With senior executives, a stay of five to seven years or longer would be an acceptable timeline.

第三项活动由学生以报纸专栏作家的身份为一个想跳槽的年轻银行职员出谋划策。下面的材料供参考。

Dear Catherine,

Quit, but not yet. First find another job that offers the same pay but more interesting work. Use your breaks and weekends to surf help-wanted websites and call prospective employers. But stay at the bank until you land one. How do you know the next job will be better? Ask questions during the job interview. Ask the interviewer for a detailed job description and ask yourself whether those duties interest you. Also ask about the promotion prospects for top-performing workers. Finally, chat with a few would-be co-workers to see how they like the job. When you switch to a more rewarding job with no change in pay, your parents can't be too angry.

Supplementary Activity

Can Job-Hopping Hurt Your Chances?

Suppose you work for a newspaper and are responsible for a column called JUST ASK. An executive concerned with his frequent job changes wants to know how to put the best face on his work history now that the job market has slowed down. Could you offer him some advice?

JUST ASK

Dear Sir or Madam,

I've made a lot of quick moves in my career, each for greater responsibility, and now that the economy has slowed, I'm concerned about how this "job-hopping" will be perceived by potential employers. Do you have any advice on how these moves can be best presented during my next search?

Thanks!

Larry

Dear Larry,

If you suspect your job history may be considered negatively by potential employers, then you should assume it will and take the initiative in addressing the issue during a search. In taking a proactive approach to confronting this potential problem, you will have greater control over the direction of the discussion, which will help you present the issue in the most favorable light possible. This approach should also be applied to other potential "objections" that may exist, such as age, lack of industry specific experience, etc.

When discussing your frequent moves it's important to demonstrate the increased responsibility you took on while helping the interviewer understand that another sudden change is not likely to happen again.

In a tight employment market, quick career moves are often the result of unexpected opportunities that can't be passed up — even at the risk of creating a perception of job-hopping. If this accurately describes your situation, highlight the challenges presented by each new job in detail, then emphasize how they helped you become better prepared to succeed in the position under consideration.

Your ability to explain this rationale effectively will be vital to your job search success. Therefore, it would be wise to spend some time creating a few key messages that can be used to discuss your work history during an interview. In addition to these messages, compile a list of questions you anticipate about your career moves then carefully draft positive answers that can be used in a discussion. This sort of preparation will prove invaluable as you move forward.

Hope this is helpful.

7. Reading II Cloze

Question 1　　an American invested company 指由美方投资的公司。若选a, investing company 意为投资公司, 与后文provides a comprehensive framework of digital services for e-Business and e-Commerce不符。

Question 2　　fast为副词, 修饰growing, 故选a。

Question 7　　If something is below a particular amount, rate, or level, it is less or lower than that amount, rate, or level. Beneath无此用法。Age below 30, 年龄小于30。Age above 30, 年龄超过30。根据上下文意思, 应选d, below。

Question 8　　on duty, 固定搭配, 意为 "上班"。

Question 11　选a, minimum, 指the least possible quantity or degree, 最低、尽可能小的数量或程度。<u>Minimum</u> 5-year HR (Human Resources) administration experiences 意思是至少5年人事管理经验。选项c不对, 应改为at least。

Question 12　选项c, command, 名词。意思是ability to control or use; mastery, 精通。如: command of four languages, 精通4种语言。

Question 13　diploma指文凭, degree指学位, 都可以和college搭配使用, 因后文有or above, 故选d。

Question 14　选d, applicants, 特指应聘者。

Key （练习答案）

>>>>>>**Reading I**

Pre-reading

I. Things people may consider in choosing their jobs:

job security	good pay
challenging work	no stress
distance from work	commuting time
opportunities to work independently	team spirit
employee shareholding program	retirement benefits
day-care service	overtime work
paid holidays	vacation time
working environment	interesting/friendly coworkers
prestigious title	job status
medical and dental plan	varied work
chance to meet important people	travel opportunities
relaxed dress code	staff appraisal system
good interpersonal relations with superiors	company insurance
equal opportunities regardless of sex	recreation & sports facilities

in-service training	promotion prospects
flexible working hours/schedule	good boss
exercise activities at lunch time	no-smoking policy
company car	expense account
friends working there	recognition

Exercises

II. 1. c   2. b   3. d   4. c   5. b

III. 1. personality   2. sponsor   3. mobility   4. personnel   5. original

     6. challenge   7. bestow   8. bounce   9. outgoing   10. reciprocal

IV. 1. led to   2. got ahead   3. as if   4. to better themselves

     5. on the basis of   6. to move upward   7. seniority   8. do-it-yourself

     9. to deal with   10. content with

V. 1. One of his traits is criticizing his wife in public.

     2. I've found he's most agreeable among colleagues.

     3. If I don't get a pay rise, I'll quit.

     4. Reducing the gap between the rich and the poor is one of the challenges facing the government.

     5. He's never been an outgoing type.

     6. By and large, the company's been doing pretty good business.

>>>>>Reading II

Exercises

I. 1. NM   2. F   3. T   4. F   5. T   6. T   7. T   8. F   9. T   10. T

III. 1. b   2. a   3. c   4. d   5. a   6. c   7. a   8. b   9. d   10. b

IV. 1. Since he came to work in the company after graduation from college, he has got ahead fast in his job.

     2. The change of supply and demand leads to the fluctuation of the rate of exchange.

     3. By and large, if nobody wants to buy our product or service, our business will have to be closed down.

4. Everything went on as usual in the stock market as if nothing had happened.

5. The company has clearly put across that since it brought in advanced technology and equipment, significant improvements have been made in the new car's fuel economy.

6. He was not content with the present plan, and kept thinking over how to improve it.

7. It's not enough for a school to have short-term aims. It should lay out long-term objectives for the school's development to better its education quality.

8. The person who takes on the job should be qualified with a good knowledge of French history and culture.

9. During the summer holidays, the library is open to the public every day except Tuesday.

10. It's not uncommon that if a company takes the lead in launching a promotion campaign, other companies may follow.

V. 1. b   2. a   3. c   4. c   5. a   6. c   7. d   8. b   9. c   10. b
11. a   12. c   13. d   14. d   15. a

>>>>>Extended Activities

B. Special Use

I.

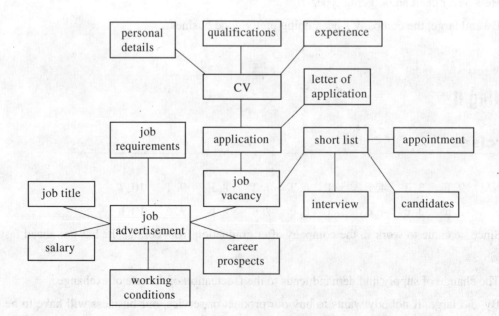

II.

The company usually advertises the job vacancy in a newspaper. The advertisement usually gives the job title and a description of the job requirements. It sometimes gives the salary and describes the working conditions and career prospects as well.

The applicant usually sends in a letter of application and a curriculum vitae or CV, which gives personal details and lists qualifications and experience. The company then makes a short list of the most suitable candidates and invites them for an interview. The company then chooses the best candidate and makes an appointment.

III.

Verb	Activity	Person 1	Person 2
employ	employment	employer	employee
interview	interview	interviewer	interviewee
train	training	trainer	trainee

C. Practical Reading

What Do You Know About the Ads?		
Item	Ad I	Ad II
Name of the recruiting units	Anglo-European PR Company	Eaton (China) Investment Co., Ltd
Job title	a role working with Director of Travel	administrative assistant
Personal qualities	1. hard-working 2. flexible 3. well-organized 4. energetic	Not Mentioned
Job duties	1. attending presentations 2. arranging meetings, travel and lunches 3. working with executives of major international companies	1. serve as a travel coordination 2. provide assistance with special projects and assignments as directed by managers 3. assist managers to prepare Power Point documents 4. assist Sales Department to maintain promotion materials and files

（续　表）

What Do You Know About the Ads?		
Item	Ad I	Ad II
Necessary qualifications for application	1. can do ten things at once 2. remain cool and calm in a crisis	1. associate bachelor degree in English/ business administration major or equivalent 2. minimum of three years related working experience 3. bilingual, with professional secretarial skills
Pay	a top salary with bonuses	1. a good corporate culture 2. competitive compensation 3. benefit package
Ways of application	call or write	send English and Chinese resumes

D. Additional Vocabulary

I.　1. actress　　　　2. waitress　　　　3. policewoman　　　4. stewardess

　　5. postwoman　　　6. doctress　　　　7. governess　　　　8. saleswoman

　　9. manageress　　　10. conductress　　11. sportswoman　　12. woman driver

　　13. workwoman　　　14. lawyeress　　　15. woman scientist　　16. woman pilot

　　17. spacewoman　　　18. businesswoman

II.　1. male model　　　2. male nurse　　　3. male typist　　　4. male secretary

　　5. male babysitter　　6. male kindergartner

F. Humor Time

　　1. Typist　　　2. Grocer　　　3. Surgeon　　　4. Tailor

Unit 5
Eating Habits

Teaching Aim （教学目的）

1. Cognitive Information （认知信息）: American and British Eating Habits; Food and Nutrition

2. Language Focus （内容重点）
   — **Key Words:** I. selection, available, nutrition, purchase, quantity, skip, consequence, consume, compile, awareness, fat, carbohydrate, fiber, cereal; II. emphasis, trend, survive, boil, fry, scramble, roast, mash, bake, steam, serve, decorate, resort, exotic, ethnic
   — **Phrases:** I. eat out, on the average, be a threat to, in a the/ (*adj.*) mood for, rich in, a variety of; II. associate with, begin with, in general
   — **Useful Structures:** used to ...

   no longer ...

   while ..., ... (clause for contrast)

   with ... (absolute structure)

   — **Grammar:** Degrees of Adjectives and Adverbs
3. Communicative Skills （交际技能）
   — **Expressions:** Ordering a Meal
   — **Reading:** Menus

Lead-in 导入

>>>>>**Listening Comprehension Tasks**

Difficult Words & Expressions

1. define: to give the precise meaning of; describe the nature or basic qualities of　给……下定义；阐释

2. a sense of belonging: 归属感

3. learned behavior: 后天行为

4. etiquette: the practices and forms prescribed by social convention or by authority　礼节

5. snack: a small amount of food or beverage eaten between meals　小吃, 点心

6. portion size: （一餐的）份额大小

7. ritual: a ceremonial form　仪式

8. norm: a standard, model or pattern regarded as typical　规范

9. sociologist: a specialist who studies human social behaviors and the development of human society　社会学家

10. component: a constituent element　组成部分

11. substitute: one that takes the place of another　替代品

12. tofu: a protein-rich food coagulated from an extract of soybeans　豆腐

13. accompaniment: sth. added for completeness　补充物

14. delicacy: pleasing and appealing food　美味佳肴

15. compliance with: 顺从, 依从

16. proscription: prohibition　禁止

17. prohibit: to forbid by authority　禁止

18. indicator: any of various statistical valu es that provide an indication of the condition　指标

19. edible: 可食用的

20. nutritional value: 营养价值

21. complex: complicated, intricate　复杂的

22. status: a state of affairs, situation　情形, 状况

23. food labelling laws: 食品标签法

24. external: relating to, existing on, or connected with the outside　外部的

25. internal: relating to, existing on, or connected with the inside 内部的

Passage Script 1

Joanne: Dr. Anderson, how would you define eating habits?

David: The term eating habits refers to why and how people eat, which foods they eat, and with whom they eat. Individual, social, cultural, religious, economic and political factors all influence people's eating habits.

Joanne: Can you tell us why and how people eat?

David: All humans eat to survive. They also eat to express appreciation, for a sense of belonging, as part of family customs, and for self-realization. For example, someone who is not hungry may eat a piece of cake that has been baked in his or her honor. People eat according to learned behaviors regarding etiquette, meal and snack patterns, food combinations and portion sizes. Etiquette refers to acceptable behaviors. For example, for some groups it is acceptable to lick one's fingers while eating, while for other groups this is rude behavior. Etiquette and eating rituals also vary depending on whether the meal is formal or informal. How people eat is determined by a variety of factors, including economic circumstances, cultural norms, and religious restrictions.

Joanne: According to your observation as a sociologist, what do people eat in their daily life?

David: The components of a meal vary across cultures, but generally include grains, such as bread, rice or noodles; meat or a meat substitute, such as fish, beans, or tofu; and accompaniments, such as vegetables. A meal is usually defined as the consumption of two or more foods in a structured setting at a set time. A common eating pattern is three meals per day, including breakfast, lunch and dinner, with snacks between meals.

Passage Script 2

Joanne: Dr. Anderson, how do people determine what food they should accept in general?

David: In each culture there are both acceptable and unacceptable foods, though this is not determined by whether or not something is edible. For example, horses, turtles and dogs are eaten, and even considered a delicacy, in some cultures, though they are unacceptable food sources in other cultures.

Joanne: What are the major influences on food choices?

David: There are many factors that determine what foods a person eats. In addition to personal preferences, there are cultural, social, religious, economic and even political factors. First, a cultural group provides guidelines regarding acceptable foods, food combinations, eating patterns, and eating behaviors. Compliance with these guidelines creates a sense of identity and belonging for the individual. Second, members of a social group depend on each other, share a common culture, and influence each other's behaviors and values. For example, a young person at a basketball game may eat certain foods when accompanied by friends and other foods when accompanied by his or her teacher. Third, there are religious proscriptions ranging from a few to many. This will affect a follower's food choices and behaviors. For example, in some religions specific foods are prohibited, such as pork among Jewish people and Muslims. When it comes to the economic influences, money, values and consumer skills all affect what a person purchases. The price of a food, however, is not an indicator of its nutritional value. Cost is a complex combination of a food's availability, status and demand. Finally, political factors also influence food availability and trends. Food laws and trade agreements affect what is available within and across countries, and also affect food prices. Food labeling laws determine what consumers know about the food they purchase.

Joanne: Can I say that eating habits are thus the result of both external factors, such as politics, and internal factors, such as values. These habits are formed, and may change, over a person's lifetime.

David: Absolutely!

Key

II. 1. d   2. a   3. c   4. a   5. b   6. c

IV. 1. d   2. a   3. c   4. d   5. b   6. b

>>>>>Spot Dictation

Eating habits refer to why and <u>how</u> people eat, <u>which</u> foods they eat, and with <u>whom</u> they eat. People eat in order to <u>survive</u> and according to learned <u>behaviors</u>, including etiquette, meal <u>patterns</u>, food combinations and <u>portion</u> sizes. A common eating pattern is three meals <u>per day</u>, with <u>snacks</u> between meals. In each <u>culture</u> there are both acceptable and <u>unacceptable</u> foods. The major <u>influences</u> that determine <u>what</u> foods a person eats involve personal <u>preferences</u> and cultural, <u>social</u> religious, <u>economic</u> and even <u>political</u> factors.

Background Information（背景知识）

1. American eating habits

For the most part, Americans want their food to be quick, convenient, and cheap — regardless of whether they buy it at a supermarket or a local fast-food franchise. For lunch, sandwiches are the commonest food. Salads are also popular. For supper, the most popular has got to be steak and baked potato. Chicken and pizza are also popular. Americans like things that are fast and easy, requiring minimal personal or economic sacrifice. Americans also value "looking good" and choose foods that "look good." Some are even willing to spend a lot of money for food that makes them "look good" — as when they eat in expensive restaurants. The characteristics of America's dominant food culture are cost, convenience, and appearance. However, a new American food ethic is emerging to challenge these dominant values. The rapid growth in demand for "alternative food products" — including organic, natural, pesticide free, hormone and antibiotic free, grass-fed, etc. — is one indicator of the new food ethic, which reflects a desire to care for the earth and its people.

2. Diet

Americans have a love-hate relationship with dieting and exercise. They purchase millions of diet books and invest in gym memberships and exercise equipment but the number of calories they consume continues to rise. The majority of US adults and 15% of US children are overweight or obese. Despite a strong interest in healthy eating, Americans continue to consume snacks and sweets at alarming rates. Americans are also unwilling to forego convenience or taste for health benefits. More and more Americans are relying on fast food, shelf stable meals, and prepared foods, rather than cooking from scratch. Consumers' food attitudes are also changing, reflected in the growing popularity of low carbohydrate products, functional foods and vegetarian and organic foods.

3. British eating habits

The British people tend to have a big breakfast before they go to work and the meal at midday is not spent with the members of the family but with workmates or schoolmates. Lunch is normally eaten between 12:30 pm and 1:30 pm. Most people finish work at five thirty. It often takes at least an hour to get home from the school or workplace, so people tend to eat their evening meal or "dinner" between 6:30 pm and 8 pm. On Sundays people don't have to work, so they usually get up very late and have a meal called *brunch*, which means a combination of breakfast and lunch. Sunday lunch is usually the best meal of the week and many of the typically British food are eaten for Sunday lunch. For example roast beef and Yorkshire pudding.

Breakfast

Generally speaking, the British breakfast is much bigger than in most other countries. Many people like to have a fried breakfast, which consists of fried bacon and eggs with fried bread and possibly fried tomatoes or black pudding. Of course not everybody wants to eat a lot early in the morning and many people prefer to just eat toast and marmalade with tea or coffee. Cereals are also very popular. The most common is cornflakes. They are made with different grains such as corn, wheat, oats, etc. In Scotland many people eat "porridge" or boiled oats. Porridge is very heavy but in winter it will keep you warm on your way to school.

Packed lunch

If you go to Britain to study English and you stay with a family you will almost certainly be given a "packed lunch" to eat for your midday meal. Some factories and schools have canteens where you can eat but the packed lunch is the most common thing to eat. A packed lunch normally consists of some sandwiches, a packet of crisps, an apple and a can of something to drink, for example, coca-cola. The contents are kept in a plastic container and you take it with you when you go to school or work.

Dinner

Things are changing and most British people eat meals from many different countries, for example, spaghetti (意大利式细面条) or curry (咖喱食品). In fact, you could even say that the British don't eat much British food. However, the most typical thing to eat for dinner is "meat and two veg". This consists of a piece of meat accompanied by two different boiled vegetables. This is covered with "gravy" which is a sauce made with the juice that was obtained when the meat was cooked. One of the vegetables is almost always potato. The British eat a lot of potatoes.

Language and Culture Focus (语言文化要点)

>>>>> **Reading I**

1. 辨析 **different than & different from:** The two expressions are all correct: "different than" is the American use and "different from" is the British use.

2. **selection** *n.*

　　1)（一般用单数）a collection of things of one kind; range. 供挑选或选购的同类物品

　　【例句】 The shop has a fine selection of cheeses.

2) the act of selecting or the fact of being selected. 挑选；选择；选拔

【例句】His selection as a presidential candidate was quite unexpected.

natural selection　物竞天择

【相关词】

selective *adj.* careful in choosing. 精挑细选的

【例句】He's very selective when he buys his suits.

3. available: *adj.* able to be had, obtained, used, seen, etc. 可获得的；可用的；可看见的

【例句】Those shoes are not available in your size.

We want to make our products available to a wider market.

Is this new timetable available yet?

【相关词】

availability *n.*

4. nutrition: *n.* the process of giving or getting food. 营养；滋养；营养物

【例句】Good nutrition is essential for good health.

the science of nutrition 营养学

【相关词】

fat 脂肪，carbohydrate 碳水化合物，fiber 纤维，vitamins 维生素

nutritious *adj.* valuable to the body as food. 有营养的；营养价值高的

nutritive *adj.* ① of nutrition. 有关营养的　②nutritious. 有营养的

5. 辨析 purchase & buy

Purchase is used in formal or business contexts. It is not very common and is used more in written English than in spoken English. **Buy** on the other hand is used both in written and spoken English.

Use of "buy":

buy sb. sth.

buy sth. for

buy sth. from sth./sb.

Related phrases with "buy":

buy (sb.) off　买通；用钱疏通

a good/bad buy　合算/不合算的买卖

【例句】That dress was a bad buy — I've only worn it once.

It's a good buy at that price!

buyer's market: 买方市场　　**antonym: seller's market**

Related phrases with "purchase":

purchasing power 购买力

make a purchase 购买

6. 辨析 quantities of & numbers of: The former can be followed by either countable or uncountable nouns while the latter can only be followed by countable nouns.

【例句】Quantities of food were spread out on the table.

Recent geological surveys have disclosed the existence of huge quantities of minerals in this area.

Quantities of radioactive materials requiring consideration of the need for an emergency plan for responding to a release.

Large numbers of vehicles had to be abandoned because of the heavy snow.

7. soda: *n.* ［C / U］苏打水；碳酸饮料 (=soda water)

【例句】a can of orange soda

Two whiskeys and sodas, please.

8. single parent: a person with a child but no husband or wife. 单亲

9. double-income families: a family in which the husband and wife both earn wages.

10. skip: to fail to attend or take part in; intentionally miss. 不出席；不参加；故意错过

【例句】I'm going to skip lunch today.

11. Americans have less time than ever before to spend preparing food: Here in this sentence, the word "ever" means "always". It is usually found together with an expression of time or in certain phrases.

【例句】He came here for a holiday several years ago and he's lived there ever since.

The prince and princess got married and lived happily ever after.

As ever, he refused to admit that he was wrong.

I will love you for ever.

The world's ever-increasing population will cause serious problems.

12. 辨析 consequence & result

Result is the most frequently used word. It can be preceded by either "good" or "bad".

Consequence usually means a "bad result".

【例句】You made the wrong decision, and now you must take the consequences (承担后果).

As a/In consequence of your laziness and rudeness, I'm forced to dismiss you.

The high level of unemployment has produced harmful social consequences.

13. eat out: to dine out.

14. on (the) average: calculated as an average. 平均

【例句】We receive 20 letters a day on (the) average.

The article "the" can be omitted.

【相关词组】

above/below average (在平均水平以上/以下)

【例句】 His school work is well above/below average.

15. **consume** *vt.*

1) to eat or drink, esp. eagerly or in large amounts. 大吃；大喝

【例句】 He's able to consume large quantities of food.

2) to use up. 消耗；消费；消尽

【例句】 Arguing about details consumed many hours of the committee's valuable time.

This is a time-consuming process.

【相关词组】

consumer 消费者

consumer durable 耐用消费品

consumer society 消费社会

consumerism 消费主义

16. **The United States Department of Agriculture (USDA) and the food industry — growers, processors, marketers, and restaurants — compile sales statistics and keep accurate records**.

【译文】美国农业部及食品工业——种植者、加工者、营销者以及餐馆——编撰销售统计数据，并作精确记录。

17. **compile:** to make (a report, a book, etc.) from facts and information found in various places. 编纂；编辑；编制；汇编

【例句】 It takes years of work to compile a dictionary.

【相关词】

compilation *n.* 汇编；编纂；编辑

compiler *n.* 汇编者；编纂者

18. 辨析 **used to & be used to**

Used to refers to a habit or a state that existed in the past. **Be/get used to** means "in the habit of".

【例句】 He used to swim in that river.

I'm used to the noise.

I shall probably oversleep as I am not used to getting up so early.

Used to can be used with "no longer" to make a contrast between the past and the present.

【例句】 Mobile telephone, which used to be a symbol for rich people, is no longer a sign of wealth.

19. **threat:** an expression of an intention to hurt, punish, etc. 威胁；恐吓

be/pose a threat to: 是/构成对……的威胁

【例句】 The existence of mass destructive weapons poses a grave threat to world peace.

【相关搭配】

empty threat: 虚张声势的威胁

under the threat of: 在……的威胁之下

【例句】 I obeyed his orders, but only under threat of punishment.

20. in a / the... (adj.) mood for: 有……的心情

【例句】 The management is in no mood for compromise over this issue.

in the mood to do sth. 有心情做某事

【例句】 I'm very tired and not in the mood to argue.

in a good/bad mood 心情好/坏

【例句】 The boss is in a good/bad mood today.

21. rich in: 富含……的

【例句】 This is a city rich in ancient buildings.

Nearly all nuts are rich in protein.

22. cereal *n.*

1) a food made from grain, esp. one such as cornflakes that is eaten at breakfast in some countries.（经加工的）谷类食品（尤指早餐时吃的，如玉米片等）

2) a plant grown to produce grain for food, such as wheat, rice, etc. 谷类植物；谷物

23. While ... (clause for contrast): The "while" clause is always used for contrast. When used this way, it means "but" or "whereas".

【例句】 Their country has plenty of oil, while ours has none.

While some people hold the idea that the computer has more advantages than disadvantages, I insist that if used improperly, the computer will do harm to us.

24. Americans' awareness of nutrition, along with their changing tastes and needs, leads them to consume a wide variety of foods — foods for health, for fun, and simply for good taste.

【译文】 美国人对营养的意识，加上他们正在变化的口味与需求导致他们消耗各种各样的食物——以健康为目的的食品、以乐趣为目的的食品，以及仅仅满足好口味的食品。

awareness: knowledge or understanding of a particular subject or situation. 意识

【例句】 environmental/political/social awareness

Health officials have tried to raise awareness (=improve people's knowledge) about AIDS

25. variety: If a group of things has variety, the things are different from each other in quality or type, so that the group is interesting or offers people a wide choice.

【例句】 She didn't like the work because it lacked variety.

Ever since then, reptiles have survived and increased in number and variety.

We are growing a new variety of wheat this year.

"A variety of" or "varieties of" means "different kinds of".

【例句】many varieties of whisky

varieties of trees

Dolphins produce a great variety of noises.

The college library has a wide variety of books.

a variety of: 各式各样的；种种的

【例句】This shirt is available in a wide variety of colors.

Everyone arrived late at the party, for a variety of reasons.

>>>>>**Reading II**

1. **Traditional British food, with its emphasis on puddings, pies, cakes, meat dishes and fried food, no longer forms a main part of most people's diet because of the trend towards lighter, more easily prepared food.**

【译文】英国的传统食物主要有布丁、饼、蛋糕、肉类和油炸食品等，但这些都不再是大多数人
选择的主要食品，因为人们倾向于更加清淡、更容易准备的食物。

with emphasis on: "with" can be used to introduce the so-called absolute construction which gives a reason or functions as an accompanying state.

【例句】With Mike away, we don't stand any chance of winning the game.

With profits up by 60%, the company has had another excellent year.

She walked to the bus stop, with a boy following her.

With the growing unemployment rate, the purchase power also declined.

With her special knowledge of politics, James would have no difficulty answering this question.

The old man sat on the bench, with his dog lying nearby.

"Emphasis" refers to the special attention given to something to show that it is very important. It is usually followed by the preposition "on".

【例句】a policy with emphasis on reducing inflation

a lecture with emphasis on parental care

Our English course lays emphasis on communicative skills.

2. **various sweet dishes mentioned in the passage**

dessert: sweet food (especially fruit) served at the end of a meal. 甜点

pudding: a solid, hot, sweet dish made with pastry, rice, bread, fat, fruit, eggs or other substances. 布丁

gooseberry fool: dessert made from crushed gooseberries and cream. 奶油醋栗泥

3. ways of cooking

fry: to cook in fat or oil. 炸，煎

【例句】 fried rice 炒饭

fried eggs 煎蛋，荷包蛋

boil: to cook or heat in boiling water. 煮

【例句】 boiled egg 煮鸡蛋

boiled potatoes

scramble: to mix the whites and the yolks of the egg, and then cook the mixture by stirring and heating it in a pan.

【例句】 scrambled egg 炒蛋

roast: to cook by dry heat in an oven or over a fire. 烤

【例句】 roast chicken 烤鸡

roast beef 烤牛肉

roast potato 烤土豆

bake: to cook in an oven without using extra liquid or fat

【例句】 baked potato in their jackets/skins 连皮烤的土豆

mash: to crush into a soft substance 捣成泥状

【例句】 mashed potatoes 土豆泥

steam: to cook by heating in steam rather than in water. 蒸

【例句】 steamed pudding   steamed rice

4. trend: A trend is a general and obvious movement or development of events, fashion, attitudes, etc.

【例句】 There is a trend towards equal opportunities for men and women.

There has been a recent trend among judges towards giving more severe punishment.

The latest figures have proved the trend of inflation.

5. different categories of food

light food: food easy to digest. 易消化的食物

convenience food and junk food: Convenience food refers to frozen, dried or tinned food which you can cook quickly whenever you want; junk food is the kind of food that is not very good for your health, but you eat because it is easy and quick to prepare. 方便食品

organic food: food which grows without the help of chemicals. 有机食品

rich food: food containing too much cream, sugar, eggs, butter, etc. 味浓油腻的食物

6. preserve: If you preserve food, you prevent it from decaying so that you can store it for a long time. There are several ways of preserving food, such as freezing, drying（制成干并脱水保存）, smoking （熏制）, or salting/pickling（腌制）.

7. kipper: salted herring that is preserved by being treated with smoke. 熏制的鲱鱼干

8. survive: If someone survives, he continues to live in spite of being in a situation in which he came close to death. 经历……后依然活着, 幸免于 If something survives, it continues to exist in spite of being nearly destroyed or made extinct (经受得住). "Survive" also can be a transitive verb, followed by a disaster directly.

【例句】Only two people survived the fire.

The project survived three changes of government.

I doubt whether the National Health Service will survive to the end of the century.

9. (be) associated with: (be) connected with.

【例句】In Peter's mind, summer is often associated with holidays.

He's working on engineering problems associated with aircraft design.

10. serve: to offer food and drink. 提供（食物）

【例句】Could you all come to the table? We're ready to serve.

What time is breakfast served in this hotel?

11. chip: a long thin piece of potato cooked in deep fat until they are hard, dry, and crunchy. 炸薯条

12. begin with: to start sth. as the first part.

【例句】The film began with the death of the dancer.

The teacher usually begins the class with some warming-up exercises.

13. porridge: a soft, sticky breakfast food made by boiling oatmeal in milk or water. 麦片粥

14. continental: of the mainland of Europe. 欧洲大陆的

【例句】The continental breakfast refers to the breakfast that features the style of the mainland of Europe.

15. various kinds of bread

toast and marmalade: 烤面包加柑橘酱

toast: bread which has been cut into slices and made brown and crisp by cooking at a high temperature

marmalade: a kind of jam-like food made from such fruits as oranges or lemons, and usually eaten on bread or toast at breakfast

cottage loaf: a loaf bread made in two round pieces with the smaller one on top of the larger one. 大小两层面团合在一起制成的农家面包

cob loaf: a round loaf of bread

roll: a small loaf of bread eaten by one person, usually with butter and sometimes with a filling of meat and cheese, etc. 面包卷, 圆面包

croissant: a piece of bread-like baked pastry, shaped like a crescent (新月), and usually eaten with coffee for breakfast. 羊角面包

hot cross buns: spiced bun, with a cross of sugar on top of it, eaten at Easter time, and especially on Good Friday. 十字小圆面包

16. **typically:** showing the most usual characteristics.

　　【例句】He's typically American.

　　　　　The dish is typically Chinese.

17. **savory:** Sometimes savoury food refers to pleasant or attractive food in taste; sometimes in British English, savory food means food with a salty or spicy flavor rather than a sweet one, such as the taste of meat, cheese, vegetables, and salt etc.

18. **in general:** usually, in most cases, generally speaking.

　　【例句】In general, people like to have decent jobs.

　　　　　In general, they want shorter shifts, and shorter working hours.

　　　　　In general, it will make them less satisfied and more envious.

　　　　　The industrial processes in general are based on man-made processes.

19. **Christmas pudding:** heavy sweet pudding containing a lot of dried fruit and often covered with burning alcohol (brandy), served hot at the end of dinner on Christmas Day. 圣诞布丁

20. **celebration:** A celebration is a special event that people organize to enjoy themselves because something pleasant has happened or because it is someone's birthday or anniversary.

　　【例句】a national celebration 国家庆典

21. **pancake:** thin soft flat cake made of flour, milk and egg. 薄煎饼

22. **Shrove Tuesday:** also called Pancake Tuesday, the day before Ash Wednesday, or the last day before the solemn period of Lent. 薄饼日，忏悔星期二，圣灰星期三的前一天或四月斋开始的前一天
Lent: the forty days before Easter. 四月斋

23. **Good Friday:** the Friday before Easter Sunday, observed by Christians to honor the crucifixion of Jesus Christ. 复活节前的星期五，耶稣受难日

24. **elaborately:** carefully planned with a large number of detailed parts.

　　【例句】prepare for the party elaborately

　　　　　Every inch of its surface was elaborately decorated.

25. **decorate:** If you decorate something, you make it more attractive or beautiful by adding some kind of ornament to it.

　　【例句】decorate a cake with icing

　　　　　The walls of the bedroom were decorated with pictures of stars.

　　　　　The streets were decorated with flags.

26. **tier:** a row, layer or level of something that has other layers above or below it. 层

　　【例句】Their wedding cake has three tiers.

27. normally: in the usual way.

【例句】The factory is now running normally again.

I don't normally drink at lunch.

Such meetings are normally held three or four times a year.

28. stuck in the icing: put in the icing. If you stick something at a place, you put it there.

【例句】She stuck the flowers in a vase of water.

Icing is a sweet substance made from powdered sugar and water or egg whites. It is used to cover cakes as a decoration.

【例句】Sweet cakes covered in chocolate icing.

29. confectionery: sweet food such as sweets, chocolates, ice cream, and cakes, etc. 甜食

【例句】a confectionery's shop 糖果点心店

30. various sweets:

toffee: a hard, sticky, chewy sweet made by boiling sugar and butter with water. 太妃糖

mint: sweet with peppermint flavor. 薄荷糖

stick of rock: a type of hard sugar sweet. 硬棒糖

candy floss: melted sugar threads spun to make a colored sticky mass, also called cotton candy. 棉花糖

31. resort: a place where a lot of people go for holidays. 游览胜地

【例句】a health resort 疗养地

a mountain resort

Brighton is one of the most popular resorts on the south coast of skiing resorts.

32. fun food: food that provides fun. 休闲食品

33. In recent years there has been an increase in the consumption of "convenience" and unhealthy "junk" foods, but also a growing interest in healthy, natural or "organic" foods.

【译文】近年来，方便食品和不健康的垃圾食品的消费有所增加，但也有越来越多的人对健康食品、天然食品或有机食品产生了浓厚的兴趣。

consumption: the eating and drinking of something or the use of fuel or energy.

【例句】Consumption of oil has declined in recent years.

The car's fuel consumption is very high.

There is a high consumption of alcohol in Britain.

34. formerly: in earlier times.

【例句】Peru was formerly ruled by the Spanish.

Formerly he worked in a factory, but now he's a teacher.

Lake Malawi, formerly Lake Nyasa, is 450 miles long.

35. exotic: If something is exotic, it is strange, unusual, and interesting because it comes from a distant country.

【例句】exotic food/dress/flowers

36. ethnic: connected with different racial groups of people, or a racial or tribal group, especially when referring to racial minorities within a particular country or city.

【例句】ethnic minorities

"Ethnic restaurants"（民族餐馆）refers to restaurants which are interestingly unusual because they are typical of some ethnic groups.

>>>>>Extended Activities

A. Function and Structure: Ordering a Meal

Dining Etiquette

Table manners play an important part in making a favorable impression. They are visible signals of the state of our manners and therefore are essential to professional success. Regardless of whether we are having lunch with a prospective employer or dinner with a business associate, our manners can speak volumes about us as professionals.

Napkin Use

The meal begins when the host unfolds his or her napkin. This is your signal to do the same. Place your napkin on your lap, completely unfolded if it is a small luncheon napkin or in half, lengthwise, if it is a large dinner napkin. Typically, you want to put your napkin on your lap soon after sitting down at the table (but follow your host's lead). The napkin remains on your lap throughout the entire meal and should be used to gently blot your mouth when needed. If you need to leave the table during the meal, place your napkin on your chair as a signal to your server that you will be returning. The host will signal the end of the meal by placing his or her napkin on the table. Once the meal is over, you too should place your napkin neatly on the table to the right of your dinner plate. (Do not refold your napkin, but don't wad it up, either.)

Ordering

If, after looking over the menu, there are items you are uncertain about, ask your server any questions you may have. Answering your questions is part of the server's job. It is better to find out before you order that a dish is prepared with something you do not like or are allergic to than to spend the entire meal picking tentatively at your food.

An employer will generally suggest that your order be taken first; his or her order will be taken last. Sometimes, however, the server will decide how the ordering will proceed. Often, women's orders are taken before men's.

As a guest, you should not order one of the most expensive items on the menu or more than two courses unless your host indicates that it is all right. If the host says, "I'm going to try this delicious sounding cheesecake; why don't you try dessert too, " or "The prime rib is the specialty here; I think you'd enjoy it, " then it is all right to order that item if you would like.

"Reading" the Table Setting

Should you be attending a formal dinner or banquet with pre-set place settings, it is possible to gain clues about what may be served by "reading" the place setting. Start by drawing an imaginary line through the center of the serving plate (the plate will be placed in the center of your dining space). To the right of this imaginary line all of the following will be placed; glassware, cup and saucer, knives, and spoons, as well as a seafood fork if the meal includes seafood. It is important to place the glassware or cup back in the same position after its use in order to maintain the visual presence of the table. To the left of this imaginary line all of the following will be placed; bread and butter plate (including small butter knife placed horizontally across the top of the plate), salad plate, napkin, and forks. Remembering the rule of "liquids on your right" and "solids on your left" will help in allowing you to quickly become familiar with the place setting.

Use of Silverware

Choosing the correct silverware from the variety in front of you is not as difficult as it may first appear. Starting with the knife, fork, or spoon that is farthest from your plate, work your way in, using one utensil for each course. The salad fork is on your outermost left, followed by your dinner fork. Your soupspoon is on your outermost right, followed by your beverage spoon, salad knife and dinner knife. Your dessert spoon and fork are above your plate or brought out with dessert. If you remember the rule to work from the outside in, you'll be fine.

There are two ways to use a knife and fork to cut and eat your food. They are the American style and the European or Continental style. Either style is considered appropriate. In the American style, one cuts the food by holding the knife in the right hand and the fork in the left hand with the fork tines piercing the food to secure it on the plate. Cut a few bite-size pieces of food, then lay your knife across the top edge of your plate with the sharp edge of the blade facing in. Change your fork from your left to your right hand to eat, fork tines facing up. (If you are left-handed, keep your fork in your left hand, tines facing up.) The European or Continental style is the same as the American style in that you cut your meat by holding your knife in your right hand while securing your food with your fork in your left hand. The difference is your fork remains in your left hand, tines facing down, and the knife in your right hand. Simply eat the cut pieces of food by picking them up with your fork still in your left hand.

When You Have Finished

Do not push your plate away from you when you have finished eating. Leave your plate where it is in the place setting. The common way to show that you have finished your meal is to lay your fork and knife diagonally across your plate. Place your knife and fork side by side, with the sharp side of the knife blade facing inward and the fork, tines down, to the left of the knife. The knife and fork should be placed as if they are pointing to the numbers 10 and 4 on a clock face. Make sure they are placed in such a way that they do not slide off the plate as it is being removed. Once you have used a piece of silverware, never place it back on the table. Do not leave a used spoon in a cup, either; place it on the saucer. You can leave a soupspoon in a soup plate. Any unused silverware is simply left on the table.

B. Special Use: Degrees of Adjectives and Adverbs

1. 形容词和副词的等级变化

英语中的形容词和副词有三个等级：原级，比较级和最高级。绝大多数形容词和副词的比较级和最高级都属于规则变化，即单音节的词以 -er 和 -est 为后缀，三音节或以上的词加 more 和 most 构成。例如：

small — smaller — smallest	great — greater — greatest
big — bigger — biggest	hot — hotter — hottest
expensive — more expensive — most expensive	
instructive — more instructive — most instructive	

含有两个音节的形容词和副词构成比较级和最高级时情况比较复杂：有些仍以 -er 和 -est 结尾。但以 -ful、-less 和 -ly 等结尾的词通常用 more 和 most。例如：

early — earlier — earliest

happy — happier — happiest

helpful — more helpful — most helpful

careless — more careless — most careless

slowly — more slowly — most slowly

有些形容词构成比较级和最高级时兼有两种变化。例如：

clever — cleverer/more clever — cleverest/most clever

英语中有少数形容词和副词的比较级和最高级属于不规则变化，请看下表：

原　级	比　较　级	最　高　级
good/well	better	best

（续　表）

原　级	比　较　级	最　高　级
bad/badly	worse	worst
much/many	more	most
little	less	least
old	older/elder	oldest/eldest
far	farther/ further	farthest/furthest

1) elder 和 eldest 常用于家庭成员中表示年长的一方。例如：

elder brother　　elder sister

但 elder 一般不与 than 连用。例如：

He is older than I.

2) farther/farthest 通常用来表示距离，而 further/furthest 常用来表示程度上更进一步。例如：

Go farther, and you will see the post office.

You should study further.

2. "as ... as" 结构

"as ... as" 结构表示 "和…… 一样"，中间用形容词或副词的原级。它的否定形式是 "not as ... as" 或 "not so ... as"，表示 "不如……"。例如：

He is as tall as Mike.

My wife loves our children as much as I do.

He is as poor as a church mouse.

He doesn't work as carefully as Mary.

如果此种结构和名词连用，要注意名词的性质。如果名词是可数名词单数或不可数名词，则位于 "as ... as" 中间，即 "as + 形容词 + 名词 + as"。例如：

Johnson is as efficient a worker as Jack.

I don't want as expensive a house as this.

He took as much cheese as he needed.

Hardly ever have I heard as impressive music as this.

如果复数名词与 many、few 连用，也采用这一顺序。例如：

This factory has as many workers as that one.

She has written as many essays as her brother has.

如果复数名词没有与 many、few 连用，则名词要位于 "as ... as" 结构前。例如：

He smokes cigarettes as expensive as he can afford.

在 "as ... as" 结构中，nearly, almost, twice, three times, half, two kilos 等词可以作为修饰语，放在该结构之前。例如：

Nowadays plastics are almost as useful as steel.

She lived nearly as long as her father.

I have twice as many books as he has.

3. "more than" 结构

"more than" 结构的基本形式是 "形容词或副词的比较级 + than"。例如：

This bag is heavier than that one.

She works harder than I do.

I have finished more work than he.

You have made fewer mistakes than I have.

"more than" 结构还有一种特殊结构，即 "the + 形容词或副词的比较级 + of 短语"。在这种带有 of 短语的比较级结构中，一定要加定冠词；遇到副词的比较级，定冠词可加可不加。例如：

John is the brighter of the two brothers.

She is the younger of the two sisters.

Of the two boys, Mike behaves (the) more politely.

1) 比较对象的逻辑一致性问题

英语是逻辑性非常强的语言，而汉语的逻辑性比较模糊。所以，中国学生受汉语的影响，在比较时容易犯一些逻辑上的错误。例如：

（×） The score of our class is better than their class.

（×） The climate of Shanghai is hotter than Beijing.

我们在使用比较结构时要防止逻辑上的漏洞。上述两句应改为：

The score of our class is better than that of their class.

The climate of Shanghai is hotter than that of Beijing.

另外，当两个单位进行比较时，它们不能相互包含。

我们不能说 The Yangtze River is longer than all the rivers in China，因为 all the rivers in China 包括 the Yangtze River。所以，我们应该说 The Yangtze River is longer than any other river in China。或者，我们也可以这样说，The Yangtze River is longer than all the rivers in Europe，因为 the Yangtze River 和 all the rivers in Europe 不相互包容。

2) 替代问题

在比较结构中，that 常用来代替前面已出现的特指名词，以避免重复；复数形式用 those。例如：

I prefer the climate of Shanghai to that of Wuhan.

The cost of oil is less than that of gas.

These TV sets are far better than those we turned out last year.

3) 修饰语的位置

形容词和副词的比较级不能用very, quite等词修饰。形容词和副词的比较级有一些固定的修饰语, 它们是even, far, many, much, still, rather, slightly, a bit, a few, a little, a lot, some, two, twice, three times等。例如:

This book is far more difficult to get.

Jane is careless, but Mary is even more careless.

I arrived a little bit earlier than usual.

Today is two degrees hotter than yesterday.

His second novel is miles worse than his first one.

如果形容词的比较级后有名词, 则修饰语也要注意与名词搭配, 即many, a few等与可数名词搭配, much, a little等与不可数名词搭配。例如:

If I had much more money, I would not be working in this nasty place.

I have many more books than George.

4. "the+最高级(+范围)"

当三个或三个以上的单位进行比较时, 要使用这种最高级的比较形式(副词的最高级形式前的定冠词the可以省略)。在这种结构中通常都有比较的范围, 一般由介词短语、定语从句或非限定短语表示。有时, 在具体的上下文中, 由于大家谈论的范围是众所周知的, 所以也可以省略。例如:

The Nile is the longest river in the world.

He studies the hardest of all.

This is the most sentimental film I have ever seen.

This is the best wine I have ever drunk.

注意: 在上面最后两个例句中, 从句要使用完成时态。

修饰形容词和副词最高级的词和短语有almost, much, nearly, next, second, third, by far, by no means, the very, one's very等。例如:

He is the second youngest in the family.

Britain is the next largest importer.

She put on her very best dress.

They are by far the slowest.

形容词的最高级也经常与one of短语搭配。例如:

Tokyo is one of the biggest cities in the world.

有时候, 比较级和最高级可以相互转换。例如:

Ellie did more work than anyone else. (= Ellie did the most work.)

Nothing in my life impressed me so deeply as my first visit to Shanghai.

(= My first visit to Shanghai impressed me the deepest.)

注意:若不定冠词 a 与 most 连用,或在没有冠词修饰的 "most + 形容词" 结构中, most 表示 "非常", 相当于 very, quite。例如:

You are most kind. (= You are very kind.)

This is a most useful device. (= This is a very useful device.)

5. 有关比较结构的特殊用法

1) "the + 比较级……, the + 比较级": 越……越

The smaller it is, the less it will cost us.

The more he has, the more he wants.

2) "比较级 + and + 比较级": 越来越……

The weather is getting hotter and hotter.

He became more and more interested.

3) "all + 比较级": 越发, 格外

He likes her all the better for her freckles. (他因为她的雀斑而更喜欢她。)

4) "none + the + 比较级": 没有更, 并不更

He is none the happier for his wealth.(他并不因富有而更加幸福。)

5) more than

① "more than + 数字" 表示 "超过", 相当于 over。

more than two hundred miles   more than ten years

② more than 表示 "十分", 相当于 quite。

It's more than enough.

He was more than pleased with their reply.

③ more than 表示 "不仅仅, 不止"。

He is more than my teacher.

④ more ... than 表示 "与其说……不如说……", 强调前者。

He is more cunning than clever. (与其说他聪明, 还不如说他狡猾。)

He is more a businessman than an artist.

(与其说他是个艺术家, 还不如说他是个商人。)

She is more a friend than a teacher.

(与其说她是个老师, 还不如说她是个朋友。)

6) less than

① less than 表示 "少于"。

less than an hour   less than two miles

② less than 表示 "毫不", 相当于 by no means。

The road was less than smooth.

③ less ... than 表示 "与其说……不如说……", 强调后者。

He is less hurt than frightened. (= He is more frightened than hurt.)

7) no more than

① not more than (即 "not any more ... than") 表示 "和……一样不", 相当于 neither ... nor ...。 例如：

Jane is no wiser than Mary. (= Neither Jane nor Mary is wise.)

He was no more wounded than you. (= Neither you nor he was wounded.)

I could no more understand his language than he could mine.

(我不能理解他的语言, 他也不能理解我的语言。)

He is no more a teacher than an engineer.

(= He is neither a teacher nor an engineer.)

② no more than 表示 "仅仅, 只有", 相当于 only。

I have no more than 5 dollars in my pocket.

No more than 50 miles has been covered. (仅仅 50 英里)

8) no less than

① no less than 表示 "和……一样"。

We pursue an open-door policy, no less in culture than in economy.

② no less than ＋数字表示确切的数字, 相当于 exactly。

They have no less than five children. (确切地说, 他们有 5 个孩子。)

9) still/much more 和 still/much less

这两个短语表示 "更不用说……" 或 "何况……"。still/much more 与肯定结构连用, still/much less 与否定结构连用。例如：

It's difficult to catch up with him, still more to surpass him.

It's not easy to catch up with him, still less to surpass him.

10) not so much ... as

not so much ... as 表示 "与其……, 不如……", 强调后者, 相当于 less ... than。例如：

He is not so much a teacher as an expert.

(= He is less a teacher than an expert.)

(= He is more an expert than a teacher.)

The situation called not so much for fight as for negotiation.

11) 其他词组：

I shall do it with the greatest pleasure. (非常乐意)

Do you mind if I close the door? <u>Not in the slightest</u>. (一点也不)

You will succeed <u>sooner or later</u>. (迟早)

Men are <u>more or less</u> selfish. (或多或少)

It is <u>none other than</u> Mr. White. (就是)

The doctor has advised him to give up smoking <u>more than once</u>. (不止一次)

<u>To make matters worse</u>, it began to blow hard. (更糟糕的是)

6. 其他含有比较意义的结构

He is four years *senior to* me. (他比我大4岁。)

I am four years *junior to* him. (我比他小4岁。)

He is *superior to* me in English. (他的英语比我好。)

I am *inferior to* him in English. (我的英语比他差。)

I *prefer* to read *rather than* talk. (我宁愿读书也不愿聊天。)

I *prefer* reading *to* talking. (我宁愿读书也不愿聊天。)

I have *the same* idea *as* you have. (我有与你同样的想法。)

My mistakes are small *compared to* this. (与你的错误相比，我犯的是个小错误。)

C. Practical Reading

本题是简单的细节查找题，只要抓住题目中的关键信息，到菜单里去"按图索骥"就可以了。具体而言，这10道题的解法如下：

1. 细节题：第一份菜单中第7道菜中有 Chow Mein，一般中餐厅可以买到，不一定非得到香港，答案是a。

2. 细节题：第一份菜单中可知，香港中餐馆供应b和c项里列举的东西，所以选项为d。菜单中的 9 ~ 12。

3. 计算题：双份的 Sweet & Sour Chicken 当然是 2.9×2=5.8, 所以答案是c。

4. 比较题：15 ~ 17中的最低价是 Plain Boiled Rice 的价格，答案是d。

5. 营业时间从菜单中可以得到，答案是a。

6. 菜单上有 before your meal 的字样，答案是a。

7. 原文有 consult our wine list 的字样，答案是c。

8. 原文提到 comes with rice 时指的是 Prawns Orientale，答案是c。

9. 特别注意题目中有 except 的地方，容易犯低级错误，主菜中只有 shrimp & steak，原文没有，答案是c。

10. 原文有 Ask your waiter about today's delights 的字样，答案是a。

Teaching Tips（教学提示）

1. 本单元背景知识1介绍了美国人的一些主要饮食习惯，背景知识2介绍了在合理膳食、运动健身等理念的影响下，美国人在饮食习惯方面发生的一些变化，这两部分可以结合Reading I相关课文内容，作为文化知识点予以穿插介绍；背景知识3介绍了英国人的饮食习惯，建议安排在Reading II课文讲解前作导入性介绍。

2. Lead-in 本单元导入部分含听力理解和听写填空两项任务。听力理解部分围绕单元主题eating habits安排了一篇访谈类的材料，从社会学的角度探讨了影响人们饮食习惯的主要因素。该篇材料有较强的学术性和专业性，语言正式，对学生有一定的难度。作为导入，在听力活动前，教师可以先和学生探讨一下 Pairwork 中第5题（ How do you think a person's life-style affects his or her eating habits? ），请学生说说除了生活方式（ life-style ），还有哪些因素会影响人们的饮食习惯。语篇篇幅较长，被分为两个部分，共设有4项听力练习。第一和第二项练习针对的是语篇的上半部分，第二和第三项练习针对语篇的下半部分，第五项练习则为针对全篇的综合性练习。第一和第三项练习均为预听活动，主要目的是让学生对所听语篇的主旨（Gist）有所了解，初步把握听音和理解上的难点所在，为接下来的听力活动做好心理和词汇上的准备。第二和第四项练习为多项选择题（ Multiple-choice Questions ），旨在考查学生对语篇主旨的把握以及辨析细节的能力。听写填空(Spot Dictation)可以作为导入活动安排在Reading II课文讲解之前进行。

3. Reading I Brainstorming: 全班学生通过自由讨论的形式，列出关于食品（肉类、海鲜、蔬菜、瓜果、甜点、饮料）的一些常用词汇。中西方饮食习惯差异很大，烹调所用材料和烹调的方法也大不相同，不是每样中式食品都能在英语中找到相对应的表达方式，这一点教师应向学生指出。

4. Reading I Pairwork: 由学生双人结对，讨论与本单元主题Eating Habits相关的5个问题。教师可引导学生从他们自己的日常饮食习惯谈起，转入生活方式的改变对饮食习惯的影响的话题。教师可让学生讨论不同年龄、职业、收入、受教育层次的人群的饮食习惯差异，探究差异形成的原因，如生活方式的不同，消费能力的不同，对营养和健康的重视程度的不同，对西方生活方式的认可和接受程度不同等。教师也可让学生对比中国人过去和现在的饮食习惯的差异，从而得出随着人们生活方式的改变，人们的饮食习惯也在不断改变的结论，自然地切入课文的主题，提高学生接下去学习课文的兴趣。

5. Reading I练习II Question 5, choice b, be particular about 意思是"考究的，挑剔的"，如：He is very particular about his food. （他吃东西很讲究/挑剔。）

6. Reading I Post-reading: 要求学生以小组为单位设计一个菜单招待宾客。此课堂活动可在学生学习过扩展性练习 Function & Structure 和 Additional Vocabulary，有一定的词汇积累后再进行。由于中餐中没有下午茶 (an afternoon refreshment consisting usually of sandwiches and cakes served with tea) 的概念，教师应予以一定文化背景知识介绍。下文供参考。

AFTERNOON TEA — A Very British Tradition

Afternoon tea was introduced in England by Anna, the seventh Duchess of Bedford, in the year 1840. The Duchess would become hungry around four o'clock in the afternoon. The evening meal in her household was served fashionably late at eight o'clock, thus leaving a long period of time between lunch and dinner. The Duchess asked that a tray of tea, bread and butter and cake be brought to her room during the late afternoon. This became a habit of hers and she began inviting friends to join her.

This pause for tea became a fashionable social event. During the 1880's upper-class and society women would change into long gowns, gloves and hats for their afternoon tea which was usually served in the drawing room between four and five o'clock.

Traditional afternoon tea consists of a selection of dainty sandwiches (including of course thinly sliced cucumber sandwiches), scones served with clotted cream and preserves. Cakes and pastries are also served. Tea grown in India or Ceylon is poured from silver teapots into delicate bone china cups.

Nowadays however, in the average suburban home, afternoon tea is likely to be just a biscuit or small cake and a mug of tea, usually produced using a teabag.

常用烹调原料：

meat	肉	beef	牛肉	lamb	羊肉
steak	牛排	chop	连骨肉，排骨	cutlet	肉条
pork	猪肉	ham	火腿	bacon	咸肉
sausage	香肠	shrimp	虾	crab	蟹
shellfish	贝类	poultry	家禽	bean curd	豆腐
noodles	面条，挂面	macaroni	通心粉	flour	面粉
broth	肉汤	cheese	奶酪	butter	奶油
jam	果酱	flavoring/seasoning/condiment			调味品
soy sauce	酱油	gourmet powder	味精	salt	盐
sugar	糖	oyster oil	蚝油	cinnamon	桂皮

vanilla	香草	mint	薄荷	chilli	红辣椒
vinegar	醋	sauce	调味汁；沙司	cooking oil	食用油
pepper	胡椒粉	mustard	芥末	salad oil	色拉油
flour paste	面酱	peanut butter	花生酱	hot sauce	辣酱
sesame oil	芝麻油	bean sauce	豆瓣酱	chilli oil	辣油
ketchup	番茄酱	anise	茴香	garlic	大蒜
ginger	生姜	onion	洋葱	caraway	香菜
starch	淀粉	curry	咖喱粉	yeast	发酵粉

饮料及酒类：

mineral water	矿泉水	orange juice	橘子汁	lemon juice	柠檬原汁
lemonade	柠檬水	beer	啤酒	white wine	白葡萄酒
red wine	红葡萄酒	cider	苹果汁	champagne	香槟酒
cocktail	鸡尾酒	liqueur	白酒，烧酒	cooking wine	料酒
Kaoliang spirit	高粱酒	Wu Chia Pee	五加皮	vodka	伏特加
whisky	威士忌	brandy	白兰地	gin	松子酒

7. Reading II Translation: Sentence 4, *Mandarin*, the official national standard spoken language of China, which is based on the principal dialect spoken in and around Beijing. 普通话，中国的官方标准语言，也可直接使用拼音：Putonghua。

8. Reading II Cloze

Question 1   A *problem* is a situation or state of affairs that cause difficulties for people, so that they try to think of a way to deal with it. A *question* is a form of words which you say or write in order to ask someone about something, for example, if you need information, or if you want to know their opinion. A *question* is also a problem or a point which needs to be discussed. 我们通常说 solve/tackle a *problem* 而 answer a *question*。

Question 6   在解释为"也"时，*too* 和 *as well* 通常放在句末或单词、词组后，如：I know the answer, *too*. If you will go, I will go *as well*. *also* 则通常放在句中，如：We *also* went to see the film. He is gentle, but he is *also* capable of fierce intellectual combat.

Question 10   此句主语是 diet，单数，所以选 b。

Question 12   *fat* 在这里作名词，意思是"脂肪"。

9. Extended Activities D 中的词汇练习可结合本书 Reading II notes: ways of cooking。

Key（练习答案）

>>>>> **Reading I**

Pre-reading

I.

Meat & Seafood	Vegetable	Fruit	Dessert & Refreshment
pork, lamb, beef, chicken, ham, turkey, fish, shrimp, oyster, bacon, steak, rib, crab, prawn, squid, lobster, cod, mussel, salmon, eel	green pepper, onion, leek, tomato, celery, garlic, cucumber, cabbage, lettuce, carrot, eggplant, mushroom, turnip, pea, potato, spinach	apple, banana, peach, orange, grape, strawberry, pineapple, lemon, plum, watermelon, apricot, cherry, coconut, pear	pudding, sandwich, cake, pasta, hotdog, cookie, toast, bun, dumpling, tart, biscuit, jelly, pie, ice-cream, pancake, pastry, hamburger

Exercises

II. 1. b   2. c   3. d   4. b   5. d

III. 1. consequence   2. statistic   3. restaurateur   4. processor   5. marketer

6. athletic   7. nutrition   8. single-parent   9. awareness   10. compile

IV. 1. variety   2. skip   3. in the mood   4. compile   5. favorite

6. survey   7. awareness   8. eat out   9. alert   10. consumes

V. 1. The employees are encouraged to purchase shares of their own company.

2. He inherited something from his father, but he soon consumed his fortune.

3. She does exercise every day so she looks very athletic.

4. Although he is over eighty his mind is still remarkably alert.

5. On the average I work ten hours a day.

6. Smoking is responsible for many cases of lung cancer.

>>>>Reading II

Exercises

I. 1. T 2. F 3. F 4. F 5. F 6. F 7. NM 8. T 9. T 10. F

III. 1. 1) c 2) a 3) a 4) b 5) a 6) d 7) c 8) d 9) b 10) d

  2. 1) d 2) a 3) f 4) b 5) g 6) e 7) c

IV. 1. The manager's assistant is responsible for handling relation and communication with our European head office.

  2. Mr. Smith's business plan became known to his competitors as a consequence of information leak.

  3. He is so busy that he works 12 hours a day on the average.

  4. He used to speak only Cantonese, but now his clients are no longer limited to Cantonese, and he has been able to communicate in English and Mandarin with clients.

  5. She eats only vegetables, fruits and low-fat foods in order to lose weight.

  6. His close analysis of the current economic situation is based on facts.

  7. Advertisements often lead people to buy things they don't need.

  8. Supper often begins with soup in Hong Kong.

  9. I prefer traditional Chinese dishes to Western ones, because Chinese dishes are rich in fiber, vitamins and minerals.

  10. We regard the French enterprise as a potential partner for cooperation.

V. 1. b 2. c 3. a 4. c 5. d 6. a 7. c 8. d 9. a 10. b

  11. b 12. d 13. c 14. c 15. a

>>>>Extended Activities

A. Function and Structure

III. 1. Diner: Waiter, please <u>show me the menu</u>.

    Waiter: <u>Here's the menu</u>, sir.

    Diner: Thank you.

    Waiter: May I take your order?

    Diner: Yes. <u>I'd like a cup of</u> fresh orange juice.

Waiter:	And what would you like after that?
Diner:	I think I'll try the roast chicken.
2. Waiter:	Have you decided on what you'd like?
Diner:	Yes. First I'll have onion soup.
Waiter:	And then?
Diner:	I'll order the lamb chops.
Waiter:	How would you like it done?
Diner:	Medium, please.
3. Waiter:	Are you ready to order?
David:	You order first, Susan.
Susan:	Order anything you like. I'm not particular about food.
David:	I'd better leave the choice to you.
Susan:	OK. Then, a glass of mineral water for me.
David:	And for me, too.
Susan:	Let us have some shrimps for a change.
David:	It sounds good, but I'd prefer some mutton today.
4. John:	Could we see the menu, please?
Waitress:	Here you are, sir.
John:	What's special for today?
Waitress:	Perhaps you'd like some mushroom soup and fried sole.
John:	OK. Mushroom soup, please.
Waitress:	And what to follow?
John:	Vegetable salad, if it's not too much trouble.
Waitress:	Not at all. Would you like it with tomato sauce?
John:	Yeah. With tomato ketchup.
Waitress:	Anything else, sir?
John:	No, thank you.

B. Special Use

1. b   2. c   3. a   4. c   5. b   6. d   7. a   8. a   9. d   10. c
11. d   12. b   13. d   14. c   15. d

C. Practical Reading

1. a   2. d   3. c   4. d   5. a   6. a   7. c   8. c   9. c   10. a

D. Additional Vocabulary

I. 1-19;   2-18;   3-29;   4-5;   5-6;   6-23;   7-25;   8-24;   9-7;   10-17;

11-30;   12-13;   13-22;   14-28;   15-14;   16-20;   17-16;   18-12;   19-11;   20-10;

21-15;   22-1;   23-2;   24-26;   25-3;   26-27;   27-4;   28-8;   29-9;   30-21

II. 1-3;   2-14;   3-1;   4-7;   5-8;   6-6;   7-9;   8-15;   9-2;   10-4;

11-10;   12-12;   13-5;   14-13;   15-11

Unit 6
Different People

Teaching Aim（教学目的）

1. 认知信息（Cognitive Information）：*The Culture of Different People*
2. 内容重点（Language Focus）

— **Key Words:** I. value *n.*& *v.*, belief, unconscious, affect, fairness, preferential, treatment, performance, disharmony, excel, caste, race, prohibit, individualism, assignment, routinely, saw, switch, knob, pervasive, estimate, construction, virtue, mildly, statement, superior; II. reserve, self-discipline, plate, pass, toe, atmosphere, bridge, appreciation, contempt, understatement, tone, Briton, frustrating, motto, interpret, non-verbal, swallow, dissatisfaction, counterpart, hostile, defensive, effect, imitate, hurry, appreciate, amorous

— **Phrases:** I. call for, base ... on, be linked to, in contrast, from top to bottom, defer to, end with; II. a sense of togetherness, make a scene, queue for, make a chat about, take an interest in, get used to

— **Useful Structures:** get sth. done

                          as + *adv*. +as possible

                          read between the lines

                          be likely/unlikely to inf.

— **Grammar:** Articles

3. 交际技能（Communicative Skills）

— **Expressions:** Expressions of "Apologizing"

— **Reading:** Identifying Source of Miscommunication

Lead-in 导入

>>>>> Listening Comprehension Tasks

Difficult Words & Expressions

1. metaphor: a figure of speech in which a word or phrase that ordinarily designates one thing is used to designate another, thus making an implicit comparison 隐喻（一种修辞手法）

2. isolate: to set apart or cut off from others 分隔

3. globalization: the state of relating to or involving the entire earth in scope or application 全球化

4. appreciate: to recognize the quality, significance or magnitude of 赏识

5. eye contact: 目光接触

6. Caribbean: 加勒比的

7. aboriginal: 土著人（的）

8. aside from: 除……之外

9. conventional: traditional 传统的

10. temple: the flat region on either side of the forehead 太阳穴

11. index finger: 食指

12. reversed: opposite, contrary 相反的，颠倒的

Passage Script 1

Now the whole world is like a village. With the advancement of hi-tech, modern transportation and communication reduce the time and distance that once kept the peoples of the world apart. In the metaphor of the global village, nations are like families and continents are like neighborhoods. People go out of the house regularly to do business and to buy what they need in the market. Now markets and businesses are global.

People feel most at home in their own families, but they also want to stay on good terms with their neighbors. As the world is becoming more like a village, the families of the world are dependent on one another. Time and space no longer isolate or protect nations and groups from each other. With the economic and trade globalization, contact among the peoples of the world is increasing. Since the world is becoming more like a village, everyone wants it to be a place they feel comfortable living in. People want to benefit from global trade and advanced technology, and they want to live among peoples who respect and appreciate one another.

However, religious, economic, and political differences continue to divide people. To meet these challenges, people everywhere need to learn about other cultures. They need to know their neighbors. They need to know how to get along with them and how to solve problems arisen from misunderstanding. To do this, it is necessary to learn how to communicate across cultures. The reality of the global village challenges all its residents to develop a broader world view and the cultural skills necessary for building relationships and solving problems across cultures.

Passage Script 2

It is true that people from different cultures use different body languages. For instance, some Indians may shake their head from side to side as a sign of agreement and active listening. In the UK, people tend to nod their head to agree and to show they are listening. Eye contact is generally regarded as a positive aspect of body language in Western cultures. But in some Caribbean cultures young people are required not to look at someone eye to eye when being talked to. In some Australian Aboriginal cultures, it is disrespectful to look at an elder or senior in the eyes. It is a sign of respect to drop one's eyes.

In Arab culture the left hand is commonly considered unclean due to associations with toilet functions, and should therefore not be offered or used for touching or eating. When in doubt in Arab environments, using the right hand for everything is a safer idea.

In some countries, Greece, Turkey and Bulgaria for example, moving the head up and down or from side to side may have additional or different meanings to those conventionally interpreted in the western countries. Specifically, in Turkey, aside from using conventional head nodding and shaking, some people may also signal "no" by moving their head up.

In the Netherlands people touch the temple with the index finger in order to indicate someone is smart or intelligent. Touching the forehead with the index finger means someone is stupid or crazy. In Russia these meanings are reversed.

Key

II. 1. c   2. d   3. b   4. a   5. c   6. d   7. a   8. b   9. c   10. c

IV. 1. T   2. T   3. F   4. T   5. F   6. F   7. T   8. T   9. F   10. T

▶▶▶▶ Spot Dictation

Each of us <u>grows up</u> in a culture that <u>provides</u> pattern of <u>acceptable</u> behavior and <u>belief</u>. We may not <u>be aware of</u> the most basic <u>features</u> of our own culture <u>until</u> we <u>come into</u> contact with people <u>who</u> do things <u>differently</u>. When an individual <u>enters</u> a strange culture, <u>all or most</u> of these familiar cues are <u>removed</u>. He or she is <u>like</u> a fish <u>out of water</u>. No matter <u>how</u> broad-minded or full of <u>good will</u> he may be, a series of <u>shocks</u> may frustrate him. This is <u>followed</u> by a feeling of <u>anxiety</u>. This is culture shock. In order to <u>get over</u> culture shock, one needs to <u>adjust himself to</u> the new situation.

Background Information（背景知识）

1. Intercultural communication

Intercultural communication, sometimes used synonymously with cross-cultural communication, seeks to understand how people from different countries and cultures act, communicate and perceive the world around them. Aside from language, intercultural communication focuses on social attributes, thought patterns, and cultures of different groups of people. Intercultural communication is also referred to as the base for international businesses as it examines how people from different cultures, beliefs and religions come together to work and communicate with each other. Demands for intercultural communication skills are increasing as more and more businesses go global. Without sound knowledge in intercultural communication businesses may unknowingly get trapped in confusion and misunderstandings. For businesses to breach the cultural barriers they encounter when stepping onto foreign lands, it is vital for them to fully understand the cultural differences that exist so as to avoid misconceptions due to intercultural communication gaps. The basic skills of intercultural communication are fundamentally general communication skills that can be used universally by all cultures and races. An example of such communication skills in the intercultural environment is to listen without judging, repeat what you understand, confirm meanings, give suggestions and acknowledge a mutual understanding. Respect in all cultures in the world is a common language and by earning it through respecting other peoples' culture and religion, the favor is returned. Other significant strategies in enhancing intercultural competence include: displaying empathy; being tolerant of ambiguity; showing sensitivity; valuing differences and gaining synergy from the differences.

2. Breaking cultural communication barriers

We live in a culturally diverse world and we will encounter individuals from different races, religions, and nationalities in our day-to-day encounters. There is often anxiety concerning unfamiliar cultures. What manners are acceptable? What will offend a person from a very different background? Knowing about other cultures will help break cultural communication barriers and develop your cross-cultural communication skills. People from different backgrounds may have varied approaches to conflict management, learning styles, family structure, religion, and most other aspects of life. When dealing with diverse people, look for similarities first. Most people have basic needs in common. Considering these things it is easy to see our essential common ground and this is where we can begin our comprehension of others.

3. Cultural stereotypes

The term "stereotype" is used today to mean a readily available image of a given social group, usually based on rough, irrational, and negative generalizations. Stereotypes often reflect the differences in socioeconomic status or religion. These differences are apparent in all races and cannot identify one specific group of people. Stereotypes supposedly give us a general overview of the whole group of people so we know what to expect and how to act. Though stereotypes contain some truth, this tiny truth cannot characterize an entire culture. It is important for us to suspend judgment, avoid misconceptions, narrow perspectives, and immature reactions. Getting the whole picture is being active, and thinking critically about people and their behavior. In the process of intercultural communication, we apply both evidence and our existing knowledge about members of a certain cultural group to reduce uncertainty involved in the context. The less we know about the other, the more we hang on to stereotypes. Often, cultural stereotypes are understood to be harmful to intercultural communication and the removal of stereotypes is believed to be a prerequisite（先决条件） for any successful intercultural exchange.

Language and Culture Focus (语言文化要点)

>>>>> Reading I

1. belief: an acceptance that sth. exists or is true, esp. one without proof. 相信, 信念; 信仰

【例句】a common belief 普遍的信念

the prevailing belief 流行的看法

religious or political beliefs 宗教或政治信仰

I haven't much belief in his ability. 我不大相信他的能力。

2. unconscious: without conscious control; involuntary or unintended; done or existing without one realizing. 未意识到的; 无意识的, 潜意识的

【例句】He was unconscious of any danger. 他不觉得有任何危险。

The blow knocked him unconscious. 那一拳把他打昏过去。

an unconscious impulse 无意思的冲动

3. fairness: the quality of treating people equally or in a way that is reasonable. 公平, 公正

【例句】They question my fairness and competence in every possible way.

There is not fairness for women in this country.

【相关搭配】

in fairness to / out of all fairness: 公平地说; 讲句公道话

【例句】In fairness to the students it must be pointed out that they did work very hard on the project.

I think out of all fairness I should say that the majority behaved very well.

It must be said in fairness that Frank played an important role in all this.

4. call for: to draw attention to the need for. 需要, 要求

【例句】Controlling a class calls for all your sill as a teacher.

The situation calls for immediate action.

5. preferential: of or involving preference or partiality; constituting a favor or privilege. 优先的; 优待的

【例句】The hotel gives preferential treatment to people who stay in it regularly.

a preferential tariff 特惠关税（率）

6. treatment: the manner in which someone behaves towards or deals with someone or sth. 对待; 待遇

【例句】receive rough treatment from sb.

suffer from cruel treatment 受到虐待

They were tired of their poor treatment by their host. 他们实在难以忍受东道主的怠慢。

7. performance: the action or process of performing a task or function. 工作情况；表现；（机器等的）工作性能

　【例句】a country's economic performance 一个国家的经济运作情况

　　　　 high performance cars 高性能汽车

　　　　 Customers are disappointed with the performance of the system.

　　　　 How is a company to measure its performance?

8. disharmony: lack of harmony or agreement. 不协调；不和谐；不一致

　【例句】social disharmony

　　　　 The new administration's economic policies are in disharmony with each other.
　　　　 新政府的经济政策互不协调。

　　　　 The choir sang in perfect disharmony.

9. base on: to use (sth. specified) as the foundation or starting point for sth. 把……建立在基础上

　【例句】base one's conclusions on facts

　　　　 Entitlement will be based on income.

　　　　 The movie is based on a real-life incident.

　　　　 The report is based on figures from six different European cities.

10. excel: (in/at sth./at doing sth.) to be very good at doing sth. 优于，擅长

　【例句】She has always excelled in foreign languages.

　　　　 As a child he excelled at music and art.

　　　　 The consumers excel at the liquor store: they buy brandy, beer and table wine at twice the national norm, possibly to take the edge off stress-filled urban living.

　有时可以做及物动词，表示"胜过"。

　　　　 The new instrument excels the old one in performance.

11. be linked to: to be related to in some way. 联系，连接；与……有关

　【例句】The video cameras are linked to a powerful computer.

　　　　 Exposure to ultraviolet light（紫外线）is closely linked to skin cancer.

　　　　 The personal development of a child is closely linked to its social development.

　　　　 (= they depend on each other).

　　　　 Televisions at home are linked to the television stations by cables.

　　　　 Some birth defects are linked to smoking during pregnancy.

12. social class: a social division based on social or economic status. 社会阶级，社会等级

　【例句】the class system 社会等级制度

　　　　 the working class 工人阶级

the middle class 中产阶级

Social classes are economic or cultural arrangements of groups in society. Class is an essential object of analysis for sociologists, political scientists, economists, anthropologists and social historians. In the social sciences, social class is often discussed in terms of "social stratification". In the modern Western context, stratification typically comprises three layers: upper class, middle class, and lower class. Each class may be further subdivided into smaller classes (e.g. occupational).

13. And in some countries, people of some castes or races are prohibited by law from full participation in society.

【译文】在一些国家，某些社会阶层或种族的人们在法律上被禁止全面参与社会活动。

prohibit *v.*

1) to stop sth. from being done or used especially by law. 禁止

synonym: forbid

【例句】a law prohibiting the sale of alcohol

Smoking is strictly prohibited inside the factory.

They are prohibited from revealing details about the candidates.

There is a rule prohibiting a truck from carrying goods on its return haul.

2) to make sth. impossible to do. 阻止；防止

synonym: prevent

【例句】The high cost of equipment prohibits many people from taking up this sport.

Heavy fog prohibited flying.

caste: hereditary class or social status. (具有严格等级的) 社会地位；社会等级制度；印度的世袭阶级

【例句】Those educated in private schools belong to a privileged caste.

This word originated in the middle of 16th century from Spanish and Portuguese *casta* "lineage, race, breed". It is now esp. used by Hindu society to indicate each of the hereditary classes distinguished by relative degrees of ritual purity or pollution and of social status. There are four basic classes or varnas in Hindu society: Brahman (priest), Kshatriya (warrior), Vaisya (merchant or farmer), and Sudra (labourer). The lowest class, the scheduled caste (formerly known as untouchables), fall outside the varna system and have historically suffered extreme discrimination.

race: a group of people sharing the same culture, history, language, etc. 人种，种族；民族

【例句】This custom is found in people of all races throughout the world.

He admired Canadians as a hardy and determined race.

14. individualism: the habit or principle of being independent and self-reliant. 个人主义

Individualism is the moral stance, political philosophy, ideology, or social outlook that stresses "the moral worth of the individual". Individualists promote the exercise of one's goals and desires and so independence and self-reliance while opposing most external interference upon one's own interests, whether by society, family or any other group or institution.

15. **assignment:** a task or piece of work allocated to someone as part of a job or course of study. （指定的）作业；（分派的）任务

【例句】What are today's assignments?

The course has heavy reading assignments but a flexible assessment system.

16. **in/by contrast (to):** the opposite of similarly, to indicate how different one thing or person is from another thing or person that you mentioned earlier. 对比之下，形成对比

【例句】Their movement, in contrast, reached a membership of 100, 000 in two years.

By/In contrast, our use of oil has increased enormously.

The day began cold and windy, in contrast to almost two weeks of uninterrupted sunshine.

The company lost $7 million this quarter in contrast to a profit of $6.2 million a year earlier.

The situation when we arrived was in marked contrast to the news reports.

In contrast to Emily, her mother was warm and welcome.

In contrast to television, the newspapers reached very different audience with very different styles. 与电视不同，不同的报纸以其不同的风格吸引不同的读者。

17. **routinely:** *adv.* of routine, to indicate sth. happening regularly and very often. 例行地；常规地

【例句】Corporations today will routinely test a product to make sure it performs adequately.

Visitors are routinely checked as they enter the building.

【相关词】

routine *n.*

1) the normal order and way in which you regularly do things. 常规，日常事务，程序

【例句】Make exercise a part of your daily routine.

We clean and repair the machines as a matter of routine.

2) (disapproving) a situation in which life is boring because things are always done in the same way. 例行公事，繁文缛节

【例句】She needed a break from routine.

adj. 1) [usually before noun] done or happening as a normal part of a particular job, situation or process. 常规的

【例句】routine enquiries/questions/tests

The fault was discovered during a routine check.

2) (disapproving) ordinary and boring. 平淡乏味的

synonym: dull

【例句】a routine job

　　　　This type of work rapidly becomes routine.

18. **get sth. done:** to cause sth. to happen or be done. 使某事物发生或处于……的状态

sth. 与 done 逻辑上存在动宾关系，done 有被动、完成的意思。

【例句】The mother get her baby hanged on her back.

　　　　The police get him defined in the room.

　　　　I'll never get all this work finished.

　　　　I must get my hair cut.

19. **from top to bottom:** going to every part of a place in a very thorough way. 从上至下地；彻底地

【例句】We cleaned the house from top to bottom.

If you say that you clean, tidy, or examine something **from top to bottom**, you are emphasizing that you do it completely and thoroughly.

20. **pervasive:** (esp. of an unwelcome influence or physical effect) spreading widely throughout an area or a group of people. 弥漫的，渗透的；普遍的

【例句】a pervasive odor 到处弥漫的气味

　　　　a pervasive atmosphere of fear 普遍的恐惧气氛

　　　　Certainly TV is the most powerful and pervasive of the media.

21. **construction:** the action or process of building sth., typically a large structure. 建造，建筑

【例句】a construction site 建筑工地

　　　　Work has begun on the construction of the new airport.

【相关搭配】

under construction 建设中，建造中

【例句】Our new offices are still under construction.

　　　　There is a large skyscraper under construction.

22. **virtue:** behavior showing high moral standards. 美德；高尚的道德；优点

【例句】Among her many virtues are loyalty, courage, and truthfulness.

　　　　a man of high virtue 道德高尚的人

　　　　Everyone has both virtues and drawbacks.

23. **defer to sb./sth.:** (*formal*) to allow (someone or sth.) to make decisions for you or tell you what to do, even if you disagree with them, because of your respect for them and/or because of their higher rank, authority, knowledge, etc. 服从，顺从（表示尊重）

【例句】I defer to (=accept) your judgment.

　　　　We defer to his opinions.

　　　　She said that she wasn't willing to defer to her husband.

I have to defer to my boss on important decisions.

【相关词】

deference *n.* [U] behavior that shows that you respect sb./sth. 尊重

【例句】The flags were lowered out of deference to the bereaved family. 降旗为遇难的家庭致哀。

24. **parent company:** an organization or company which owns or controls a number of subsidiaries. 母公司，总公司

【例句】Policy considerations were determined largely by the parent company.

25. **He presented the potential problems of the equipment as mildly as possible and ended his report with a statement that if management decided to sell the equipment in the United States, he would do everything possible to market it.**

【译文】他尽可能温和地陈述设备的潜在问题，并在报告结束时这样写道：如果管理层决定在美国销售此设备，他将尽一切可能营销它。

mildly: in a mild or gentle manner 温和地，适度地

【例句】protest mildly 温和地抗议

He had suffered mildly from the illness since he was 23.

He kept his voice mildly curious.

26. **as+*adv.*+as possible**

as ... as的用法：

as ... as意为"和……一样"，表示同级的比较。使用时要注意第一个as为副词，第二个as为连词。其基本结构为：as+*adj./adv.*+as。

【例句】This film is as interesting as that one. 这部电影和那部电影一样有趣。

Your pen writes as smoothly as mine. 你的钢笔书写起来和我的一样流畅。

其否定式为not as/so+*adj./adv.*+as。

【例句】This dictionary is not as/so useful as you think. 这本字典不如你想象的那样有用。

若有修饰成分，如twice, three times, half, a quarter等，则须置于第一个as之前。

【例句】Your bag is twice as expensive as mine. 你的袋子比我的贵一倍。

as ... as的常见句型：

1) as ... as possible

【例句】Please answer my question as soon as possible. 请尽快回答我的问题。

2) as ... as usual/before

【例句】She looks as pretty as before. 她看起来和以前一样漂亮。

一些带有as ... as结构的常见短语归纳：

【例句】as busy as a bee 像蜜蜂一样忙碌

as easy as ABC 像ABC一样容易

as deep as a well 像井一样深

as light as a feather 像羽毛一样轻

as soft as butter 像黄油一样软

as rich as a Jew 像犹太人一样富裕

27. **statement:** an account of facts, views, or plans; a definite or clear expression of sth. in speech or writing. 陈述，说明；报告；声明；说法

【例句】the statement of an idea 一种想法的陈述

This is merely a statement of fact. 这仅仅是陈述事实。

Soon afterwards he made his first public statement about the affair.

His statement was correct.

I could not deny the truth of this statement.

28. **superior**

1) *n.* a person higher in rank or status, esp. a colleague in a higher position. 上级；长官

【例句】obeying their superiors' orders

2) *adj.* (to): higher in rank, status, or quality. (在职位、地位、等级等方面)较高的；上级的

【例句】a superior officer

The new model is superior to every other car on the road.

29. **disloyal:** falling to be loyal to a person, country, or organization to which one has obligations. 不忠实的；不忠诚的

【例句】be disloyal to one's friend

He was accused of being disloyal to the government.

>>>>>Reading II

1. **The British are said to be reserved in manners, dress and speech. They are famous for their politeness, self-discipline and especially for their sense of humor.**

【译文】据说英国人在礼仪、着装和言语方面生性矜持。他们的礼貌、自律，尤其是幽默感闻名于世。

reserved: unwilling to show feelings or express opinions. 矜持的

【例句】cold and reserved letters 态度冷漠、言语不多的信件

British people are very reserved, quiet, and always discreet.

英国人生性矜持，举止安详，行事审慎。

self-discipline: the ability to control yourself without needing other people to remind you what to do.

自我约束，自律

【例句】a man of self-discipline

We should help children develop self-discipline rather than spoil them.

sense of humor: 幽默感

2. **stand on one's toes:** to offend somebody by stepping on his toes. 踩到某人的脚.

3. **numerous:** great in number; many. 数量众多的，举不胜举的

【例句】numerous reasons　　numerous examples

4. **atmosphere:** the feeling or mood that one has in a particular place or situation; a feeling between two people or in a group of people. 气氛，环境

【例句】The hotel has a good reputation for its friendly and welcoming atmosphere.

5. **a sense of togetherness:** a warm and happy feeling you have when you are with other people, especially your family and friends. 凝聚力，亲如一家的感觉

【例句】Our family has a strong sense of togetherness.

6. **bridge difference:** to fill the gap between different people and make it easier for them to communicate.

bridge *v.* to reduce or get rid of the difference between two things

【例句】The differences between our two cultures can be bridged if we continue to communicate.

7. **appreciation:** recognition of the good qualities of someone or sth. 欣赏

【例句】appreciation of modern art 对现代艺术的欣赏

【相关词】

appreciate: to be grateful.

【例句】I would appreciate it if you paid in cash.

Your support is greatly appreciated. 非常感谢你的支持。

I don't appreciate being treated like a child.

8. **contempt:** the feeling that someone or sth. is worthless or deserving scorn. 鄙视，蔑视

【例句】contempt for the truth 对真理的蔑视

He would often look at me with total contempt.

9. **understatement:** the presentation of sth. as being smaller or less important than it really is. 保守的陈述，留有余地的陈述

【例句】They were speaking with the deliberate understatement of professional people.

他们以专业人员的那种故意留有余地的口吻在说话。

10. **tone:** quality in the voice which shows a particular feeling or mood. 语气，口吻

【例句】a firm tone of voice 坚定的口吻

an encouraging tone 鼓励的口吻

in cold and sarcastic tones 冷漠讽刺的口吻

11. **praise:** the expression of approval or admiration for someone or sth.

　【例句】Three competitors were singled out for special praise.

　　　　三位参赛者被挑选出来给予特别的表扬。

12. **Briton:** a person who comes from Great Britain or who is a citizen of the United Kingdom. 英国人，大不列颠人

13. **read between the lines:** to find the hidden meanings. 看出字里行间的言外之意

　【例句】If you read between the lines, you will discover that the letter is really a request for more money.

14. **frustrating:** causing someone to have feelings of annoyed disappointment or dissatisfaction. 令人沮丧的

　【例句】The current situation is very frustrating.

　　　　It's frustrating to have to wait for so long.

15. **motto:** a short sentence or phrase that expresses the aims and beliefs of a person, group or institution. 格言, 座右铭

　【例句】My motto is "Live and let live."

　　　　我的座右铭是"得饶人处且饶人"。

　　　　The school motto is "to strive, to seek, to find."

　　　　学校的校训是"奋斗、探索、发现"。

16. **the British culture is a high-context culture:** In Britain, the cultural message has to be understood according to the background and context on which it depends. 英国的文化是高度依赖情景来理解的文化。(high-context culture 的含义参考本单元 Business World)

17. **Words are not enough, you have to know the background and context to understand the message and interpret tone, expression and non-verbal behavior.**

　【译文】语言本身表达的信息远远不够，你必须知道交际的背景和语境来理解对方信息，解读对方的语气、表情和非言语行为。

　interpret: to understand the meaning of sth.

　【例句】I interpret his silence as a refusal. 我把他的沉默理解为拒绝。

　　　　The result of the election is being interpreted as a serious setback for the government.

　　　　选举的结果被认为是政府遭受的一次严重挫折。

　non-verbal behavior: a kind of behavior or communication that does not involve the use of language. 非语言行为

　【例句】Art, like gesture, is a form of non-verbal expression.

　　　　艺术和手势一样，是一种非语言的表达方式。

18. be likely to do: If someone is likely to do something, they will very probably do it. 很有可能做某事

【例句】Tickets are likely to be expensive.

These services are likely to be available in the years to come.

不久的将来就可能有这些服务了。

19. swallow bad service: to put up with bad service and accept it patiently. 忍受糟糕的服务

swallow: to accept (an insult, etc.) patiently or without opposition. 忍受

【例句】Do they really think we can swallow that?

20. make a scene: to loudly show your anger or strong emotions in public. 当众吵嘴, 大吵大闹

【例句】Please don't make a scene here.

Please don't talk so loudly. You're making a scene.

Rather than make a scene, I kept quiet.

21. dissatisfaction: a feeling that you are not pleased and satisfied. 不满意

【例句】in a tone of deep dissatisfaction 极为不满的语调

Many people have expressed their dissatisfaction with the food and service.

There is widespread dissatisfaction with the existing political system.

民众对现行的政治体制存在着广泛的不满。

22. counterpart: a person or thing that has a similar function or position in another place or organization. 对应方

【例句】The Chinese foreign Minister held talks with his German counterpart.

中国外交部长和德国外交部长进行了会晤。

Canada's Prime Minister is the counterpart of the US President.

加拿大总理相当于美国总统。

23. hostile: very unfriendly or aggressive and ready to argue or fight. 充满敌意的, 不友善的

【例句】He used to be a reserved and hostile person.

他以前是一个沉默寡言、对一切充满敌意的人。

She was surprised and puzzled, but not hostile. 她只是惊诧, 但并没有敌意。

24. defensive: someone who is defensive acts in a way that is intended to hide their weaknesses, esp. when people are criticizing him. 防御性的, 自卫的

【例句】a defensive attitude 防御性态度, 守势

Why is he so defensive about his wife? 他为什么总是这样护着他的妻子?

Don't ask him. He is getting defensive. 不要去问他。他什么都不会说。

25. have effect: to produce the result that is intended. 见效

【例句】His protest had no effect.

26. queue: to wait in a line of people.

【例句】queue up for the bus 排队等公共汽车

queue for the tickets 排队买票

queue up for sb.'s autograph 排队等某人的亲笔签名

27. **imitate:** to copy the way a person speaks or behaves in order to amuse people. 模仿

【例句】imitate one's voice 模仿某人的声音

His handwriting is difficult to imitate.

She knew that people used to imitate her and laugh at her behind her back.

28. **hurry someone:** to make someone do sth. more quickly without enough care.

【例句】Don't hurry me. I need time to think about it.

I don't want to hurry you into making an unwise choice.

我不想催你做出不明智的选择。

29. **make a chat:** to talk in an informal and friendly way, usually about things which are not very serious or important. 闲聊，聊天

30. **take an interest in:** to be keen to learn or hear about sth. 感兴趣

【例句】take an interest in the project

None of them took the slightest interest in music.

他们中没有人对音乐有丝毫的兴趣。

31. **get used to:** to be familiar with sth. because you do it or experience it very often.

【例句】We are used to the noise from the traffic now.

I'm not used to eating so much at lunch time.

I found the job tiring at first but I soon got used to it.

You'll soon get used to the climate here.

32. **amorous intentions:** an idea or plan that shows or involves sexual desire and love towards sb.

【例句】an amorous glance 含情脉脉的一瞥

>>>> Extended Activities

A. Function and Structure: Apologizing

1. Sometimes Chinese do not consider westerners' apologies to be sincere although the westerners involved were being sincere in the western way of honestly and directly expressing feelings of regret. So then the question becomes, what do the Chinese on the receiving end of the apology consider to be sincere? The conclusion is that for an apology to be considered sincere, it must follow a proper

form. Words of regret are not always sufficient. The person apologizing must express a higher degree of respect to the offended party to restore the balance in the relationship. This may require some concrete sign of respect for the offended person (or country) and a sign of humility on the part of the person (or country) wishing to apologize. Westerners sometimes use a cursory apology to move past the troublesome event and on to the next thing. This is offensive to a Chinese who is paying attention to the form and not just the words of the apology. The Westerner thinks he has done enough by saying "I'm sorry" but to the Chinese these words are empty unless accompanied by proper communication of respect and humility. Communicating respect for others and humility of self is not a strong point in the American communication repertoire. This is especially true if the person apologizing is accustomed to being in a high status or dominant position in relation to the person (or country) to whom he is apologizing.

Generally, American apologies have one or more of the following three elements, in addition to "I'm sorry":

- an excuse — I was looking at an old map.
- an offer of repair — I'll compensate the victims.
- a promise about future actions — It'll never happen again.

Chinese tend to interpret the offer of an excuse as a sign of insincerity. An excuse does not improve an apology as it does for Americans; it weakens it.

2. Working together as we often do, under pressure, conflicts are inevitable. At times, we hurt each other, sometimes by accident, and sometimes by intention. Delivering apologies is a skill critical to maintaining our relationships and to repairing these hurts. Here are some tips for making effective professional apologies.

Ask for permission

It's possible that your intended recipient isn't willing or ready to receive an apology. Ask for permission. Realize that you really are asking for a gift — the gift of receiving your apology.

Expect nothing

Apologies must be unconditional. Expectations of reciprocity, mutual concession, or forgiveness undermine your apology. Often expectations are experienced as demands.

Apologize for mistakes, not intentions

Apologizing for accidents of execution or plan can help; apologizing for something done intentionally, and which you'd likely do again in similar circumstances, isn't likely to work. Such apologies seem insincere, and often are. "I'm sorry I had to lay you off" won't help.

Offer no excuses

When we consider ourselves responsible for the pain of others, we sometimes say, "I didn't mean to," or, "That was not my intention". Any assurances that their pain wasn't a primary objective of your actions are in vain. Instead, apologize for your negligence, or your thoughtlessness, or your failure to find an alternative.

Acknowledge pain

Acknowledge their pain, and your inability to grasp it fully. And acknowledge your own pain. Of course, sincerity is required.

Take full responsibility

Acknowledge that you are 100% responsible for your own actions, which you now regret. Allocating responsibility to others defeats the purpose of the apology, especially when you allocate some of it to the person you're apologizing to.

Tell what you've learned

If you've learned something from the incident, consider revealing it. Knowing that you're less likely to repeat your transgression can be a comfort. Whatever the form of your apology, think carefully before asking for forgiveness. Asking for forgiveness can seem like a demand, and that compounds your offense. Only forgiveness freely given has true meaning.

B. Special Use: The Use of Article

1. 冠词的种类

英语中的冠词用在名词前面起修饰作用。冠词主要有两类：不定冠词(indefinite article) a / an 和定冠词(definite article) the。但有时名词前面也可以不用冠词或省略冠词，我们把这种用法称为零位冠词(zero article)。

2. 不定冠词a / an 的用法

1) 当可数名词单数在上下文中第一次出现时，a / an可与之连用，表示不确定的人或物。例如：

Yesterday I met an old friend in the department store.

2) 用于类指，表示一类人或物。例如：

A child needs care. (= Children need care.)

3) 表示某一个人或事物。例如：

There is a visitor to see you. (某个参观者)

It was an April in my childhood.

He came on a Friday.

A Mr. Smith is waiting outside. (某个叫史密斯的人，我不认识他)

比较：Mr. Smith is waiting outside. (我认识他)

4) 表示每一个，相当于each, every 或per。例如：

four times a day   sixty kilometres an hour   five pounds a kilo

5) 表示一个, 相当于one。例如:

If you have an umbrella, lend me one.

A stitch in time saves nine.

a dozen   a hundred   a thousand   a million

注意a与half的搭配:one and a half kilos, one kilo and a half, half a kilo。

有时a / an含有一阵或一次的意思。例如:

A heavy rain was falling.

A silence followed the heated discussion.

I want to have a shower/rest/walk.

6) 表示同一个或同一种。例如:

Birds of a feather flock together.

We are of an age.

7) 表示某些疾病。例如:

I have got a cold

He has got a headache.

3. 定冠词the的用法

1) 与可数名词单数连用, 表示一类人或物。例如:

The horse is a useful animal.

Galileo invented the telescope.

The whale is in danger of becoming extinct.

2) 用于民族名或职业名的复数形式前表示全体成员。例如:

The Chinese are courageous and industrious.

3) 和形容词或分词连用, 泛指一类人或事物。例如:

the sick   the dead   the old   the young

4) 与乐器和娱乐场所连用。例如:

play the piano   go to the theater

5) 用于上文已经提到的名词。例如:

His bike struck a tree. You can still see the mark on the tree.

6) 用于上下文中, 表示对话双方都明了的人或事物。例如:

Shut the door, please. (你知道是哪一扇门。)

What is in the paper? (你知道是哪一份报纸。)

Ann is in the garden. (你知道是哪一个花园。)

Please pass the wine. (你知道是哪一瓶葡萄酒。)

Has the postman come? (指天天给我们送信的邮递员。)

7) 经常与有修饰语的名词连用,表示特指。例如:

The girl in blue is my desk-mate.

The old man I met on the road is my father's teacher.

8) 经常和独一无二的普通名词连用。例如:

the earth   the sky   the equator

* 用于形容词或副词的最高级前。例如:

the best policy   the most expensive one

9) 经常与first、second等序数词,next、following、last等一些表示顺序的词以及only等有限定意义的词连用。例如:

the first week   the next day   the following sentence

the last one   the only way

10) 与一些表示时间和空间的词连用。例如:

the beginning   the middle   the end   the past

the present   the top   the bottom   the back

the centre   the inside   the outside

11) 经常与表示江河、海洋、山脉、岛屿、沙漠等专有名词和以复数形式出现的国家名词连用。例如:

the Mississippi   the Atlantic   the Thames

the Alps   the Rockies   the Netherlands

the Philippines   the Sahara

12) 用于"名词+ of +名词"的结构中,表示同位关系。例如:

the city of Shanghai   the Gulf of Mexico

the United States of America   the Cape of Good Hope

the north of China   the Tower of London

the Duke of York

13) 与报纸、组织和轮船名等连用。例如:

The New York Times   the UN   the Titanic

14) 与身体部位连用。例如:

He hit me on the head.

He took her by the arm.

15) 与姓氏的复数连用,表示一家人。例如:

the Smiths (=Mr. Smith, Mrs. Smith and their children)

16) 与单数形式的姓氏连用,以区别同名同姓的人。例如:

— We have two Mr. Smiths. Which one do you want?

— I want the Mr. Smith who sends this letter.

4. 零位冠词的用法

1) 用于泛指意义的复数名词。例如：

I like horses.

She likes flowers.

2) 用于泛指意义的抽象名词或不可数名词。例如：

Men fear death.

Paper is made of wood.

3) 表示独一无二的职务。例如：

He is elected monitor of the class.

He is chairman of the English Department.

He is elected president.

They appointed her manager.

但当这些名词不表示职务，而表示有关的人时，我们用冠词。例如：

The monitor has just left.

The president is going to visit China.

4) 用于家庭成员的称谓。例如：

Father is ill.

Mother, where are you?

5) 用于呼语。例如：

When shall we hand in our articles, professor?

When shall I come to see you, doctor?

6) 用于洲名、国名、城市名、路名、人名等。例如：

Asia	Europe	China	Beijing
Shanghai	New York	Tokyo	Fifth Avenue
Smith	Tom	Mary	Turner Street

7) 用于一日三餐。例如：

We have breakfast at eight.

I was invited to dinner.

He is having breakfast.

8) 用于表示时间的一些名词。例如：

at noon	at night	at dawn	at midnight	at sunset

Morning is the best time for study.

9) 用于球类运动。例如:

He plays golf.

10) 用于节日。例如:

National Day   Children's Day   Christmas   Easter

11) 用于某些疾病的名称。例如:

He's got bronchitis/diabetes/anaemia/dysentery/insomnia.

12) 用于表示学科的名称。例如:

English is my favorite subject.

I don't like physics.

13) 用于表示交通或运输的手段。例如:

by bike   by boat   by bus

by car   by plane   by train

14) 在 turn 和 go 之后的名词作主语补足语(表语)时不用冠词。例如:

He turned traitor.

He has gone socialist.

15) 用于复合结构中。例如:

He stood there, book in hand.

16. 表示虽然的 "as ..." 结构中, 位于句首的主语补语常不用冠词。例如:

Child as he was, he had to make his own living.

Boy as he is, he has invented a lot of things.

5. 名词与冠词的搭配比较

1) bed, church, court, hospital, prison, school, college, university

通常当这些词具有约定俗成的含义时, 不用冠词。例如:

go to bed (to sleep)   go to hospital (as patients)

go to church (to pray)   go to prison (as prisoners)

go to court (as litigants / witness)

go to school / college / university (to study)

同样, 我们说

get home from school/college/university   leave school

leave hospital   be released from prison   in bed

in hospital   at church   at school   in court

当这些词用于其他特殊意义时, 要加冠词。例如:

He goes to the school sometimes to give lectures. (不是去上学。)

2) work, office

work 与介词搭配表示"干活"时，通常不用冠词。例如：

on his way to work   at work

He is hard at work on a picture.

但 office 表示"办公"时，需要加冠词。例如：

He is at/in the office.

office 不与冠词连用时，通常表示职务。例如：

be out of office (= to be no longer in power)

3) word, legend

word 表示消息时，为不可数名词，不与 a 连用。例如：

Word came that there would be no flight on Tuesday. (消息)

I would like to say a few words. (话)

但我们用 have a word with sb. 表示与某人说句话。

另外，Legend has it that 表示"据传"，但是我们说 It's not a true story. It's a legend。

4) man, nature

man 指"人类"时，前面不用冠词。例如：

Man is descended from apes.

nature 指自然界时，也不用冠词。例如：

Man should live with nature instead of making war against it.

5) sea

当我们说 go to sea 时，我们一般指的是海员出海；be at sea 指的是在大海上航行。sea 与冠词连用通常表示海边的意思。例如：

go to the sea 去海边   be at the sea 在海边

live by / near the sea 住在海边

6) in front of, in the front of

这两个词组中文都解释为"前面"、"前部"，但 in front of 强调在外部，in the front of 强调在内部。例如：

There is a tree in front of the house. (在房子的外面)

There is a blackboard in the front of the classroom. (在教室的里面)

7) in possession of, in the possession of

这两个词组的意思都是"拥有"，但 in possession of 是主动含义，in the possession of 是被动含义。例如：

The house is in the possession of his father. (被动)

He is in possession of a large house. (主动)

8) in charge of, in the charge of

这两个词组的意思都是"负责"，但in charge of是主动含义，in the charge of是被动含义。例如：

Mr. Wang is in charge of our class.（主动）

The country is in the charge of the military government.（被动）

9) 冠词和并列的名词连用

当冠词分别与并列的名词连用，表示两个不同身份的人。例如：

the teacher and the artist（两个人，一个是教师，一个是艺术家）

当只有一个冠词用于并列的名词前，表示一个人，双重身份。例如：

the teacher and artist（一个人，既是教师，有时艺术家，双重身份）

C. Practical Reading

练习I是一个阅读归类题。学生阅读一些关于东西方文化差异具体表现的描述性文字，再把它们分别归纳到Type of Logic（逻辑模式）、Expression of Agreement and Disagreement（反对和赞成的表达）、Communication of Information（信息的沟通）、Expression of Honesty（如何表达坦诚）、Expression of Self（自我的表达）、Thinking Orientation（思维定势）、Appreciation of Individuality（对个性的评价）、View of Business Relationship（对商业关系的看法）、Way of Conflict Resolution（解决冲突的方式）、Time Sense During Meetings（关于会议的时间观）以及Perception of Conflict Results（对冲突结果的认知）等各项下。与一般篇章阅读理解不同，这些描述不是以完整的句子结构形式出现，多为词组或片语，表述简练，可能会给学生的理解造成一定的困难。此外，也要提醒学生在理解的基础上同时掌握一定的归类技巧。很多表述在结构上具有平行性，如比较级、反义词的使用，关键词的反复出现，类似的构词方式（如：I-oriented; usually sender-oriented 和 We-oriented; generally receiver-sensitive）等。

练习II是一个阅读讨论题。学生先阅读两个简单的商务案例，再口头指出哪些文化上的差异造成了双方沟通上的误区。这两个案例均属东、西方文化间的冲突（a US sales representative *vs.* his Vietnamese partners in the first case; a western businessman *vs.* his Chinese partner in the second case），学生可以比对练习I中列出的各项文化差异，非常容易地找到答案。教师还可以布置学生在课后利用因特网资源学习更多各国商业文化间差异的知识。

1) http://www.worldbusinessculture.com/ provides culture-focused country profiles which contain information on a range of topics of immediate commercial relevance to anybody working in a global organization or studying international trade.

2) http://www.cyborlink.com/ provides information about understanding the uniqueness of

cultures around the world and how to apply the skills of cultural understanding to become more successful in the global business environment.

3) http://www.chinese-culture.net/html/chinese_business_culture.html shows how to understand unique Chinese business culture and etiquette.

4) http://www.kwintessential.co.uk/etiquette/doing-business-in.html provides tips on international business values, etiquette, customs and protocol for business people travelling abroad.

这里再提供两个案例资料，教师可以根据学生具体情况予以补充。

1. To help her company establish a presence in Japan, Susan wants to hire a local interpreter who can advise her on business customs. Kana Tomari has superb qualifications on paper. But when Susan tries to probe about her experience, Kana just says, "I will do my best. I will try very hard." She never gives details about any of the previous positions she's held. Susan begins to wonder if the resume is inflated.

2. Elspeth is very proud of her participatory management style. On assignment in India, she is careful not to give orders but to ask for suggestions. But people rarely suggest anything. Even a formal suggestion system doesn't work. And to make matters worse, she doesn't sense the respect and camaraderie of the plant she managed in the United States. Perhaps, she decides gloomily, people in India just aren't ready for a woman boss.

Teaching Tips （教学提示）

1. 在安排学生进行Lead-in听力训练之前，教师可先结合背景知识1部分的内容，让学生谈谈跨文化交流以及跨文化交流技能的培养对当代国际商务、贸易发展的影响和深远意义。背景知识2可以结合Pre-reading中相关讨论题予以介绍。背景知识3可以穿插在Post-reading活动中讲解。

2. Lead-in 本单元导入部分安排了听力理解和听写填空两项任务。听力理解部分包含两个语篇，共4项听力练习。第一篇听力的主题是全球化背景下跨文化交流的重要性，第二篇听力通过一些有趣的例子,介绍了不同文化背景下身体语言所传递的不同意义。听力练习的编排和以往各单元一样,第一和第三项练习均属预听活动,主要目的是在进行精听训练之前,让学生对所听语篇的主旨(Gist)有所了解,初步把握听音和理解上的难点所在,为接下来的听力活动做好词汇和心理上的准备。第二项练习为多项选择题(Multiple-choice Questions),第四项为正误辨析题(True or False),两项练习侧重考察学生理解、辨析语篇细节和关键信息的能力。教师应鼓励学生养成边听边作笔记的习惯,笔记的重点在于语篇的逻辑层次和关键信息点。听写填空(Spot Dictation)注重与文化休克有关的动词短语和名词,可以作为导入活动安排在Reading II课文讲解之前进行。

3. Reading I Brainstorming 全班学生通过自由讨论的形式,列出他们所知道的可以用来描述民族特性的词汇。我们一般对来自某一特定地区、文化或国家的人会持有一套固化的看法(stereotypes),教师可以用提问的方式来引导学生给出他们的答案:What do you think of/What can be said about/ What do you think is typical of/ What is your general impression of/ What can best describe people from (the city of XXX, northern China, Japan, France, Britain, Italy, Germany ...)。此处只需罗列出一些常用的单词或词组即可,无需具体展开。

4. Reading I Pairwork 由学生双人结对,讨论与本单元主题 the Culture of Different People 相关的五个问题。讨论题1、2 和 3 可以作为 Brainstorming 的延伸,学生可以从 national traits, customary practices, ethical values, religious beliefs, physical appearance, social etiquette, business customs, dietary habits, consumption habits, lifestyle, outlook on the world and life, perspectives on money, love, marriage, family, friendship, job-hopping, social welfare, charity, education ...等多角度多方面具体展开,谈谈他们对来自不同国度的人们的印象和感受。一般而言,学生的这些印象和感受往往来自网络、电影、电视、书本、报纸杂志等媒体,也有来自亲身的体验或家人、朋友的经历。教师在学生完成前3题的讨论后,也可以布置学生在课后思考以下问题,为进行Post-reading活动打好伏笔。

➤ Are those generalized impressions/stereotypes we have about people from other cultures usually true or false?

➤ Are those generalized impressions /stereotypes usually helpful or harmful in cross-cultural interactions?

5. Reading I Post-reading 本单元课文介绍了大量文化差异性和文化多元化现象,为培养学生 critical thinking 的能力,本活动通过问卷调查和集体讨论等方式导入了cultural stereotypes的概念,旨在激发学生对cultural stereotypes 对跨文化交流的影响进行更为全面、客观的思考。教师可以结合以下材料和背景知识3的内容对学生的讨论予以引导和评介。

People of all backgrounds and cultures are susceptible to stereotyping individuals from other groups. Stereotypes tend to be oversimplified general impressions of any particular group of people. Some tags seem harmless enough, but when negative cultural stereotypes come into play there is potential for great harm.

How do cultural stereotypes form?

Two factors that seem to lead to stereotyping behavior are past experiences and the environment. Stereotypes do not develop suddenly but are formed over a period of time. They are made up of bits and pieces of information that we store and use to make sense of what goes on around us. As we grow up, we absorb the statements of cultural differences from our parents, teachers and friends, which become our own stereotypes. The mass media, such as TV, magazines, newspaper, books and Internet, also play an important role in spreading and consolidating the stereotypes. The stereotypes are relatively steady, which can be right for a long time. Nevertheless, they can be influenced by some historic events like the change of international political relations. A good example is how we think of Japanese. We Chinese first thought they were wise, diligent and initiative. But after their invasion, the stereotypical impression on this nation turned into totally opposite — aggressive and extremely ethnocentric. The established stereotypes which used to be true might also change as time goes by. For example, the stereotype that Chinese people tend to refuse praises from other people in order to show their humility was true in the past. However, being influenced by the western cultures, the situation has changed now. It is common to see Chinese people say "thank you" when you compliment them.

The effects of cultural stereotypes on intercultural communication

Positive   If the stereotypes are in coincidence with the truth, the benefits are apparent. They can be the first step toward learning more about another people or culture. When talking with a person from a different culture, we may feel anxious that we have little idea of his likes and dislikes. At this moment, the stereotypes can help us know another individual or group that we are not familiar with easier and faster. As a result, their possible reactions and behaviors can be predicted before we communicate with them. For example, never will we ask the privacy — age, salary or marriages — of a westerner we first meet, because we have stereotyped that they might feel offended by such questions. Thus the possible unpleasantness or even conflicts can be avoided. The primary reason that people stereotype in workplace is to relieve anxiety. It is of human nature to feel anxious when situations are ambiguous or behavior is unpredictable. By stereotyping or by constructing categories which human beings can be placed into, this anxiety is relieved, and we regain a sense of control and predictability.

Negative   Often stereotypes are problematic because they are oversimplified and exaggerated, based on half-truth or distortions about a group of people. They bring about widely false perception on the people we will communicate with. For instance, in America, the white commonly think African-Americans are violent. Reports constantly show white people are attacked by them. As a result, the white become so scared that they keep a distance from them. Second, stereotypes often lead to self-fulfilling prophecies — people see in foreigners what they expect to see, preventing some people of stereotyped groups from succeeding in certain activities or fields. Besides, as an extension of ethnocentrism, stereotypes are one of the obvious barriers to intercultural communication, contributing to racism as well as the confrontation between cultures.

Breaking the myth   Stereotypes are present in almost every aspect of daily life. It can be age-related ("Youngsters today have no respect for their elders"), sexual in nature ("Men want just one thing") or cultural ("Americans are more brash and loud than the English"). A recent US National Institutes of Health study found that common national stereotypes, such as "Americans are pushy while the English are more reserved", were baseless. A survey of 40, 000 adults from 49 cultures showed that the Swiss were most open to new ideas in art and music (the opposite is commonly believed), that the British were not as introverted as previously thought, and that the Czechs did not need anger management classes but, in fact, came across as a modest and humble group.

Changing your mindset   Perception is all in the mind, but people's viewpoints can be changed in simple ways. It is important for individuals to examine the assumptions they make about others and to ask themselves where those assumptions come from. Asking questions such as "where is the evidence for this?" can be helpful. Are your assumptions based on personal experience, on things you heard from others, from the TV or movies or heard at school? Could some of your negative impressions of others be wrong? Getting to know individuals personally can help change negative views and stereotypes.

6. Reading IICloze 介词，关系代词，连词填空为主，详细信息请参考相关的词典和语法书。以下是简单的注释。

Question 1　　born with... 意为"与生俱来的"，其他与上下文不符。

Question 2　　修饰nothing的定语从句只能用that引导。

Question 3　　因为instead of和replaced by后面不可跟介词短语，in contrast只能作状语，故只能选

rather than。

Question 4 　倒装句，只能选Nor。

Question 5 　定语从句，先行词是culture，只能选which。

Question 6 　build sth. up意为develop; create or form gradually, 符合上下文；make up sth. 意为to combine together to form something; constitute构成，与上下文不符。

Question 8 　so far后面不能接宾语，正确答案是as far as与... is concerned相配。

Question 9 　beyond 意为 "超出……范围"，此处指 "不知不觉地"。

Question 10 　by means of 意为 "通过……"，其他与上下文不符。

Question 11 　adopt意为 "采用"，accept意为 "接受" 都不宜与反身代词合用，adapt oneself to意为 "使自己适应……"。

Question 12 　with的宾语，定语从句先行词是people，只能选whom。

Question 13 　once意为 "一旦"，其他与上下文不符。

Question 14 　what引导的从句作getting的宾语，what在宾语从句中作want的宾语，其他与上下文不相配。

Question 15 　与accepting只能是as, accept ... as ... 意为 "承认是；接受为"。

Question 16 　与后面的themselves with...相配的只有identify, identify oneself with 意为 "将自己认同于……"。

Question 17 　arise from意为 "来自……" 其他于上下文不符。

Question 18 　adjustment意为 "调整"，与make相配。

Question 19 　what引导主语从句，意为The thing or things that。

Question 20 　towards与attitude相配，意为 "对……的态度"。

Key（练习答案）

>>>>>**Reading I**

Pre-reading

I.

romantic, practical, polite, rude, talkative, reserved, sincere, hypocritical, emotional, phlegmatic, open-minded, narrow-minded, flexible, dogmatic, egalitarian, class-conscious, innovative, stereotyped, conservative, liberal, bohemian, conventional, industrious, lazy, humorous, humorless, arrogant, modest, prudent, aggressive, subtle, frank ...

Exercises

II. 1. d   2. b   3. a   4. a   5. c

III. 1. routinely   2. disharmony   3. race   4. fairness   5. performance   6. superior

   7. prohibit   8. estimate   9. virtue   10. affect   11. mildly   12. construction

IV. 1. has been/is linked to   2. pervasive   3. based ... on   4. ended with   5. superior(s)

   6. defer to   7. called for   8. In contrast   9. assignment   10. preferential

V. 1. Despite hours of talks, the government and the union are still in disharmony.

   2. It is estimated that four million viewers watched that program.

   3. In order to find evidence, the police searched the house from top to bottom.

   4. Their economy has expanded enormously in the last five years, whereas ours, by/in contrast, has declined.

   5. He was prohibited from driving for a year because of drunk driving.

   6. Contrary to popular belief, the economy of the country developed as smoothly as possible last year.

>>>>>Reading II

I. 1. F   2. T   3. F   4. F   5. T   6. T   7. F   8. T   9. F   10. NM

III. 1. b   2. d   3. a   4. d   5. a   6. c   7. b   8. d   9. c   10. a

IV. 1. American values uphold independence and individualism, whereas Asian values tend to respect and defer to their parents' opinion.

   2. The price of a product is based on the production cost and the expected profit.

   3. He was really unconscious of what he was doing.

   4. Wages are linked to prices in a number of countries.

   5. There should be preferential treatment for the smaller developing countries.

   6. He was from a caste superior to others'.

   7. The firm excels at producing women's watches.

   8. In contrast to other groups and societies, the Greenpeace does not accept funding from governments or firms.

   9. They are particularly wasteful because they have got used to such cheap energy.

   10. I'm ashamed of you! How can you make a scene in the restaurant like that!

V. 1. c   2. d   3. a   4. d   5. c   6. a   7. b   8. b   9. d   10. c

   11. b   12. a   13. a   14. c   15. b   16. a   17. b   18. d   19. b   20. a

>>>>> Extended Activities

A. Function and Structure

I. 1. Mary: I'm very sorry, but I can't find the dictionary you lent me.

Sue: That's OK.

Mary: I feel so awful about it. Let me buy you a new one.

Sue: Oh, no. Don't be silly. Just forget about it.

2. (*at Susan's home*)

John: I'm afraid I spilled coffee on the tablecloth.

Susan: Oh, don't worry about it.

John: It was very careless of me, I'm afraid. I wish there was something I could do.

Susan: Don't mention it. I never did like it.

3. Kim: Please forgive me, Cathy. I've just ruined your record. It was quite by accident.

Cathy: That's all right.

Kim: I feel so awful about it. I'll make it up to you. Let me buy you a new one.

Cathy: Oh, just forget about it.

4. (*in an office*)

Secretary: I'm awfully sorry that I haven't got all the documents ready for you this morning. It must have been very embarrassing. I do beg your pardon.

Mr. King: Well, I was a bit upset at first, but as it turned out it didn't really matter.

Secretary: That was entirely my fault. I should have finished them before you attended the meeting.

Mr. King: It wasn't really all your fault. You had so much to deal with at the time. Anyway, don't worry about it any more.

5. (*in Manager's office*)

Manager: I'm really sorry for keeping you waiting, Mr. Edwards. I was answering an overseas call.

Mr. Edwards: No problem. You must be a very busy manager.

Manager: Well, what can I do for you?

Mr. Edwards: I checked into my room this morning. I found the bathroom is in a total mess. The shower doesn't have hot water and there's no towels, no soap, not even toilet paper.

Manager: I can tell you how sorry I am to hear that. We do apologize for the inconvenience. You see, the hotel has just opened and the kinds haven't been worked out yet.

Mr. King: I understand. That's OK.

Manager: I'll have the shower fixed and the toilet items sent to your room immediately. We
            shall ensure <u>that won't happen again</u>.

B. Special Use

1. /	2. a; The	3. an; an; the	4. an	5. a
6. the; the; the	7. the; the	8. /; a; the	9. /; The; /; a	10. the
11. The; /; the	12. the; /; the	13. The; the; the	14. the; the; the	15. the; the; /
16. the; the; a; /	17. A	18. /	19. /; a	20. A; an

C. Practical Reading

Cultural Values Expressed	West (America & most European countries)	East (China and Most Asian countries)
Type of Logic	a	m
Expression of Agreement and Disagreement	j	u
Communication of Information	b	p
Expression of Honesty	e	s
Expression of Self	g	i
Thinking Orientation	c	k
Appreciation of Individuality	f	l
View of Business Relationship	v	d
Way of Conflict Resolution	r	n
Time Sense During Meetings	t	o
Perception of Conflict Results	h	q

D. Additional Vocabulary

Country	People	Language
China	Chinese	Chinese
Japan	*Japanese*	*Japanese*
France	French	French

（续　表）

Country	People	Language
America	*American*	*American English*
Germany	German	*German*
Australia	Australian	*English*
Greece	*Greek*	*Greek*
Sweden	*Swedish*	*Swedish*
Great Britain	*English*	*English*
Italy	*Italian*	*Italian*
India	Indian	*Hindi, English*
Canada	*Canadian*	English, French
Spain	Spanish	*Spanish*
Portugal	*Portuguese*	*Portuguese*
Russia	*Russian*	*Russian*
Brazil	Brazilian	Portuguese
Egypt	*Egyptian*	*Egyptian*
Austria	Austrian	German
Ireland	*Irish*	*Irish*
Denmark	*Danish*	Danish
Korea	*Korean*	*Korean*
Malaysia	*Malaysian*	*Malay, English, Chinese*

Unit 7
Body Language

Teaching Aim（教学目的）

1. Cognitive Information（认知信息）: Cultural Differences of Body Language
2. Language Focus（内容重点）

— **Key Words:** I. appoint, despite, easygoing, relax, carefree, gesture, signify, customary, etiquette, impact, circumstance solution, lean, deject, intent, indifference, impatient, terminate, breath, sigh, relief, posture, subtle, stake, negotiation, vital, hostile; II. apart, protrude, flex, arc, fortify, interrogate, suspicious, awkward, insulting

— **Phrases:** I. be guilty of, be appointed to, prior to, lack of, go away, resort to, stake one's claim; II. measure off, hold up, point at, at arm's length, take ... to be ..., on guard, to be the opposite to, in public, cause offence to

— **Useful Structure:** It is noted/unlucky that ...

It is normal/common/vital (for sb.) to ..., a sign of relief

if he were to inf. ..., it would inf. ...

— **Grammar:** Numerical Expressions（II）
3. Communicative Skills（交际技能）

— **Expressions:** Making Invitations

— **Reading:** Program Schedule

Lead-in 导入

>>>>> Listening Comprehension Tasks

Difficult Words & Expressions

1. consciously: intentionally, subjectively 有意识地

2. indispensable: essential 必需的

3. social interaction: 社交

4. aware: having knowledge of 意识到的

5. square: straight 笔直的

6. dart: to cause to move swiftly and abruptly 使迅速、突然地移动

7. subtle: not immediately obvious, abstruse 微妙的，难以琢磨的

8. posture: a position of the body or of body parts 姿势

9. facial expression: 脸部表情

10. isolation: the quality or condition of being separated from others 孤立

11. amplify: to make larger or more powerful 增强，放大

12. modify: to qualify, adjust 修正

13. subvert: to overthrow completely 彻底推翻

14. verbal utterance: 口头表达

Passage Script 1

Body language is a way that you communicate with others through body movement. It is something you do all the time, sometimes consciously and sometimes unconsciously.

Your body is like a radio that cannot be turned off. The messages that your body sends out is an indispensable element in your social interaction. Sometimes you are aware that the way you act has an influence on the other party and you try to act the way you want the other person to see you. Sadly, all too often, your body is not saying what you want it to. You think your body is doing one thing when in fact it is doing the opposite. For instance, you are putting on an act of confidence. You know you have to stand straight with your shoulders square. Unfortunately, your eyes are darting in every direction, showing you are nervous.

Body language is very subtle and can only be read by looking at the whole body — the face, the posture and the gestures. Facial expressions, especially around the eyes and mouth, can tell a lot more than you imagine. Looking at one of these in isolation is misleading since they all combine into an overall message. Your body movements can amplify, modify, confirm, or subvert any verbal utterance.

Passage Script 2

There are two elements for you to understand body language:

1. The message that you send from your body

2. The message that you receive — and interpret — from someone else

Knowing both of these is going to give you a tremendous advantage over anyone around you.

The first step to success is to learn what your own body has been telling everyone for years. Knowing this is going to greatly benefit you. It will tell you exactly what other people think of you, whether you like it or not. It is better to know; otherwise, you will blindly go through life not knowing the truth. Understanding body language will help you make subtle changes that will improve your chances of success.

The second step is to learn what others are telling you. Remember, the body tells the truth. It makes no difference if the other person is saying something or not. You will know the truth. This is a great advantage to you in any situation, especially in a business setting.

Learning body language is fun. Watching what others are doing and saying and measuring the responses of the people they are talking to is a great form of entertainment. Learning should be fun. The more entertaining it is, the easier it is to learn. The more you learn, the more successful you will become.

Key

II. 1. c　2. d　3. b　4. a　5. c　6. d　7. d　8. a　9. c　10. b

III. 1. T　2. T　3. F　4. F　5. T　6. T　7. T　8. F　9. T　10. F

>>>>>Spot Dictation

Body language is <u>nonverbal</u> communication <u>by means of</u> facial expressions, eye <u>behavior</u>, gestures, <u>posture</u>, and the like. Body language expresses <u>emotions</u>, feelings, and <u>attitudes</u>, sometimes even revealing the true messages <u>which</u> are opposite to <u>what</u> is <u>conveyed</u> by spoken language. Between <u>60 and 70 percent</u> of all meaning in <u>human communication</u> is derived <u>from</u> nonverbal behavior. Some nonverbal expressions are <u>understood</u> by people in <u>all cultures</u>, <u>while</u> other expressions are <u>particular to</u> specific cultures. Although they are generally not <u>aware of</u> it, many people <u>send and receive</u> non-verbal <u>signals</u> all the time.

Background Information（背景知识）

1. The importance of body language

We are social beings and we cannot live without each other. As soon as we are in contact with others, we are communicating. For this we can make use of spoken and written language. In these ways we make the content of a message clear to each other. However we can also communicate without words. This kind of communication tells us something about the relationship between people. Often this is more important than getting the content of the message across. When we connect with a person, we have to make it clear to each other how the content of a spoken message needs to be interpreted. To make the meaning of our words clear we use body language. Body language is a language without spoken words and is therefore called non-verbal communication. Body language is used all the time and usually occurs unconsciously. We start forming impressions of people we meet from the moment we set eyes on them. A large part of the initial impression that we create comes from our body language. Our posture, facial expression, eye contact, and gestures speak louder than the words we say. We all interpret body language all the time on a subconscious level.

2. Different interpretations of body language

It is important to note that body language has different meanings in different cultures. How we can interpret body language depends on the situation, the culture, the relationship we have with the person as well as the gender of the other. This means that there is not one signal that has the same meaning all over the world. If you do not take this into account, you may get yourself in some serious trouble!

3. The expression of feelings

Body language is used especially to express feelings. For instance, if we do not like someone, it is often difficult to say that directly to the person. However we can make it clear either intentionally or unintentionally through body language. The opposite is also true. We may say that we ARE angry through words yet our body language may be saying loud and clear that we are NOT. This can be very confusing for the receiver. This is usually described as giving out double messages — one message in words and an opposite message in body language. It is also difficult to lie or cover up our feelings through body language. People may give their true feelings away by not being aware of their body language. Researches have shown that most people pay more attention to, and believe more readily, their impression of how a person acts through body language than what is said through words.

Language and Culture Focus (语言文化要点)

>>>>>Reading I

1. **be guilty of:** to be responsible for behavior that is morally wrong or socially unacceptable.

　　【例句】Politicians of all parties are guilty of ignoring this serious problem.

　　　　　Whoever wrote this is guilty of appalling bad taste.

2. **It is noted that ...:** "Note" in this structure means "notice" or "observe".

　　【例句】It is noted that this law will come into effect within 10 days.

　　　　　Note the way this writer uses the present tense for dramatic effect.

　　　　　Note how he operates the machine and try to copy him.

In the structure " it is noted that ...", "that" clause is the real subject while "it" is the formal subject. In English sentences there are two principles: to place new information toward the end of a sentence and to reserve the final position for the more complex parts of a clause or sentence. The former principle is called end-focus (句尾焦点), the latter, end-weight (句尾重心). These two principles work together to present the new and important information in communication. Many past participles can be used in the structure. For example, It was said (reported, rumored, announced, arranged, decided, stressed, expected, etc.)... Adjectives can also be used in this structure: It is strange(natural, obvious, true, possible, likely, unusual, etc.)...

If the following adjectives are used in this structure: It is essential (appropriate, desirable, fitting, imperative, important, vital, impossible, necessary, obligatory, proper, etc.), the "be-type" subjunctive mood is always used.

　　【例句】It is essential that all the facts be examined first.

　　　　　It is necessary that he come back without delay.

　　　　　I thought it advisable that an armed guard stand in readiness.

It was appropriate that this tax be abolished.

It is imperative that this mission not fail.

3. appoint: ［as, to］ to choose for a position or job. 任命；委任

【例句】We have decided to appoint a new official.

She has been appointed as sales director/to the post of sales director.

They appointed him chairman.

I have been appointed to deal with this matter.

【相关词组】

make/keep/cancel an appointment

by appointment 要事先预约

【例句】He will only see you by appointment.

4. despite: in spite of.

【例句】He came to the meeting despite his illness.

Demand for these cars is high, despite their high price.

5. prior to: (*formal*) before. 在……之前

【例句】All the arrangements should have been completed prior to our departure.

6. It is normal/common/natural ... (for sb.) to do sth.: 某人做某事很正常/普通/重要

In this structure "it" is the formal subject and the real subject is the infinitive. The logical subject of the infinitive is introduced by "for sb.".

【例句】In the West it's becoming normal for couples to live together before they are married.

It is very common for new fathers to feel jealous of the baby.

It is not natural for a child of his age to be so quiet.

7. easygoing: taking life easily; tending not to worry or get angry. 脾气随和的；温和的

【例句】Our teacher is very easygoing; she doesn't mind if we turn up late.

8. relax *vt./vi.*

1) to make or become less active and worried. 放松；（使）轻松

【例句】Sit down and relax!

The music will help to relax you.

2) to make or become less stiff or tight. （使）松弛

【例句】His muscles relaxed.

She relaxed her hold on the wheel. 她没有把紧方向盘。

【相关词】

relaxed *adj.*

1) (of a person) free from worry; easy in manner. （人）轻松的；自在的；无拘无束的

【例句】He looked relaxed and happy.

2) (of surroundings or situation) comfortable and informal; restful. (环境)舒适的; 随便的

【例句】a relaxed atmosphere

relaxation

1) *n.* [U/C] rest and amusement. 消遣; 娱乐

【例句】He plays the piano for a bit of relaxation. It's one of his favorite relaxations.

2) the act of becoming or making less stiff or severe. 松弛; 松懈; 放松; 放宽

【例句】the relaxation of controls on government spending

9. **carefree:** free from anxiety; having no worries or problems. 无忧无虑的; 快乐舒畅的

【例句】After finishing our exams we all felt happy and carefree.

10. **gesture**

1) *n.* the use of movement of the body, esp. of the hands, to express a certain meaning. 手势; 姿态

【例句】She shrugged her shoulders in a gesture of impatience.

He made an angry gesture.

2) *n.* an action that is done to show one's feelings or intentions. 姿态; 表示

【例句】We invited our new neighbors to dinner as a gesture of friendship.

Their offer to renew the peace talks is a conciliatory gesture.

3) *vt./vi.* to call or direct with a movement of the body. 用手势表示; 用动作示意

【例句】She gestured to the waiter to bring some more coffee.

He gestured me over with a movement of his head.

11. **signify:** to be a sign of; represent; mean. 表示, 表明, 代表; 意味着

【例句】What does this strange mark signify?

His speech may signify a shift in his foreign policy.

12. **customary:** established by custom; usual or habitual. 习惯上的; 通常的; 惯例的

【例句】It's customary to wear formal clothes on these occasions.

13. **etiquette:** the formal rules; proper behavior. 礼节; 礼仪

【例句】The rules of etiquette are not so strict nowadays.

medical/legal/professional etiquette 医学界/法律界/专业界的行为规范

14. **impact:** [on] an esp. strong or powerful influence or effect. 影响; 作用

【例句】The full impact of these changes has not yet been felt.

The computer has made a great impact on modern life.

His speech made a considerable impact on everyone.

15. **circumstance:** a fact, condition, or event concerned with and influencing another event, person, or course of action. (一般用复数) 情形; 条件; 情况; 状况

【例句】We can't judge what he did until we know all the circumstances.

This rule can only be waived in exceptional circumstances.

【相关搭配】

in/under no circumstances 决不；无论如何都不

【例句】Under no circumstances must you leave the house.

in/under the circumstances 在这种情况下；既然这样

【例句】I wanted to leave but then my uncle died, so under the circumstances I decided to stay.

The result was the best that could be expected in the circumstances.

16. Take this typical situation ...: Take this typical situation as an example/instance ...

17. solution: an answer to a difficulty or problem. 解决；解决方法

【例句】There's no good solution to this problem.

He finally came up with a solution.

18. lean:

1) *vi.* to bend from an upright position. 倾斜；弯曲

【例句】The trees leant in the wind.

He leant forward/down/over to hear what she said.

2) *vi.* to support or rest oneself in a bent or sloping position (against, on). 倚靠；斜靠

【例句】She leant against his shoulder.

He leant on the back of the chair.

3) *vt.* to place so as to be supported from the side of a sloping position. 斜靠；靠置

【例句】Lean the ladder against the wall.

He leant his bike against the post.

19. dejected: having or showing low spirits; seeming sad or disappointed. 沮丧的；忧郁的

【例句】a dejected look/person/expression

20. intently: with fixed or eager attention. 专心致志地

【例句】He listened to the teacher intently.

【相关词】

intent *adj.* ［on/upon］showing fixed or eager attention. 专注的；专心于……的

【例句】an intent stare

be intent on one's work

21. indifference: lack of interest. 漠不关心；不在乎

【例句】The government's indifference to social inequality resulted in a large scale riot.

【相关词】

indifferent *adj.* 不感兴趣的；不关心的；不在乎的

【例句】I was so excited to see snow that I was indifferent to the cold.

His manner was cold and indifferent.

22. impatient: *adj.* annoyed because of a situation one cannot control, especially when he has to wait for sth. 不耐烦的；无耐心的；急躁的

【例句】After an hour's delay, passengers were becoming impatient.

I'm coming — don't be so impatient.

【相关词】

impatience *n.* 不耐烦；无耐心

【例句】The teacher's impatience with his slower students was beginning to show.

patient *adj.* 耐心的；有毅力的

【例句】He was very patient with me when I was ill and crazy.

【相关搭配】

have no patience with 没有耐心

【例句】She has no patience with time-wasters.

lose patience (with) 失去耐心

【例句】I'm beginning to lose patience with you.

have the patience to do sth. 有耐心做某事

【例句】I wouldn't have the patience to sit sewing all day.

23. terminate: *vt./vi.* to come or bring to an end. (使)结束；(使)终止

【例句】The next train terminates here.

Your contract has been terminated.

【相关词】

termination *n.* 结束；终止

24. go away: (of a problem, unpleasant feeling, etc.) to disappear. (问题、不愉快的感觉等)消失

【例句】His stutter (口吃) went away once his mother was home.

25. breathe a sigh of relief: 松了一口气

"A sigh of relief" is a set phrase, meaning letting out a sigh with a feeling of comfort when something frightening, worrying, or painful has ended or has not happened. Besides the verb "breathe", it can also be used with prepositions such as "with" or "by", and can be modified by "loud", "deep", "audible", etc.

【例句】You could hear the students breathing a collective sigh of relief when the final bell rang.

She breathed a sigh of relief when she found out she had passed her exams.

Everyone in the convoy breathed a deep sigh of relief.

Donna jumped up with a loud sigh of relief.

With a glad sigh of relief, I joined the chorus of nods.

Invariably, most of those same hands were raised again, accompanied by sighs of relief.

There was an almost audible sigh of relief as they all stood around the foot of the column.

26. **If his superior enters his office, it is unlikely that the boss would take an obvious ownership posture but would resort to more subtle gesture such as putting his foot on the lower drawer of his desk or placing his foot hard against the legs of the desk to stake his claim of the ownership.**

【译文】如果他的上级走进他的办公室，他不太会摆出明显的主人翁姿态，但会借用更细微的手势，例如将他的脚放在办公桌下方的抽屉上，或将脚用力踩在桌脚上以申明其主人身份。

posture *n.*

1) the general way of holding the body. 姿势；姿态；体态

【例句】Humans have a naturally erect posture.

2) attitude. 态度

【例句】The government's posture on this new trade agreement seems very unhelpful.

27. **resort to:** to make use of; turn to (often sth. bad) for help. 采取；诉诸；求助于（通常为不好的事物）

【例句】When polite requests failed, he resorted to threats.

He resorted to stealing when he had no more money.

They would resort to violence means if their requests are not satisfied.

28. **subtle:** not easy to notice, understand or explain. 微妙的；细微的

【例句】subtle difference in meaning

His attempt to offer us a bribe was not exactly subtle.

29. **stake:** to risk the loss of sth. on a result, esp. because one is confident of success. 打赌

【例句】The prime minister is staking his reputation on a successful outcome to the arms talks.

I've staked all my hopes on you.

【相关词组】

stake (out) a/one's claim (to): 提出（对……的）要求；声明对某物拥有所有权

【例句】He staked a claim to the land where he'd found the gold.

With her latest novel, she stakes her claim to greatness.

at stake: at risk 濒临险境

【例句】The company is on the verge of bankruptcy, and hundreds of jobs are at stake.

30. **Such gestures can be quite annoying if they are found during negotiation, and it is vital for you to make the person change to a different position, because the longer he stays in the leg-over-chair or feet-on-desk position, the longer he will have an indifferent or hostile attitude.**

【译文】这些姿势如果在商谈中表现出来会相当烦人，让他改变姿势是关键，因为他将腿搭在椅子上或把脚踩在桌上的时间越长，就越表明他持有一种漠不关心或敌意的态度。

negotiation: official discussions between the representatives of opposing groups who are trying to reach an agreement, especially in business or politics. 商议 , 谈判

【例句】The negotiations with the company had reached a crucial stage.

　　　　This follows private negotiations between the landowner and the leisure centre.

　　　　He is trying to involve community leaders in negotiations on reform.

31. **vital:** extremely important and necessary for something to succeed or exist. 生死攸关的 , 重大的 , 至关重要的　**synonym: crucial**

【例句】The work she does is absolutely vital.

Notice the prepositions used with "vital" and the sentence patterns of this word:

1) vital to

【例句】These measures are vital to national security.

2) vital for

【例句】Regular exercise is vital for your health.

3) It is vital （that）...

【例句】It is vital that you keep accurate records.

4) It is vital to do sth.

【例句】It is vital to keep accurate records.

　　　　It is vital to be honest with your children.

32. **hostile:** showing extreme dislike or disapproval; unfriendly. 怀有敌意的 ; 不友好的

【例句】a hostile crowd　　　　　　hostile gesture

　　　　They are hostile to us.

【相关词】

hostility *n.* 敌意 ; 敌对状态

【例句】There is now open hostility between the two countries.

>>>>Reading II

1. **gesture:** the use of the movement of the body, especially of the hands or head to express a certain idea or emotion. 手势 ; 姿势

【例句】He made an angry gesture with his fist.

　　　　She shrugged her shoulders in a gesture of impatience.

　　　　She held one hand over her eyes in a gesture of pain.

　　　　English people do not use as much gesture as Italians.

"gestural" is the adjective. For example: gestural expressions.

2. **An angler in Britain will demonstrate the size of a fish he has caught by holding his two hands, palms facing each other, the appropriate distance apart in front of him, but an angler from certain parts of Africa will measure off the size along his left arm with his right hand.**

【译文】英国的垂钓者会举起双手，掌心相对，两手掌间保持适当的距离，以此比划钓到鱼的大小；但非洲某些地方的垂钓者会用右手在左臂上比划鱼的大小。

3. 辨析 angler & fisherman

angler: someone who fishes with a fishing rod, especially as a hobby. Its verb is "angle".

【例句】He loves to go angling on a fine summer day.

fisherman: a person who catches fish, but he takes it as a job rather than a hobby.

4. **names for different parts of a hand**

palm: the inside surface of the hand between the base of the fingers and wrist. 手掌

【例句】She placed the money in his palm.

thumb: the short thick finger that is set apart from the other four fingers. 大拇指

index finger: (also called forefinger) the finger next to the thumb. 食指

middle finger: the longest finger, in the middle of the five fingers of the hand. 中指

ring finger: the fourth finger of the hand on which a wedding ring is usually worn. 无名指

little finger: the smallest finger on the hand, which is the farthest from the thumb. 小指

Names for Different Parts of a Hand

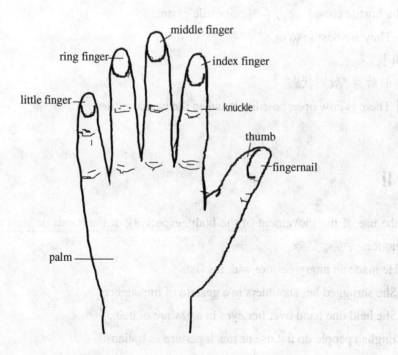

fingernail: the hard flat piece that covers the end of a finger. 指甲

knuckle: a finger joint, especially the one joining the finger to the hand. 指节，掌指关节

5. **appropriate:** correct, suitable, or acceptable for a particular situation or occasion.

【例句】His bright clothes were hardly appropriate for such a solemn occasion.

I think this is an appropriate moment to raise the question of my promotion.

"Inappropriate" is its opposite.

【例句】It seems inappropriate to end our lesson with a joke.

6. **apart:** If two people or things are a particular distance apart, there is a space or distance between them.

【例句】He stood with his legs apart.

The two boxers stood apart, waiting for the sign to start fighting.

They planned the trees wide apart.

He and his wife are living apart.

7. **measure off:** to find the size, length, amount or degree of sth. 测量出

【例句】He measured off three yards of rope.

He measured off six yards of cloth.

He measured off the height of the cupboard.

8. **numeral:** a symbol or group of symbols used to represent a number.

【例句】In Arabic numerals, the year is written 1983; but in Roman numerals, it is written MCMLXXXIII.

9. **hold up:** If you hold up your hand or something you have in your hand, you move it upward into a particular position and keep it there.

【例句】Ralph held up his hand.

The soldier held up the rifle.

10. **Switzerland:** a republic in Central Europe. Its capital is Bern.

11. **point at:** If you point at something, you show it to people by holding out your finger or an object such as a stick, so that if people look in the direction of your finger or the stick, they will see what you are showing.

【例句】She pointed at the house and said, "This is where I live".

He pointed at her and shouted, "Don't move!"

12. **protrude:** to stick out. 伸出

【例句】He saw a gun protruding from the man's pocket.

13. **The gesture for "come here" is made in Britain with the index finger, which is held, pointing upwards, at eye level and flexed towards the body; in Greece, the hand and forearm describe**

an arc away from the body towards the ground; in Egypt the hand is held at arm's length, palm downwards, and the fingers are then flexed.

【译文】在英国，"过来"的手势是向上举起食指与视线持平，然后手指向自己的身体方向勾动；在希腊，对应的手势则是手和前臂弯拢成一个弧形，从自己的身体向地面方向运动；在埃及，该手势是手和手臂举平，手掌向下，所有手指向里勾曲。

14. **flex:** If you flex your muscles or part of your body, you bend, move or stretch them for a short time in preparation for physical exercise or work.

   【例句】He eased his boots off and flexed his toes in front of the stove.

   The runners flexed their muscles as they waited for the race to begin.

15. **forearm:** the lower part of the arm between the wrist and the elbow. 前臂

16. **arc:** part of a curved line or circle. 弧度

   【例句】The sun appears to move in an arc across the sky.

17. **at arm's length:** If you hold or carry something at arm's length, you hold it at a distance from your body.

   【例句】He held the paper at arm's length.

   If you keep someone at arm's length, you avoid being friendly with him and keep a safe distance.

   We all understand the necessity of keeping Mike at arm's length.

18. **considerable:** fairly large or great in amount or degree.

   【例句】A considerable number of people object to the government's attitude to immigration.

   The building suffered considerable damage as a result of the fire.

19. **take...to be:** to consider...to be, understand... to be.

   【例句】I took your nodding to be a sign of approval.

20. **precisely:** accurately and exactly.

   【例句】The train leaves at ten o'clock precisely.

   Let's explain to you precisely what I'm going to do.

21. **to be the opposite to:** to be most different from.

   【例句】Indifference is taken to be the opposite to enthusiasm.

   Black is the opposite to white.

22. **intend:** to plan or decide, to have something in one's mind as a plan or purpose.

   【例句】I intend to do the job.

   I intend to report it to the police.

   She had intended to catch the early train, but she didn't get up in time.

   "Intended" can be used as the adjective to indicate something expected.

【例句】What is the intended result?

Everything they do and say is intended to promote sales.

23. **misinterpretation:** wrong understanding or explanation.

【例句】misinterpretation of the teacher's directions

misinterpretation of the results of the experiment

24. **disastrous:** causing a disaster.

【例句】a disastrous marriage/mistake/failure

The new system has had a disastrous effect on productivity.

In 1973, famine came in the wake of disastrous floods.

25. **consequence:** result.

【例句】The high level of unemployment has produced harmful social consequences.

The safety procedures had been ignored with disastrous consequences.

26. **fortified:** strengthened against possible attack, more able to resist an attack. 加强的

【例句】a fortified castle/city/town

【相关词】

fortify: *v.*

1) to build towers, walls etc. around an area or city in order to defend it. 加强   **synonym: strengthen**

【例句】The town was heavily fortified.

2) ［usually passive］to make food or drinks more healthy by adding vitamins to them. 强化

【例句】fortified breakfast cereals

27. **coastal area:** area near the coast or sea. 沿海地区

【例句】coastal cities 沿海城市   coastal resort 海滨游览胜地

coastal waters 沿海水域   coastal defenses 沿海防御工事

coastal fishing 近海捕鱼

28. **the Eastern Mediterranean:** the eastern part of the Mediterranean Sea. 东地中海

29. **on guard:** Someone who is on guard is on duty or in a state of watchful readiness to protect or defend.

【例句】There are soldiers on guard at the gate.

30. **unidentified:** We use "unidentified" to describe something or somebody whose name, nature or origin is unknown.

【例句】unidentified flying object (UFO) 不明飞行物

An unidentified man was seen near the scene of the murder.

31. **interrogate:** to question formally to get information, especially for a long time and perhaps with the use of threats or violence.

【例句】The police interrogated the prisoner for several hours.

They said they had been interrogated for 20 hours about the political demonstration.

The police were ready to interrogate him.

32. suspicious: If you are suspicious of/about someone, you feel or show that you do not trust him.

【例句】We are suspicious of her intentions.

I'm a bit suspicious about the package that has been left in the corridor.

His strange behavior made the police suspicious.

The policeman on duty became suspicious of the youth and asked him why he was standing there.

33. open fire: to start shooting.

antonym: hold fire

【例句】The general ordered his men to hold fire.

cease fire: to stop shooting.

34. tragic: very sad, unfortunate because it involves death, suffering or disaster.

【例句】a tragic accident

the tragic death of the actress

35. awkward: causing difficulty or uncomfortable feelings; inconvenient or embarrassing.

【例句】awkward questions

a long awkward silence

It's an awkward time to call you.

36. For instance, an Englishman speaking in public would find it very natural if he wished to request his audience to be silent, to hold up both his hands on a level with his head, with the palms facing outwards.

【译文】例如,英国人在公众场合发言时,如果他想要求听众保持安静,会很自然地举起双手,与头部持平,掌心向外。

in public: in the presence of strangers or of many people.

【例句】He repeated in public what he had said in private.

【相关搭配】

in private: secretly, not in the presence of people.

【例句】Could we talk to you in private?

I don't mind what people do in private.

37. request sb. to do: formally or politely ask sb. to do.

【例句】We request all the members of the club to attend the annual meeting.

The gardener requested visitors not to pick up flowers.

38. **If he were to do..., it would cause...:** This sentence is the typical use of the subjunctive mood to imply that something is unlikely to happen in the future or it is not expected to occur. In the subordinate clause, we normally choose the verb form "were to do" (were can be used with any person) or "should do"; in the main clause, we use the verb form "would do".

【例句】If it were to rain tomorrow, the opening ceremony would have to be postponed.

(Actually it is unlikely to rain or I don't wish it to rain.)

If we were to miss the 10 o'clock train, we would get there till after lunch.

(Actually, it is unlikely to happen and we can't miss the train.)

If someone were to threaten me, I would call the police.

(I don't want to be threatened.)

If he were to tell us everything, we would try to solve his problem.

(He is unwilling to tell us everything.)

39. **cause offence to sb.:** to cause displeasure to sb., to make someone upset.

40. **insulting:** If you insult someone, you offend him by doing something rude, usually by speaking rudely to him or treating him with no respect. "Insulting" is the adjective used to describe this kind of behavior.

【例句】insulting language　　insulting gesture

>>>>>Extended Activities

A. Function and Structure: Making Invitations

1. The point at which a casual comment becomes a firm invitation varies from culture to culture. In the US, if an American says: "We must get together some time", a firm invitation has not been made. However, if that person names a specific date and time, for example:"How would you like to come to dinner on Tuesday at 6 : 00?" and his friend accepts, the American host assumes that a firm commitment has been made and expects his friend to arrive on Tuesday at 6 : 00 pm.

2. You should accept an invitation in the same medium the invitation was sent. If the invitation to a party or function was a formal card, which was posted to you, then it will follow that your acceptance should be a formal card that you post. It is thought to be inappropriate to email or telephone your acceptance if the invitation was formally sent and it's always best to send your acceptance as soon as possible. As with accepting an invitation, declining an invitation should be made in the same medium. If you cannot make the date, you may wish to state why and arrange

another time to meet.

3. Because invitations are sometimes agreed upon in informal conversation and will probably not be followed by a written invitation, many people carry pocket calendars in which to mark the date of the engagement and the host's telephone number (should cancellation be necessary due to an emergency). When a written invitation is received, the guest is expected to telephone or write to the host to accept or decline the invitation. At the time of acceptance, guests notify the hostess of any medical or religious restrictions against foods such as pork or beef, or beverages containing alcohol, etc. Once an invitation has been accepted, the commitment to attend is regarded as a firm obligation, to be respected by both guest and host even if other invitations for the same time are received later. In addition, it is assumed that guests will accept no other invitations for a later hour on the same evening they are invited for dinner.

4. Unless the host indicates otherwise, an invitation offered to a guest is only for that person. Americans usually prepare for a specific number of guests and often plan to have a similar number of male and female guests. Therefore for a dinner guest to arrive with one or two unannounced friends is considered impolite and embarrassing to the hosts who may not have prepared enough food for extra people, or who may not have enough room for them at the table. When a social, rather than business invitation is extended to a married person, the assumption is that the spouse is invited as well. The guest should ask the host if there is any question about this.

5. Some expression of thanks is considered appropriate when hospitality has been extended and received. Guests express appreciation in various ways:

- *After receiving dinner hospitality,* guests often present a gift to the hostess. This is considered a nice gesture, but not a necessary one. Many international visitors give something distinctive from their home land, such as postage stamps or coins to emphasize the special cross-cultural spirit of the evening.

- *A written "thank-you" note or a telephone call* to the hostess delivered or made within one week after the engagement is the most common and often most welcomed expression of appreciation.

B. Special Use: Numerical Expressions (II)

1. 序数词与定冠词the

序数词前通常都有定冠词the。例如：

the fortieth day   the twentieth visitor

但遇到下列情况时，序数词不与the连用：

1) 序数词表示又一个或又一次。例如：

A second girl came into the room.

He tried for a third time.

2) 序数词作路名。例如：

Excuse me, would you please tell me where Second Street is?

Fifth Avenue is famous for its expensive commodities.

3) 序数词表示排名。例如：

He stands first in his class.

4) 序数词作副词。例如：

He came first.

2. 倍数词的使用

1) 分数 (fraction) 的表达法

分数的分子用基数词表示，分母用序数词表示。分子如果是1，序数词为单数；分子如果是1以上的数字，序数词为复数。例如：

a/one third　　　two thirds　　　three fourths

我们也可以用"基数词 + in/over + 基数词"来表示。例如：

one over three　　　nine over ten　　　one in ten

读整数带分数时，先读整数部分，整数部分与分数部分用and连接。例如：

one and a half　　　　three and a quarter　　　five and two sevenths

2) 倍数词与比较结构

倍数词用于比较结构时，必须位于more than或as...as之前。例如：

I have twice as many books as he has.

My room is three times larger than his.

该结构也可以转换成包含数词的名词短语。例如：

My living-room is half as large as yours.

=My living-room is half the size of yours.

China is twenty times as large as Japan.

=China is twenty times the size of Japan.

They have twice as many ships as we have.

=They have twice the number of our ships.

He is twice as old as you.

=He is twice your age.

3) half的用法

① half与名词搭配

half作为限定词，后面可以直接跟名词。例如：

half my earnings

I have read half the book.

half也可以作代词，用于"half of + 名词"结构。例如：

half of my earnings

I have read half of the book.

half a mile, half an hour在美国英语中也可以说成a half mile, a half hour。

注意下面的表达方式：

one day and a half（跟在后面，用单数）

one and a half days （单位超过一，用复数）

one and half a day

② half还可以做副词。例如：

A good beginning is half done.

My homework is not yet half done.

4) double的用法

① double与名词搭配

double作形容词与名词搭配时，名词有时用单数形式。例如：

double room   a man of double identity

double还可用作限定词修饰名词。例如：

He is double her age.

The ship has double the capacity of that.

② double本身也可以作名词和动词。例如：

Twenty is the double of ten. （名词）

The students of the school doubled in one year. （动词）

3. 有关数字的习语

我们有时用数词表示的并不是确切的数目，而是"大量"、"许多"的意思。例如：

It broke into a dozen pieces.

I have tried scores of times.

A thousand thanks for your help.

We have tried a thousand and one ways.

There are thousands of apples in our garden.

The weather changes twenty-one times a day here.

许多固定的说法都包含数词。例如：

in one's teens （在某人十多岁时）

in one's thirties （在某人三十多岁时）

in the eighties （在80年代）

Ten to one he forgets it. （十之八九）

English is second to Chinese in its number of speakers. （仅次于）

America is second to none in natural resources. （不亚于……）

The crew were rescued at the eleventh hour. （=at the very last moment）

The editor made several eleventh changes in the magazine.
（=last-minute changes）

The guests departed by twos and threes. （三三两两）

I like English from the first. （从一开始）

It looked like an island at first sight. （乍看起来）

He was nine years old when he went abroad for the first time. （第一次）

If you want me to trust you, first of all, be honest. （首先）

I have known him, first and last, for five years. （总共）

C. Practical Reading

　　娱乐新闻（entertainment news）主要的信息是日期、时间、地点、节目、演出单位、价格、交通等。注意这里的"地点"一项不用place一词，而是用venue（来源于法语 venir，原意是 to come，做名词指 the place in which the alleged events take place）。要完成这类阅读材料后的题目，关键是将上述项目进行归类。例如："节目"这个项目里总共有6类：

　　1. Concert 音乐会

　　2. Classical Vocal Performance 古典声乐演出

　　3. Chinese Local Opera 中国地方戏曲

　　4. Ballet 芭蕾舞

　　5. Peking Opera 京剧

　　6. Evening Party 晚会

　　只要有了这种简单的归类，要解决后面的题目也就易如反掌了。比如第一道题就是问节目类型的。从上面的归类项中，我们知道ballet, Chinese Local Opera, 以及Symphony（交响乐）三种节目都有，只有rock and roll是干扰项。所以答案是b。同理，第二道题目问的是本月能有几次欣赏symphony的机会。根据上面的分类，我们会很快找到关键词symphony与Concert和Orchestra（交响乐团）有关，共有Dec. 7和Dec 10~11两次，这也正是本题的答案，也是b。其他问题以此类推。

Teaching Tips（教学提示）

1. Lead-in 本单元导入部分安排了听力理解和听写填空两项任务。听力理解部分包含两个语篇，共3项听力练习。第一篇听力介绍了身势语的基本定义，以及身势语在我们日常沟通交流中所起的作用；第二篇听力介绍了理解身势语的两大要素，以及理解身势语的重要性。听力练习的编排和以往各单元一样，第一项练习属预听活动，主要目的是在进行精听训练之前，让学生对所听语篇的主旨（Gist）有所了解，初步把握听音和理解上的难点所在，为接下来的听力活动做好词汇和心理上的准备。第二项练习为多项选择题（Multiple-choice Questions），第三项为正误辨析题（True or False），两项练习侧重考察学生理解、辨析语篇细节和关键信息的能力。在进行听力理解活动之前，教师可以结合背景知识部分的内容，简单介绍body language这一概念和正确理解body language所传递的信息在人际交往中的重要意义。听写填空(Spot Dictation)注重介词、形容词短语、从句和交际方面的动词、名词等的听写，可以作为导入活动安排在Reading II课文讲解之前进行。

2. Reading I Brainstorming 学生通过讨论，列出他们所知道的关于communication的各种方式。为了进一步对学生加以引导，教师可1）请学生谈谈最喜欢用什么样的方式和不同的对象交流（What is your favorite way to communicate with your parents/friends/teachers/classmates... ）；2）请学生说说他们能用多少种不同的方式向别人传递某一个特定的信息（e.g. I'm interested/bored/annoyed... ）。

3. Reading I Pairwork 学生双人结对讨论一些关于body language的常识。教师可根据讨论题第3、4、5题教参中给出的参考答案，并结合 Background Information 中提供的信息为学生进一步介绍相关知识。

4. Reading I 练习IV Question 7中 I resorted to standing outside her window and calling up to her. 意思是"我只得采取站在她窗外，大声喊她的办法了"。call to, 向……喊。如：We can hear various birds calling to one another in the park.

5. Reading I Post-reading 要求学生分组活动，边按指示做出相应的肢体动作，边尝试解读这些动作，讨论它们各自代表的含义。教师也可把教材上的动作指令复印并裁剪开来，分发给若干学生，一人一条，请拿到指令的学生轮流到讲台前把各个动作表演出来，让其他学生猜一猜，他们各自做的是哪个动作或他们可能想表达的意思。

sitting with legs crossed, foot kicking slightly — 双腿交叉而坐，脚轻轻踢动。
standing with hands on hips — 双手置髋部，直立。

sitting, legs apart — 双腿分开而坐。
arms crossed on chest — 两臂交叉置胸前。
walking with hands in pockets, shoulders hunched — 双手插袋, 耸肩, 踱来踱去。
hand to cheek — 手托腮部。
touching, slightly rubbing nose — 触摸并轻揉鼻子。
rubbing the eye — 搓揉眼睛。
hands clasped behind back — 双手紧扣, 放在背后。
head resting in hand, eyes downcast — 头枕在手上, 眼睛向下看。
rubbing hands — 搓揉双手。
sitting with hands clasped behind head, legs crossed — 双手反枕在脑后, 跷着二郎腿。
open palm — 手掌摊开。
pinching bridge of nose, eyes closed — 双眼紧闭, 掐捏鼻梁。
tapping or drumming fingers — 轻叩手指。
patting/fondling hair — 轻拍或抚弄头发。
tilted head，direct eye contact — 头微微翘起, 直接目光交流。
limited or no eye contact — 无或很少有目光交流。
relaxed brow — 眉宇舒展。
tension in brow — 眉头紧锁。
stroking chin — 抚摸下巴。
looking down, face turned away — 向下看, 脸转过去。
biting nails — 咬指甲。
pulling or tugging at ear — 拽耳朵。
fidgeting with hands or objects（e.g. pen）— 心不在焉地把玩手或其他物件（如钢笔）。
fingers interlocked placed behind the head leaving elbows open and armpits exposed — 十指互扣, 放在脑后, 胳膊肘向外, 露出腋窝部分。

教师应向学生指出，在不同的场景下，对同一个肢体动作的理解会有很大的差异（对此学生在活动中自己应已有所体会）。verbal language 和 non-verbal language 两者相辅相成，使沟通更为顺畅。

> However, some non-verbal signals have several meanings. Crossed arms can indicate defensiveness, or simply a comfortable position. Touching the nose can suggest doubt in what the person is hearing. Or it could be a response to an itch or soreness from a recent cold. Likewise, an unbuttoned jacket can signify openness and cooperation. It could also be an overweight person trying to fit into an old jacket. The key is that a non-verbal signal is not a complete message. The body language should match the verbal expressions. It should also match the context of the situation.

6. Reading II　　Exercise III　　Vocabulary

Question 10 insulting tongue, 这里 tongue 指 "说话方式"，如：have a quick/sharp/glib tongue 口齿伶俐/说话尖刻/油嘴滑舌；speak with a double tongue 说话模棱两可；watch your tongue 说话要当心。

7. Reading II　　Exercise V　　Translation

Question 3　　in ... circumstances = under ... circumstances。

Question 10　　a heavy smoker 烟抽得很凶的人。heavy 在这里的意思是 "indulging to a great degree, 过量的, 放纵达到很大程度的"，又如 a heavy drinker, 酒瘾极大的人。

8. Reading II　　Exercise VI　　Cloze

Question 4　　此处选 d。close enough, close 用作副词，可以表示 "接近地"，如：follow close behind me; sit close to his mother。而 closely 通常表示 "紧密地；严密地"，如：English and German are closely related. It's a closely guarded secret.

Question 5　　此处选 c。zone, 因为前文有 three "personal space" zones 一说，后文又有 the "wrist zone" 和 fingertips zone 相对应。

Key（练习答案）

>>>>>Reading I

Pre-reading

I.

Verbal	Non-verbal words; sentences; speech
conversation; intonation; stress; e-mails; letters; notes; faxes; phone calls; memos; reports...	body movement; gesture; posture; clothing; eye contact; facial expression; clapping hands; shaking hands; waving hands; smiling; frowning; shrugging; shaking head; rubbing nose; fondling hair; biting nails; stroking chin; tapping fingers; crossed arms...

II. 3. The face is the most expressive part of your body. If you are feeling anxious then your facial expression may lead you to appear aloof, disapproving, or disinterested. Your smile is one of the strongest tools you have in meeting new people. It will help you appear warm, open, friendly, and confident. Our eyes give clues to our emotions. A direct stare implies intensity. It may also mean romantic interest, aggression, or fear. Making very little eye contact can either convey shyness or submissiveness. The middle ground of a gaze says that you are interested, secure, and at ease.

   Your hands are also very expressive. Open gestures tend to make you appear open and honest. By pointing your finger, or moving your hands closer together, you can draw emphasis on what you are saying. Used in moderation, hand gestures can make you seem enthusiastic and committed to your topic. Making too many gestures can make you appear nervous and uncontrolled. Wringing your hands or touching your sleeves, face, etc. can make you appear tense, nervous, and sometimes dishonest.

4. One's culture, gender, mood, past experiences, age, religion, nationality, race and the conversational situation etc.

5. The most effective selling technique is to use non-verbal communication, subtle messages conveyed without words. These include posture, facial expressions, gestures, mannerisms and your appearance. People buy based on their senses, and everything that you can do to positively affect their senses can and will affect your ability to sell to them. Psychologists claim that the impact you make on others depends on what you say (7%), how you say it (38%), and by your body

language (55%). Since how you sound also conveys a message, 93% of emotion is communicated without actual words. It's often not what you say that influences others; it's what you don't say. The signals that you send non-verbally suggest attitude, understanding, empathy and ethics. The moment you meet a prospective client, they judge you by what they see and feel. The process takes less than 10 seconds but the impression is permanent. Whether you make or break a sale can literally depend on the silent signals that you send during this first contact.

Exercises

II. 1. b   2. b   3. c   4. a   5. d

III. 1. hostile   2. signify   3. impact   4. customary   5. dejected   6. indifference
   7. impatient   8. resort to   9. terminate   10. prior to   11. easygoing   12. vital

IV. 1. are guilty of   2. easygoing   3. in fact   4. go away   5. a sign of relief
   6. signifies   7. resorted to   8. was appointed   9. to stake his claim   10. impact
   11. reflect   12. Despite

V. 1. She found his manner towards her distinctly hostile.

   2. The government's posture on this new trade agreement seems very unhelpful.

   3. How much money he earns is none of your concern/no concern of yours.

   4. The etiquette is not so strict nowadays.

   5. All the arrangements should have been completed prior to our departure.

   6. Your contract has been terminated.

Post-reading

Body Language	Your Interpretation
sitting with legs crossed, foot kicking slightly	boredom
standing with hands on hips	readiness, aggression
sitting, legs apart	open, relaxed
arms crossed on chest	defensiveness
walking with hands in pockets, shoulders hunched	dejection
hand to cheek	evaluation, thinking
touching, slightly rubbing nose	rejection, doubt, lying
rubbing the eye	doubt, disbelief

（续 表）

Body Language	Your Interpretation
hands clasped behind back	anger, frustration, apprehension
head resting in hand, eyes downcast	boredom
rubbing hands	anticipation
sitting with hands clasped behind head, legs crossed	confidence, superiority
open palm	sincerity, openness, innocence
pinching bridge of nose, eyes closed	negative evaluation
tapping or drumming fingers	impatience
patting/fondling hair	lack of self-confidence; insecurity
tilted head/direct eye contact	interest
limited or no eye contact	lying, uninterested, distraction
relaxed brow	feeling comfortable
tension in brow	confusion, tension, fear
stroking chin	trying to make a decision
looking down, face turned away	disbelief
biting nails	insecurity, nervousness
pulling or tugging at ear	indecision
fidgeting with hands or objects （i.e. pen）	boredom, having something to say
fingers interlocked placed behind the head leaving elbows open and armpits exposed	open to ideas, feeling comfortable

>>>>> **Reading II**

Exercises

I. 1. F　2. F　3. T　4. NM　5. T　6. F　7. F　8. T　9. NM　10. F

III. 1.a　2. b　3. b　4. c　5. c　6. d　7. c　8. a　9. d　10. a

IV. 1. He was guilty of misjudgment so that the loss was great.

2. We received no notice from the sales manager prior to Monday.

3. We need employees able to work independently in different circumstances.

4. I didn't mean to cause any offence to any people, and I was just stating my opinion.

5. The project had to be delayed for lack of funds.

6. It is unlikely that the player is to win because his rival is rather competitive.

7. The owner of the factory forced his workers to work overtime every weekend.

8. The new office boy is not polite enough, so Susan held up one warning finger at him.

9. The wine-merchant pointed at the bottle of wine and claimed that it was made over a century ago.

10. That senior official is a heavy smoker, but he never smokes in public.

V. 1. b 2. a 3. a 4. d 5. c 6. b 7. d 8. a 9. c 10. b 11. b 12. c 13. a 14. d 15. c

>>>>>Extended Activities

A. Function and Structure

I. 1. Tom: <u>What about</u> a drink?

   Jack: <u>OK</u>.

2. Sam: I've got two tickets for tonight's fashion show. Would <u>you be interested in it</u>?

   Diana: Oh darn! <u>I'd love to</u>, but I have to work for tomorrow's history quiz.

   Sam: What a pity!

3. Mary: <u>How about</u> coming over for dinner this Sunday?

   Sue: <u>That's very kind of you</u>. Thank you.

4. Jim: We're having a farewell party for Miss King tomorrow evening. We'd <u>like to invite you to come</u>, too.

   John: <u>Thank you very much for the invitation</u>, but I don't think I can. Some friends are coming over for dinner tomorrow evening.

   Jim: I see. That's too bad. We're counting on having you come.

5. Christine: <u>Would you like to</u> have lunch next week?

   Mr. Ernst: <u>Sounds great</u>. When exactly?

   Christine: Is Wednesday convenient for you?

   Mr. Ernst: I'm afraid I can't <u>make it</u> on Wednesday.

   Christine: That's a pity. <u>How about</u> Friday, at twelve o'clock?

   Mr. Ernst: Yes. <u>That's fine</u>. I'll look forward to it.

B. Special Use

1. c   2. a   3. b   4. d   5. b   6. a   7. d   8. c   9. c   10. b

C. Practical Reading

1. b   2. b   3. d   4. a   5. b   6. c   7. d   8. b

D. Additional Vocabulary

H	P	Q	Y	W	I	S	H	W	E	L	L	Y	D
U	A	V	M	W	R	Y	G	T	J	T	I	M	G
G	C	N	R	E	E	H	C	Z	A	G	A	L	F
X	F	J	D	L	Z	R	G	B	M	H	H	T	V
R	F	G	K	C	A	B	N	O	T	A	P	W	K
E	O	R	H	O	L	H	T	B	N	L	X	I	J
G	D	O	Z	M	W	A	H	D	U	G	S	T	T
A	D	D	R	E	S	S	Y	D	S	T	S	C	
R	T	J	R	L	T	H	V	P	M	T	S	A	E
D	W	R	E	D	A	V	W	A	V	E	T	O	P
L	O	M	C	K	J	E	A	W	R	A	J	T	S
D	T	N	E	M	I	L	P	M	O	C	K	L	E
X	W	H	I	E	A	I	R	B	C	M	L	R	
W	O	Y	V	S	T	M	J	W	E	O	X	A	Y
J	K	G	E	D	M	S	L	P	H	S	W	C	L
L	V	M	G	X	Y	S	A	L	U	T	E	G	V

Unit 8
Manners

1. Cognitive Information（认知信息）: Different Manners in Different Cultures

2. Language Focus（内容重点）

— **Key Words:** I. global village, arrange, community, guidebook, corresponding, custom, behave, feed, sleeve, executive, signal, ease, sole, height, exceed, deal, essential, bow, causal, illustrate, cool, reserved, impersonal, geographical link, wink, clasp; II. present, gymnastic ability, challenge, content, process, entertain, counterpart, energy, formality, offend, admire

— **Phrases:** I. on time, allow... for, give advice on, get to understand sth./sb., roll up, take off, get down to, regard as, take it easy, of its own; II. get...wrong, other than, chew over, on business, pick up, side by side with, get into difficulties, make/break a deal

— **Useful Structures:** V-ing used as adverbial of attendant circumstance（伴随情况状语）
　　　　　　　　　　on doing sth., ...
　　　　　　　　　　the more... the less...
　　　　　　　　　　be worth the effort

— **Grammar:** Simple Present and Past Tenses of Verbs

Lead-in 导入

>>>>> Listening Comprehension Tasks

Difficult Words & Expressions

1. courtesy: polite behavior 有礼貌的举止行为

2. considerate: having or showing regard for the needs or feelings of others 体谅的, 体贴的

3. in kind: 以同样的方法

4. police (*v.*): to regulate, control or keep in order 约束, 管制

5. hang out: 外出游玩、闲逛

6. generous: liberal in giving or sharing 大方的, 慷慨的

7. bossy: given to ordering others around 喜欢发号施令的; 跋扈的

8. put sb. down: 羞辱, 轻视

9. personal property: 个人财物

Passage Script 1

This is a lecture on manners. Manners are something used every day to make a good impression on others and to feel good about oneself. Nobody was born with good manners. No matter where you are — at home, work, or with friends — practicing good manners is important.

Good manners are more than opening doors and writing "thank you" notes. While opening doors for others and writing notes are nice, true courtesy goes deeper. Being polite and courteous means considering how others are feeling.

If you practice good manners, you are showing those around you that you are considerate of their feelings and respectful. You are also setting standards for others' behavior and encouraging them to treat you with similar respect.

Generally speaking, the way you look at someone or move your body can send messages. You should look someone in the eye when you or they are talking. It is not polite to whisper in front of other people. Don't eavesdrop. If someone is whispering in front of you, don't sink to their level and be rude by listening in. If people wanted you to be part of or hear the conversation, they would be including you. Never tell someone's secrets. No one likes to be laughed at. You may be hurting someone's feelings by laughing at them when they trip or burp. Some things, especially gross or unappetizing things, should not be discussed when people are eating. Don't discuss things that may make other people uncomfortable over the dinner table. If you can't reach the food, you'd better ask someone near you to pass the food; don't lean across their plates to grab it. Always remember it's rude to argue all the time.

Passage Script 2

Having good manners will serve you well, not just around friends and families, but also in a work environment. Many of the things you do to be polite in casual settings are just as polite in work situations. For example, using your telephone manners, saying "please" and "excuse me", shaking hands and introducing yourself when meeting someone new, paying attention to people when they are talking, and appearing neat and clean.

However, work situations often call for an even higher level of manners than those you use in casual situations. For example, jeans and T-shirts may be fine for hanging out with friends or going to the movies, but you may be expected to dress more professionally at work. You may answer the phone with a simple "hello" at home, but at work, you may be required to state your name, the company's name, and offer to help, "This is Jigsaw International, Anita Smith speaking. May I help you?"

Good manners show the best you have to offer and encourage others to be their best. Practicing these manners on a daily basis makes for a more pleasant career and life. Remember the followings:

- Be thoughtful
- Be cheerful
- Be generous
- Be cooperative
- Be helpful

- Don't be bossy
- Don't put people down or say rude things
- Respect other's privacy
- Take care of personal property

Key

II. 1. F   2. T   3. T   4. T   5. F   6. F   7. T   8. F   9. F   10. T

III. 1. Although it may seem as though some people were born knowing the right thing to say and do, they developed their good manners the same way everyone else did — through practice and consideration of others. And with patience and practice, you too can make good manners seem effortless.

5. No one likes to be laughed at. You may be hurting someone's feelings by laughing at them when they slip up.

6. Ask someone near you to pass the food; don't lean across their plate to grab it.

8. Some things, especially gross or unappetizing things, should not be discussed when people are eating. Don't discuss things that may make other people uncomfortable.

9. Don't eavesdrop. If people wanted you to be part of or hear the conversation, they would be including you. If someone is being rude and whispering in front of you, don't sink to their level and be rude by listening in.

IV. 1. d   2. b   3. b   4. c   5. a   6. d   7. b   8. d   9. b   10. d

⫸⫸⫸⫸Spot Dictation

Good manners display <u>respect</u>, care, and <u>consideration</u>. Good manners can <u>vary</u> widely between different <u>cultures and nations</u>. In China, a person <u>who</u> takes the last <u>item</u> of food <u>from</u> a common <u>plate</u> or bowl <u>without</u> first <u>offering</u> it to others <u>at the table</u> may be <u>seen as</u> insulting the generosity of the <u>host</u>. In America a guest is <u>expected</u> to eat <u>all</u> of the food <u>given</u> to them, as a compliment to the <u>quality</u> of the <u>cooking</u>. However, it is still <u>considered</u> polite to <u>offer</u> food from a common plate or <u>bowl</u> to others at the table. An <u>exchange</u> of business <u>gifts</u> might <u>take place</u> on very <u>special</u> occasions, but <u>in general</u> the British do not <u>expect</u> gifts or practice the custom. If <u>gift-giving</u> is your <u>preferred</u> method of showing <u>appreciation</u>, keep it <u>tasteful</u> and <u>modest</u> in price. Good manners make good <u>first impressions</u>, and can <u>impact</u> how well people <u>like</u> you.

Background Information（背景知识）

1. The rules of etiquette dictate the proper way people should behave in society. Each culture has its own unique set of rules. The culturally-savvy business person understands the rules of business and social etiquette when interacting with people from different cultural backgrounds. Doing business with international clients requires more than just financial acumen（敏锐）. A lack of knowledge about a customer's culture can lead to misunderst-anding, frustration and potential embarrassment. The building of successful business relationships is a vital part of any international venture, and such relationships rely heavily on an understanding of each partner's expectations and intentions. As global business continues to expand and bring people closer, the most important element of successful business outcomes may be the appreciation and respect for what is known as cultural diversity.

2. Proper etiquette in today's business world goes well beyond basic table manners and common courtesies (allowing an esteemed colleague or superior to precede you through a doorway, for example). Think of all the elements that go into making a first impression. The list is lengthy. There is your manner of dress, your professional appearance, the color of your dress or tie, your body language, handshake, posture, amount of eye contact on introduction, where you put your hands, how you accept a business card and how you present yours as well as the actual content of the card — and you haven't even sat down to begin talks. Many experienced international business travelers will advise you "when in Rome, do as the Romans do". While this may work if you are trying to figure out which fork to use or whether to bow or shake hands, it is, in most cases, far easier said than done. Here are four guiding principles of international interactions:

   • Don't set yourself up as the arbiter（仲裁人）of acceptable behavior for someone from another culture.

   • Do your homework so you don't give unintentional offense through ignorance of the culture.

   • Don't undermine yourself by taking offense when none was intended, when the other persons were simply behaving according to their cultural norms.

   • Be aware of cultural differences. You can't expect to be successful in the international arena by behaving the same way you do on your home turf（活动范围）.

3. You can learn some interesting aspects of international business etiquette in this unit and here are more for your reference.

   • Only in the Germanic countries will the people be as eager to get down to business as in the United States of America. Almost anywhere else in the world, but especially in Asian and Latin countries, it's important to first get to know the person with whom you're dealing to build a bond of trust. Three F's of business in Asian cultures are family, friends and favors.

- If you have no idea how someone from another culture communicates either verbally or non-verbally, you can't possibly negotiate effectively. All Asian cultures put a great deal of emphasis on the concept of face. In order to save face, theirs or yours, you will seldom get a direct answer, especially if it's "no". You will hear "yes" a great deal, but that doesn't signify agreement, only acknowledgement. Pay heed to your volume, vocal quality, tone of voice and posture because they indicate good breeding. Learn to listen and remember that, when in doubt, modesty is the best policy.

- Never call someone by the first name unless you are specifically asked to do so; virtually nowhere else are people as informal in the manner of address as in the United States. Don't forget the honorifics or titles that go with the name. They are usually a point of pride. In Germany you might use a whole string of titles to address someone, and in Italy it's an honor to be addressed by your profession.

- Differing attitudes toward time are the major source of annoyance in international interactions. How far in advance appointments and bookings must be scheduled, and to what extent punctuality is stressed or ignored are all important considerations to remaining in control during negotiations. It can be totally unnerving when a task-oriented, linear American, who considers time a commodity to be managed, is confronted with a relationship-oriented Arab, Asian, or Latin, who considers time as flowing and flexible, beyond human control, and to be accepted whatever happens and regardless of who may interrupt and how frequently the interruptions may occur. It pays to develop some flexibility to avoid angry outbursts.

Language and Culture Focus (语言文化要点)

>>>>>Reading I

1. **global village:** The development of technology, such as the Internet, has greatly promoted communication. The distance between people in different corners of the world seems to be considerably shortened and they seem to live in a global village. 地球村

2. **arrange:**

   1) *vi./vt.* to make preparations; plan or settle in advance. 筹划；安排

【例句】I've arranged for a taxi.

We must arrange about dinner.

Let's arrange a meeting for next Friday.

He called at 9 : 00, as arranged.

We have arranged to meet them at the hotel.

I've arranged for a doctor to meet with him.

We still have to arrange where to meet.

I've arranged with the electrician to call tomorrow.

2) *vt.* to put into a correct, pleasing or desired order. 整理；安排；布置

【例句】The books are arranged on the shelves in alphabetical order.

【相关词】

arrangement *n.* 安排；筹划；准备

【相关搭配】

arranged marriage 包办婚姻

make arrangements for 安排

【例句】We must make arrangements for the wedding.

3. **on time:** arriving or happening at the correct time or the time that was arranged. 准时；按时

【例句】The buses are never on time.

right/bang/dead on time 准时；一分不差

【例句】Our train arrived bang on time.

4. **allow...for...:** to be sure that you have enough time, money, food, etc. available for a particular purpose.

【相关搭配】

allow sth. for sb./sth.

【例句】I've allowed half a bottle of wine for each person.

allow sb. sth.

【例句】Allow yourselves plenty of time to get to the airport.

At the weekend I allow myself (= I permit myself the special pleasure of having) a box of chocolates.

You are allowed one book each.

5. **community:** *n.* a group of people living together and/or united by shared interests, religion, nationality, etc. 社区；社会；团体；界

【例句】the international community 国际社会

the academic community 学术界

the black community 黑人社区

community center 社区活动中心

6. **... several guidebooks appeared giving advice on international etiquette.:** In this sentence, "giving advice on international etiquette" is an adverbial of attendant circumstance（伴随情况状语）, which further interprets the meaning of the main clause.

【例句】I phoned again, making sure I had the right number.

He walked out of the room, slamming the door behind.

She was in London for two years, working as a tourist guide.

She went out, saying she would be back in an hour.

A *guidebook* is a special book about a city, area, etc. that gives details about the place and its history.

7. **At first many people thought this was a joke, especially the British, who seemed to assume that the widespread understanding of their language meant a corresponding understanding of English customs.**

【译文】刚开始许多人，尤其是英国人，认为这是个玩笑，他们似乎认定对英语广泛的理解便意味着对英国习俗的相应了解。

corresponding: *adj.* matching or related. 相应的；相当的；一致的；对等的

【例句】There has been a decline in the value of the pound and a corresponding increase in the strength of the dollar.

Profits for the first three months are 50% higher than in the corresponding period of last year.

8. **custom:** ［U/C］an established and habitual practice. 风俗；习惯

【例句】Social customs vary greatly from country to country.

When in a country, it is better to its customs well.

Customs（海关）is a different word, which means a place where customers' belongings are searched when leaving or entering a country.

【例句】As soon as I had got through customs, I jumped into a taxi.

9. **get to know/see/understand, etc.:** gradually begin to know, see, understand, etc. 逐渐了解/明白/理解等

【例句】I'm sure the kids will soon get to like each other.

They got to understand his intention only with the time passing on.

It'll take a while for you to get to know everyone.

After a while, I got to understand him.

10. **be well fed and watered:** to eat well and drink well.

feed: to give food to a person or an animal.

【例句】Have you fed the cat?

She was too weak to feed herself.

Several children were feeding bread to the ducks.

They were fed well on their mother's home cooking.

11. take off

1) to remove (esp. clothes). 脱下；脱去（尤指衣服）；拿掉

【例句】Take your coat off.   antonym: put on

He took off his clothes and got into the bath.

These clothes can be taken off for cleaning.

2) (of a plane, etc.) to rise into the air at the beginning of a flight. （飞机等）升空；起飞

【例句】The plane will soon take off.

3) to have a holiday from work. 休假；歇假

【例句】I'm taking Thursday off because I'm moving house.

Take a few days off; you are too tired.

It's difficult for me to take time off (work) during the summer.

He took off two weeks in September.

12. roll up: to fold the sleeves or legs of sth. that you are wearing upwards, so that they are shorter. 卷起

【例句】His sleeves were rolled above his elbows.

13. sleeve: the part of a piece of clothing which covers your arm or part of your arm. 袖子

【例句】a dress with long sleeves

【相关搭配】

have sth. up your sleeve: 有锦囊妙计

【例句】Come on, what have you got up your sleeves?

【相关词】

sleeveless *adj.* 无袖的

14. get down to: to begin to give serious attention to. 开始认真对待

【例句】It's hard to get down to work after a nice holiday.

I really must get down to filling in my tax form.

15. regard sb./sth. as: to consider sb./sth. as. 把某人/某物看作

【例句】She is generally regarded as one of the best writers in the country.

Regard can also be used as a noun in the following phrases.

【相关词组】

in this/that regard 在这个方面

【例句】The company is owned by its staff, and in that regard it is very unusual.

with regard to 关于

【例句】With regard to your recent application, I am afraid we are unable to offer you the job.

have no regard for 不考虑

【例句】You have no regard for my feelings!

give one's regards to 代我向某人致意

【例句】Please give my best regards to your parents.

16. take it easy

1) to relax and not do very much （also take things easy）.

【例句】Take things easy for a few days and you should be all right.

After the operation, I was told to take things easy for a month or two.

I'm going to take it easy this weekend.

2) (spoken) used to tell someone to become less upset or angry.

【例句】Just take it easy and tell us exactly what happened.

Hey, take it easy! Nobody's saying you're not good at your job.

17. executive

1) *adj.* having the power to carry out government decisions and laws. 行政上的；有行政能力的

【例句】the executive department 行政部门

2) *n.* a person in an executive position. 主管；行政人员

【例句】a young advertising executive

18. signal *vt.*

1) to express, warn, or tell as if by signal or signals. 用信号示意

【例句】Both sides have signaled their willingness to start negotiations.

The police signaled the traffic to move forward slowly.

The thief signaled his friends that the police were coming.

2) to mark. 标志

【例句】The defeat of 1066 signaled the end of Saxon rule in England.

19. ease *n.*

1) the state of being comfortable and without worries or problems 舒适；安逸；悠闲

【例句】He is rich and lives a life of ease.

Give her a drink to put her at her ease.

2) the ability to do sth. without difficulty. 容易；不费劲

【例句】They are expected to win the election with ease.

The government is very concerned about the ease with which the terrorists got onto the plane.

【相关搭配】

feel at ease 感到自在

stand at ease 稍息 （*cf.* attention 立正）

20. sole:

1) *n.* the bottom surface of the shoes.　鞋底

2) *adj.* the only one.（仅用于名词前）唯一的；仅有的

【例句】the sole American in the room

3) *adj.* not shared with anyone else.（仅用于名词前）专有的；独占的；唯一的

【例句】He has sole responsibility for sales in China.

21. height *n.*

1) the highest degree. 极度；极点

【例句】It's the height of stupidity to go sailing when you can't swim.

　　　　She always dresses in the height of fashion.

2) a high position or place. 高处；高地

【例句】We looked down from a great height to see the whole town below us.

　　　　I'm afraid of heights. 我恐高。

3) the quality or degree of being tall or high. 高；高度

【例句】What's the height of the Empire State Building?

　　　　The corridor is at the height of 10 meters.

　　　　During the floods, the river rose to the height of the main road beside it.

4) the main or most active point. 主要点；最活跃的点

【例句】at the height of storm/the tourist season

　　　　The crisis/famine was at its height.

22. exceed: to be greater than. 超过；超出

【例句】His income will very likely exceed 1 million this year.

　　　　His expenditure always exceeds his income.

　　　　The truck driver was fined for exceeding the speed limit.

23. deal: an agreement or arrangement. 协议；交易；安排

【例句】do/make a deal (to do sth.) 达成交易（做某事）

　　　　wrap up/complete a deal 完成交易

24. of one's own: belonging to oneself. 自己的

【例句】He left the company to start a business of his own.

　　　　This is a book of my own, but we can share it at class.

25. on meeting: Used with V ＋ -ing, the preposition phrase "on doing" is the equivalent of the clause introduced by "as soon as" or "the moment...". The preposition "upon" can also be used in this phrase.

【例句】On hearing the news, she jumped with great joy.

(=As soon as she heard the news, she jumped with great joy.)

On arriving at a business meeting, a manager shakes hands with everyone.

(=As soon as a manager arrives at a business meeting, he shakes hands with everyone.)

26. essential:

1) *adj.* extremely important and necessary in order to do sth. correctly or successfully. 绝对重要的；必不可少的

【例句】If you are going walking in the mountains, strong boots are essential.

Good food and plenty of exercise are essential for a healthy life.

【相关搭配】

It is essential that ...

【例句】It is essential that the oil be checked every 10, 000 km.

It is essential that students do the exercises.

It is essential to do sth.

【例句】It is essential to read the footnotes to understand the whole book.

2) *adj.* the most important, typical or noticeable. 最重要的；最典型的；最显著的

【例句】The essential character of the village has not changed in over 300 years.

The essential difference between men and apes is intelligence.

3) *n.* sth. necessary for life or for doing sth. else. 必需品；不可缺少的东西

【例句】The charity provides homeless people with essentials like food and clothing.

27. When it is handed to a person in a superior position, it must be given and received with both hands, and you must take time to read it carefully, and not just put it in your pocket!

【译文】当给级别高的人递名片时，必须用双手给或接，而收到的名片必须花时间仔细阅读，不能随手放进口袋！

superior *adj.*

1) of higher rank or class. 上级的

【例句】I'll report you to your superior officer!

2) better in quality or value. 质量或者价值更好的

【例句】Of the two books, I think this one is superior to that one.

3) of high quality. 上等的；优秀的

【例句】This is a very superior make of car.

superior craftsmanship

antonym: inferior

28. bow

1) *n.* an act of bending forward the head or the upper part of the body, esp. to show respect. 鞠躬

【例句】He gave a deep/low bow.

take a bow: to come to the stage to receive praise (applause) at the end of a performance. 谢幕

2) *vi.* 〔before/to〕to bend the upper part of the body forward, as a way of showing respect, admitting defeat, etc. 躬身；鞠躬

【例句】He bowed to/before the Queen.

Muslims bow to Mecca when they pray.

3) *vt.* to bend one's head forward. 低头；俯首

【例句】He bowed his head in shame/stood with his head bowed in shame.

29. casual *adj.*

1) showing or feeling little interest. 漫不经心的；随随便便的

【例句】His casual manner annoyed me.

She tried to sound casual, but her excitement was obvious.

2) without a clear aim, plan or intention; not serious or thorough. 漫无目的的；不认真的

【例句】I took a casual glance at the article.

It's not a real lecture, but a few casual remarks.

30. cool: calm and not easily excited. 冷静的；沉着的；不易激动的

【例句】We need someone with a cool head.

If you hear the fire bell, keep cool and don't panic.

31. reserved *adj.*

1) (typical of people) who do not like to talk about themselves or show their feelings; shy. 沉默寡言的；含蓄的；矜持的

【例句】Bob is very reserved — you never know what he is thinking.

2) kept for the future or special use. 预定的；保留的

【例句】reserved seats/tables

32. impersonal: not showing or including personal feelings. 客观的；不牵涉个人感情的；无人情味的

【例句】an impersonal letter

a large impersonal organization

33. geographical link: geographical connections, that is, the relationship in terms of places where one or one's relatives live(s) or used to live.

34. When in Rome, do as the Romans do: When one is in a strange country or place, one should follow the local customs. 入乡随俗

35. wink: to close and open one eye quickly, usu. as a sign between people. 向……使眼色；眨眼示意

【例句】He winked mischievously at Erica.

He winked an eye at his companion.

36. clasp: to grip firmly in or with the hand; grasp. 紧握；紧抱

【例句】Mary leaned forward, clasping her hands around her knees.

She stood with her hands clasped tightly together.

He clasped the child in his arms.

The two men clasped hands warmly.

⟫⟫⟫Reading II

1. Nobody actually wants to cause offence but, as business becomes ever more international, it is increasingly easy to get it wrong. There may be a single European market but it does not mean that managers behave the same in Greece as they do in Denmark.

【译文】没有人想冒犯别人，但随着商业交往的国际化，人们在交往中越来越容易犯错。虽然欧洲市场只有一个，但这并不意味着希腊和丹麦的经理人会有同样的举止行为。

2. get...wrong: to make a mistake about sth. 搞错

【例句】I think she got his name wrong. 我想她把他的名字搞错了。

He acknowledges that he got his timing wrong. 他承认把时间算错了。

I often got things wrong in those days.

3. Greece: a small European country where Western civilization started about 2, 500 years ago. Athens (雅典) is the capital and the largest city of Greece. 希腊

4. automatic: done without conscious thought, especially as a habit. 自动的

【例句】automatic response

automatic gesture 无意识的姿势

The movements needed to ride a bicycle soon become automatic.

5. everyone present: everyone who is at the meeting. Here "present" is a post-modifier, which means "in this/that place". 出席的，在场的

【例句】members present at the meeting

There is a photographer present at the meeting.

On arriving, he shook hands with all of the people present.

一到场，他就与所有与会者握手。

When used in this sense, "present" is in contrast with "absent". But when "present" is used as a pre-modifier, it means "existing/current" or "being considered now".

【例句】the present conditions 现在的条件

the present system

the present chairman

What's your present address?

6. This can be a demanding task and, in a crowded room, may require gymnastic ability if the farthest hand is to be reached.

【译文】这可能是非常需要技巧的任务。在拥挤的房间里，要伸手够到最远处的手，可能需要高超的体操技巧。

7. a demanding task: Something that is demanding needs a lot of time, energy, attention, and efforts. 费力的任务，难做的事

【例句】It's a demanding job. 工作很难做。

A new baby and a new job can be equally demanding.

8. crowded: completely full, filled with people. 拥挤的

【例句】a crowded bus/street/pavement/urban area

The bar was very crowded with people.

The department store is crowded with shoppers.

9. ... may require gymnastic ability if the farthest hand is to be reached.: to shake hands with people who is the farthest away in a crowded room, a manager has to stretch out his arm as far as he can like a gymnast.

"Gymnastic" is used to describe things relating to gymnastics, which is the training and practice of physical exercises with equipment such as bars, mats, and ropes, in order to develop one's strength, co-ordination and agility.

【例句】gymnastic ability/skill

10. Northern European: people who live in North Europe.

11. Scandinavian: native or inhabitant of Scandinavia (Denmark, Norway, Sweden and Iceland).

12. be fond of: to have a strong emotional feeling or a great liking for someone or sth.

【例句】She has many faults, but we're all very fond of her.

Many young nephews are fond of playing practical jokes.

Mary is fond of shopping.

She's fond of Shakespeare's plays.

【相关词组】

be into: [spoken] to like doing a particular activity or be interested in a particular subject.

【例句】I know she's really into sports, so I thought I'd ask her to come skiing with us.

A lot of his relatives are into very weird New Age stuff.

be keen on: (especially British) to like or be very interested in an activity or idea.

【例句】I know he's keen on opera. Let's take him to see La Traviata (茶花女).

I'm quite keen on the idea of having a fancy dress party.

13. **physical demonstration of friendliness:** signs of friendliness shown through body language or gestures such as handshake, embrace, or smile, etc.

14. **In Europe the most common challenge is not the content of the food, but the way you behave as you eat. Some things are just not done. In France it is not good manners to raise tricky questions of business over the main course.**

    【译文】在欧洲,最常见的问题不是吃什么,而是吃东西时的行为举止。有些事情是不能做的。在法国,上主菜的时候问一些令人难以回答的问题是不礼貌的。

15. **challenge:** A challenge is something new and exciting or difficult which you have the opportunity of doing and which requires great effort and determination if you are going to succeed. 挑战

    【例句】She was willing to accept the challenge of the unknown. 她打算接受未知的挑战。

    They are now facing a great challenge. 他们面临巨大挑战。

    I'm looking for a job with a bit more challenge. 我要找一个更有挑战性的工作。

    One of the greatest challenges facing the present government is how to create new jobs and new industries.

16. **... is not the content of food:** ... is not what we eat. Here "content of food" refers to something contained in the food; or the substance or ingredient of the food.

    【例句】food with a high fat content

    No other food has so high an iron content. 没有其他食物的含铁量更高。

17. **raise tricky question:** to ask questions that are difficult to answer.

    tricky: difficult to handle or deal with; full of hidden or unexpected difficulties.

    【例句】a tricky question/problem

    I'm in a rather tricky position. Can you help me out?

    The problem may prove rather tricky for the government.

18. **the main course:** the main part of the meal. A course is a part of the meal that is eaten separately from other parts of the meal. 主菜

    【例句】We had a three-course dinner: chicken soup, roast beef, and ice cream.

    She has eaten course after course.

    The first course was soup with delicious crusty rolls.

Usually a typical and formal western meal may consist of the following courses:

appetizers: sth. (such as juice and soup) eaten or drunk at the beginning of a meal to increase the desire for food. 开胃小吃或饮料

main course: including entrees, which refers to a small meat dish such as fish, chicken, steak, shrimp, or lamb chops, etc., and vegetables, such as potatoes, beans, carrots, onions, etc.

dessert: sweet food (such as apple pies, ice cream, cheese, and cake, etc.) served after the main part of a meal. 甜点

19. **Business has it place:** Business should be talked about at the proper time and place.

20. **...the cheese course:** Cheese can be served as a separate course (also called dessert) after the main course. Here the author means business can only be talked about after the cheese course. 奶酪（作为一道菜）

21. **... other than the business deal you are chewing over in your head.:** absolutely not the business deal that you have been thinking about all the time during the dinner.

    other than: apart from, except. 除了

    【例句】She never discussed it with anyone other than David.

    There was nothing we could do other than wait.

    We can't get there other than by boat.

    He doesn't eat pork, but other than that he'll eat just about anything.

    We know he once lived here, but other than that we don't know much about him.

    chew over: to think about (a question, problem, etc.) carefully. 细想，仔细考虑

    【例句】I'll chew it over for a few days and then let you have my answer.

    In discussions, we chewed over problems and worked out possible solutions.

22. **process:** a series of human actions or operations which are performed or carried out intentionally in order to achieve a particular result. 步骤，程序

    【例句】the process of learning to read

    the electoral process

    the process of collecting information

23. **business entertaining:** business party given to provide food and drink. 商务宴请

24. **entirely:** completely. 完全地

    【例句】I entirely agree with you.

    In the early years, the school was attended almost entirely by "problem" children.

    It was entirely the work of these women's organizations.

25. **on business:** for work. 因公（出差）

    【例句】I'm here on business. 我来这儿办事。

    When traveling on business, I take my tiny travel sewing kit. 出差时，我随身带针线包。

    She's in New York this week on business. 她这周去纽约出差。

26. **If you have the energy...:** If you are still vigorous after having so much food ...

    Here "energy" is the power of effort and attention that you have in order to achieve something. 精力

    【例句】It would be wiser for you to direct your emotional energy into social activities.

27. **a lively discussion:** If something is lively, it is conducted in an active, enthusiastic, and cheerful

way with lots of interesting and exciting things. 活跃的讨论

【例句】a lively song

a lively mind

The subject produced a lively debate in Parliament.

We had a lively conversation.

28. **pick up the bill:** to pay the bill. 付账

【例句】They went, leaving us to pick up the bill for the materials.

The football club should pick up the bill for the damage since their fans are responsible for it.

29. **apparently:** seemingly, obviously, clearly.

【例句】Apparently she never got my letter after all.

She was standing by the window, apparently quite calm and relaxed.

30. **entertain sb. with sth.:** to give someone food and hospitality, for example, by inviting them to your house. 以……招待某人

【例句】We always entertain our guests with parties and delicious Chinese food.

The cinema often entertains the local film fans with free films.

31. **the same enthusiasm as:** "Enthusiasm" is a great eagerness to be involved in a particular activity, because it is something you like or enjoy or something of great interest. 热爱

【例句】her enthusiasm for the theatre

She shows boundless enthusiasm for the work. 她无限地热爱她的工作。

【相关词】

enthusiastic *adj.* 热心的；感兴趣的

【例句】The retired worker is very enthusiastic about neighbourhood affairs.

We use "the same ... as" to refer to something in common.

【例句】You've made the same mistake as last time.

I've still got the same car as I had before.

I found she was staying in the same hotel as I was.

32. **counterpart:** a person or thing that has the same function or position as another in a different system or organization. 相对物，对应方

【例句】The English Merchant Bank made a deal with its American counterpart, the Wall Street Investment Bank.

The Minister of Defense is meeting his American counterpart in Washington today.

The Foreign Minister met his counterpart last week.

33. **notable for:** deserving to be noticed or given attention; important, excellent, interesting and remarkable. 以……著名

【例句】This area is notable for its pleasant climate. 此地以天气怡人著称。

The policy has been more notable for its ultimate failure than for its short-term success.

34. **formality:** the formal style; careful observance of rules and correct, serious behavior used, for example, in official situations or when one is talking to someone important. 礼节；正规形式；遵守礼节

35. **outsider:** a person who is not accepted as a member of a particular social group or a particular organization. 局外人 **antonym: insider**

【例句】To an outsider, this looks like an idyllic life (田园般的生活).

We will have to invite an outsider to chair the meeting.

36. **title:** a word or name such as "Mr.", "Lord", "Lady", "Doctor", "Professor", "General", etc., given to someone to be used before their names as a sign of social rank or profession to show respect. 称呼

37. **Herr Doktor or Frau Direktorin:** (German) Mr. Doctor or Mrs. Director.

38. **offensive:** Something that is offensive upsets or embarrasses people and causes offence because it is rude, insulting or unpleasant. 冒犯的, 无礼的

【例句】I find him extremely offensive.

He likes to tell crude jokes that are offensive to ladies.

The advertisement is highly offensive to women.

"Offend" is the verb, which means to cause offence or upset or embarrass somebody by doing something rude.

【例句】They took care never to offend their visitors.

I was very offended that you forgot my birthday.

39. **architect:** a person who plans or designs new buildings and is responsible for making sure that they are built properly. 建筑师

【例句】Who was the architect of St. Paul's Cathedral?

40. **exist side by side:** If two things develop or exist side by side, they are happening in the same place at the same time. 并行存在的

【例句】The two bottles stood side by side on the table.

Two interdependent communities evolved side by side.

All these virtues exist side by side with the real vices.

If two people are side by side, they are sitting or walking next to each other.

【例句】They stood side by side on the platform.

She was walking side by side with Romeo.

If people work side by side, they work closely together.

【例句】We have worked side by side for many years.

Student and tutor learn side by side.

41. **disaster may be only a syllable away:** sth. unfortunate may occur if you say the wrong word or make a slip of the tongue. 祸从口出

42. **the more..., the more...:** This is the structure of "parallel increase".

【例句】The smaller it is, the less it will cost us.

The more he has, the more he wants.

The harder the shrub is to grow, the higher its price is.

The sooner we start, the more quickly we'll get there.

The higher the standard of living, the greater the amount of goods consumed.

43. **be likely to do:** If someone or something is likely to do something, it is expected to happen or will probably happen. 可能

【例句】He's likely to arrive a bit late.

They're likely to lose the election.

A butcher will not be likely to preach vegetarianism.

These services are likely to be available to us all before long.

44. **get into difficulties:** to get into trouble, to be in a difficult situation in which you are struggling. 陷入困境

【例句】When sales slowed down, the company got into difficulties.

45. **It is worth the effort.:** If we say that something is worth a particular activity, amount of effort, time, or money, etc., we mean that anyone who does the activity, puts in the effort, spends the time or money, etc., is likely to benefit or gain something from it. 值得……

【例句】The building is well worth a visit. 这栋建筑值得一游。

He felt it wasn't worth the effort. 他感到这不值。

It was worth every penny. 这不值一文。

We may not succeed, but it's worth a try.

It was a great evening, and definitely worth all the hard work.

46. **contract:** a formal written agreement, having the force of law, between two or more people or organizations. 合同

【例句】a building contract 建造合同

contract of employment 雇佣合同

47. **light-hearted:** entertaining, cheerful and amusing, not at all serious. 轻松愉快的

【例句】light-hearted remarks

a television comedy that takes a light-hearted look at life in prison

Let me finish with a light-hearted question.

48. **comment:** a statement or opinion about sth. 评论；意见

【例句】He thanked me, but made no comment.

He made several unfavorable comments about their candidate.

49. **aperitif:** a small alcoholic drink that one has before a meal. 开胃酒

50. **admire:** to think of or look at something with pleasure, respect and approval. 赞赏；钦佩；称赞

【例句】 I admire the way she handles her staff.

You may not like him, but you've got to admire his persistence.

She is always looking into the mirror, admiring herself.

I admire your cleverness and courage.

51. **make or break the deal:** to result in a success or failure in a business agreement. 做成/做不成生意

>>>>> Extended Activities

A. Function and Structure: Asking for, Giving and Refusing to Give Permission

In our daily interaction, we must ask for the OK from other people before we enter on something that involves other people in — either our action may put them to possible inconvenience or simply we mean to volunteer a favor, for example, by helping a lady with something heavy or leading a blind man across the street. By doing so, we are showing a sign of proper respect for their authority, independence or pride. In order to get consent to what we ask permission for, we had better accompany our request with some explanations: *Do you have any objection if I have a day off? I've to take my son to the dentist tomorrow.* Of course, if we have to refuse to give permission, an explanation is always appreciated: *I'd rather you didn't. The room is air-conditioned.*

B. Special Use: Simple Present and Past Tenses of Verbs

1. 一般现在时

1) 表示现在或说话时刻的状态或动作。例如：

What time is it now?

China is a developing country.

This credit card belongs to me.

I feel uncomfortable.

How much does it cost?

I wish you a happy Christmas.

Now VOA presents music from Hawaii.

2) 用于动作演示。例如：

Now I put the sugar into the cup.

Now I put the cake mixture into the bowl and add some butter.

3) 表示事物的客观存在或特征、性能等。例如：

Shanghai lies in the east of China.

London stands on the Thames.

Computers work at great speed.

The machine runs smoothly.

Hydrogen is the lightest element in the world.

注意：用该时态表示事物的特征时，我们常用主动语态表示被动意义。

Such books sell well. 这种书很好卖。

This kind of cloth washes easily. 这种布料很容易洗。

The clock winds at the back. 这钟是在背面上发条。

4) 表示普遍真理、谚语或俗语。例如：

The moon turns around the earth.

Light travels faster than sound.

Time and tide wait for no man. 岁月不等人。

Knowledge is power. 知识就是力量。

5) 表示经常或反复发生的习惯性动作。例如：

Mike often goes to his office by underground.

He always sleeps with the windows open.

Mrs. White teaches English.

Whenever I come across a new word, I look it up in the dictionary.

一般现在时用于此种意义时，可以与 always, ever, frequently, hardly ever, never, occasionally, often, rarely, seldom, sometimes, usually, generally, from time to time, every day 等频度副词 (adverb of frequency) 连用。这些频度副词一般放在 be 动词或第一个助动词之后，或实义动词之前。例如：

Tom is always late for class.

He never makes any mistakes when he writes.

We rarely go dancing at weekends.

I have never been abroad.

6) 表示已经计划好的，或已排在议事日程上的将来事件，并含有不可变更的含义。例如：

Tomorrow is my birthday.

The train leaves at ten a.m.

7) 在一些状语从句中用现在时表示将来。例如：

When I grow up, I will be a teacher.

I will stay here till he comes.

You will be highly appreciated if you give me a lift.

2. 一般过去时

1) 表示与现在无关的、发生在过去的某个状态、动作、经历或历史事件。例如：

He gave up the opportunity to go to America after the terrorist attack.

Susan began to work in a toy company in 1997.

O. Henry was born in 1862 and followed several occupations in his early years.

一般过去时常与过去时间状语连用。例如：

We got to know each other in 1991.

She called you a moment ago.

在一定的上下文中，过去时间状语也可以省略。例如：

I bought this book in London.

Did you have a nice sleep?（现在已经醒了，睡觉是刚才的动作。）

I didn't know you would teach us English.（现在我知道了，但刚才我不知道。）

I didn't expect to receive this letter so soon.（我以前没有想到过会那么早收到这封信，但现在我知道了。）

2) 表示过去经常发生的动作。

一般过去时表示过去经常发生的动作或习惯，必须借助频度副词，否则一般过去时只能表示过去发生的某一个动作。例如：

She went there to see her aunt.（过去的一次动作。）

She went there every week to see her aunt.（过去经常发生的动作。）

He never drank wine.

Henry smoked forty cigarettes a day till he gave up.

我们也可以用 used to 来表示过去经常发生的动作。used to 只能用于过去时，表示过去经常做某事，但现在不做了，后跟动词原形。例如：

He used to go there to see his aunt.

He used to help me.

He used to have a pen friend.

I used to go to school by bus.

3) 用于从句中与主句的过去时态保持一致。例如：

She told us that school started the next day.

I didn't know you were here.

但若从句中表述的是一个普遍真理或不变的事实,从句中的动词不必遵循时态一致原则,应使用一般现在时。例如:

He believed that the sun is the center of the solar system.

The teacher told us that knowledge is power.

4) 用来表示客气和礼貌。例如:

Could you tell me where the nearest post office is?

I wondered if you could give me a lift.

5) 用于一些固定结构中。例如:

I would rather you went now.

It's time you had a rest.

6) 一般过去时中动作的先后顺序。

在一般过去时中,如果两个或两个以上的动作依次发生,我们通常用and连接。And通常放在最后一个动词的前面。例如:

She addressed and sealed the letter. 她写好地址,然后封上信封。

She went into the room, turned on the light and took off her coat.

当然,除了用and连接动作之外,我们也经常用when, before, after等时间状语从句和过去完成时来表示动作的先后。例如:

He went to bed after he finished his homework.

Before he went to bed, he finished his homework.

When he got to the cinema, the film had been on.

C. Practical Reading

产品目录Catalog (Cat)的核心内容一般包括产品名称、编号、规格、型号、品质、价格等信息。教师应要求学生一些相关的词汇,并看懂目录中各个项目的信息,特别要强调对细节信息的理解与查找。这类题目虽然不难,但要求学生仔细对照,才能准确答题。

1. nylon: 尼龙

2. zipped pouch: 带拉链的小袋子

3. detachable shoulder straps: 可拆卸的肩部背带

4. vented for wet items: 让潮湿物品通风

5. reinforced base: 加厚的底部

6. hand grip: 手柄

7. padded shoulder straps: 有衬垫的肩部背带

8. polyester webbing: 涤纶网

9. water resistant: 防水的

10. drawcord: 拉绳

11. snap closure: 可闭合的搭扣

12. hanging loop: 吊环

Teaching Tips （教学提示）

1. **Lead-in** 本单元导入部分安排了听力理解和听写填空两项任务。听力理解部分紧扣单元主题 Good Manners 安排了两个听辨训练语篇，共4项练习。第一篇听力设有三项练习。第一项练习 属于预听活动，主要目的是在进行精听训练之前，让学生对所听语篇的主旨（Gist）有所了解， 初步把握听音和理解上的难点所在，为接下来的听力活动做好词汇和心理上的准备。第二项练 习为正误辨析题（True or False），侧重考察学生理解、辨析语篇细节和关键信息的能力。第三项 练习教师可以让学生在指出相关单句错误之处的基础上，对所听到的语篇进行复述，以加强对 所听语篇的理解和记忆。练习四是一个完型填空（Cloze）训练。教师特别要向学生指出，和学 生以往熟悉的听写填空(Spot Dictation)要求不同，并不是听到什么填写什么，学生在书上看到 的文字材料和他们所听到的语音材料并不一样。学生在听音前，先要快速预读文字材料的内容， 把握语篇的主题，并根据空格前后的语法结构、词语固定搭配、词语间的并列对比结构以及上 下文语义的连贯等对空格内容进行积极地预测，明确听音时记忆的重点。在进行听音时，摆脱 书面文字的干扰，把注意力放在听辨、理解、记忆语篇的主旨，关键信息点，以及语篇的逻辑层 次上，同时做好笔记。听音完毕后，再根据自己的理解和笔记的帮助，完成练习。教师应根据学 生实际能力，对学生进行一定的听力笔记技能的辅导。听写填空(Spot Dictation) 主要听写相关 的动词，名词和介词，可以作为导入活动安排在Reading II课文讲解之前进行。

2. **Reading I Brainstorming** 学生通过自由讨论的形式，列出他们认为在特定的场景下属于不礼貌的 行为。来自不同文化背景的人对礼貌的定义各不相同,例如：

> When being complimented, an English-speaking person would readily accept the compliment by saying something like "Thank you" to show his appreciation of the praise, but a Chinese speaker would try to deny the truth of the compliment. Before entering a house in some Asian countries it is

necessary to take off one's shoes. In European countries, even though shoes sometimes become very muddy, this is not done. A guest in a Chinese house never finishes a drink. He leaves a little to show that he has had enough. In England, a guest always finishes a drink or eats up his food to show that he has enjoyed it.

但是不管在东方还是西方文化中，许多基本的社会礼仪准则还是一致的。对别人关心、尊重、宽容、友好，这些行为无论在哪种文化中都是受到欢迎和赞赏的。除答案中提到的一些行为，日常生活中常见的不礼貌行为还有：

➤ spitting and littering up in the street;

➤ laughing at people in trouble;

➤ jumping the queue or pushing to the front of the line;

➤ refusing to give one's seat to an old or disabled person;

➤ asking people, women in particular, their age;

➤ interrupting when other people are talking;

➤ omitting to pay proper respect to company, on entering or leaving a room, or paying it only to one person, when more are present;

➤ entering a room with the hat on, and leaving it in the same manner;

➤ sitting still on the entrance of your instructor, strangers, or parents;

➤ laughing loudly when in company, and drumming with feet or hands;

➤ swinging the arms, and all other awkward gestures, especially in the street, and in company;

➤ leaning on the shoulder, or chair of another person, and overlooking persons who are writing or reading;

➤ throwing things instead of handing them;

➤ crowding others in a passage or running against their elbows;

➤ staring at people earnestly in the face without any apparent cause.

3. Reading I Pairwork   由学生双人结对，讨论与本单元主题 Different Manners in Different Cultures 相关的一些话题。众所周知，礼貌具有明显的文化特征。简而言之，中国式礼貌的最大特点是"夫礼者，自卑而尊人"。现在这个礼貌准则中"卑"的成分逐渐被"自贬"和"自谦"取代。(Self-denigration has been at the core of the Chinese notion of politeness for over two thousand years. The Chinese, in order to show modesty, will go to such lengths as to underrate what he himself has achieved and deny the truth of a complimentary remark.) 而前往境外旅行的游客在出发前应该了

解一些目的国（target country）的文化历史、风土人情、风俗禁忌、气候地理等情况，以确保旅行愉快并顺利地进行。

4. Reading I Exercises IV Question 2 中，diagram 指 a plan, sketch, drawing, or outline designed to demonstrate or explain how something works or to clarify the relationship between the parts of a whole， 为演示或解释某物或为澄清整体各部分之间关系而设计的图示、图解。

Question 7 中 sort out 可解释为：

1) to deal effectively with a problem.

【例句】I think we've sorted out our difficulties with the printer.

2) to think and come to a conclusion about a problem or difficulty. .

【例句】All the outstanding issues have been sorted out.

3) to put sth. into order.

【例句】It took weeks to sort out the library.

4) to separate sth. from the mixture it exists in, or from another group of things.

【例句】Sort out the best apples for eating and the rest for cooking.

在本句中，sort out 取第三条解释，意思是 "我必须整理好我桌上的那堆文件"。

5. ReadingI Post-reading　设有两项任务。任务1）由学生完成一个关于商务礼仪的小测验。教师可先让学生根据他们的一般常识自行完成，然后比较各自的答案。对学生有歧义的问题，教师可先让学生陈述自己的理由，然后根据给出的参考答案予以分析和解释。应该指出的是，教师用书中给出的参考答案多基于西方礼仪，可能和时下中国商场上流行的一些做法有不同之处。教师还可准备一些实物，如餐巾等，请学生演示小测验中提到的部分场景，以加深学生的印象和认识。任务2）主要目的是让学生说说他们熟悉的一些中国礼仪和风俗。中国地域辽阔，各个地方的风俗习惯也不尽相同，教师应向学生指出这种地域文化的差异性。下文供教师参考。在进行本活动之前，教师也可参考本书 Unit 6, Practical Reading 中提供的相关网络资源信息，让学生课前作一定的背景知识阅读，为课堂活动做好准备。

☐ When invited for dinner, it is considered to be proper etiquette to sample every dish served. Always leave something on your plate at the end of the meal or your host might think that you are still hungry.

☐ A gift should always be wrapped, but avoid plain black or white paper because these are the colors of mourning. Present the gift with both hands as a sign of courtesy and always mention that this is only a small token of appreciation. Do not expect your gift to be opened in your presence. This indicates that it is the thought that counts more than the material value.

☐ Never give a clock, handkerchief, umbrella or white flowers, specifically chrysanthemums, as a gift, as all of these signify tears and/or death.

☐ Never give sharp objects such as knives or scissors as they would signify the cutting of a relationship.

☐ Lucky numbers are 6 and 8 (especially in a series, such as 66 or 888). An unlucky number is 4.

☐ If a Chinese person gives you a compliment, it is polite to deny it graciously. Modesty is highly valued in China.

☐ Do learn a few words of Chinese. This shows an interest in your host's language and culture. It also is a very good icebreaker.

6. Reading II Exercises VI Cloze

Question 4　选 c. Upon。此处 upon 用来指 something that happens immediately after you have done something or at the same time. 例如：Upon entering the cabin, she sat down. 她一进小木屋就坐了下来。On 也可以这样用，如：On entering the room, she saw him. 她一进这个房间便看到了他。

Upon 和 on 一般可通用，但有以下区别：表示日期时，一般只用 on, 不用 upon; 在某些习语中，upon 和 on 不能互相替换，如：upon my word; once upon a time; on no account; 在句末或分句末的动词不定式后往往用 upon, 不用 on, 如：nothing to defend upon。

Question 5　选 a. lower。此处 lower 用作动词，意思是"降低", to move down, 如：Her hand lowered. 她的手垂了下来。

Question 6　此处选 a. sign, 指"标志", something that suggests the presence or existence of a fact, condition, or quality. 如：A high forehead is thought to be a sign of intelligence. 选项 b. signal 指"信号", an indicator, such as a gesture or colored light, that serves as a means of communication, 如：A red light is usually a signal of danger. 选项 c. mark 指"标记", a visible trace or impression, such as a line or spot, 如：It is dangerous to swim beyond this mark. 选项 d. notice 指"通知", a formal announcement, notification, or warning, 如：Can you be ready at short notice?

Question 8　此处选 a. maintaining。Be sensitive to 意思是"对……敏感", 此处 to 作介词用，故后跟动词 -ing 形式。

Question 10   此处选c. lose。Lose (one's) face指丢脸，失面子；save（one's）face指挽回面子。

Question 11   result in & result from

If something *results in* a particular situation, it causes that situation to happen or to exist. e.g. The use of such techniques could result in disastrous ecological changes. / Such behavior may result in the executive being asked to leave.

If something *results from* a particular event or action, it is caused by that event or action. e.g. Inflation results from an excess of demand over supply. / Nothing has resulted from his efforts.

Question 14   relationship & relation

In some contexts, the words are interchangeable. For example, we can also refer to the "relationship between smoking and heart disease" (though *relation* is the better choice) and "the relationship of parent to child". We can speak of something in relationship to or in relation to something else. In other contexts, the words are not interchangeable. We cannot, for example, refer to a person as a "relationship"; a person is a relation. And we cannot refer to a situation or the connection between two people as a "relation"; it is a relationship. Context determines the choice. Generally when we refer to the *situation* that exists between two people, it is a relationship, not a relation.

Key（练习答案）

>>>>>Reading I

Pre-reading

I.

behavior	situation
yawning	while somebody is talking to you
smoking	in a crowed room
talking loudly	at movies

（续　表）

behavior	situation
using cellular phone	in a quiet reading room
laughing and whistling	when someone slips on a banana peel

Exercises

II. 1. c   2. b   3. a   4. c   5. c

III. 1. insult   2. corresponding   3. strict   4. behave   5. ease   6. widespread

7. reserved   8. custom   9. exceed   10. signify   11. impersonal   12. illustrate

13. executive

IV. 1. reserved   2. illustrated   3. getting to   4. the custom

5. Take it easy ... relax   6. corresponding   7. get down to   8. exceeded

9. roll up   10. was taken off (=removed from sale)   11. allowed

12. of his own   13. regarded as   14. essential   15. clased

V. 1. Both sides have signaled their willingness to start negotiations.

2. He didn't feel completely at ease in the strange country.

3. She went to the United States three years ago. Thereafter we had no further communication.

4. The cost of the damage exceeded our worst fears.

5. She always dresses in the height of fashion.

6. Our employees should not behave rudely towards customers, however unreasonable they may be.

Post-reading

Task 1   Business Etiquette Answers

1. No. Introduce the more important person first. You should address your client and say "Mr. Brown, I'd like you to meet our Vice President of Development, Ms. Smith." (Alternative answer — introduce the client as the more important person!)

2. Yes. When your client steps out of the car, he or she will be on the curbside and therefore won't have to deal with getting out in traffic or sliding across the seat.

3. d. It's more polite not to call attention to the fact that you can't drink champagne.

4. d. Leave it on your chair. Definitely don't put it on the table — what if you have crumbs on it?

5. b and c. Sort of a trick question. The most important guest should get served first.

6. b. Make eye contact with all of the individuals you're talking with.

7. b. Indicating where your guest should sit will make her feel more comfortable.

8. b, c, or d. Just don't grab it first unless you're playing one of these roles.

9. a. You've waited 30 minutes. Expect an apology later, though.

10. d. Call and set up another appointment. And don't forget to apologize for your error. Imagine how you'd feel if it were you!

>>>>>Reading II

Exercises

I. 1. F   2. F   3. T   4. T   5. NM   6. F   7. T   8. T   9. F   10. T

III. 1. b   2. d   3. a   4. d   5. d   6. a   7. c   8. b   9. c   10. a

IV. 1. The career advisor gave several college students some advice on choosing their careers after graduation.

2. They made a $55 million deal with a Japanese automobile company to sell the land.

3. After working with him for some time, I get to know him better.

4. You really must get down to work, or you will be fired.

5. It's nice to lie down and take it easy after a hard day's work.

6. He seldom talks with me other than to report his work to me.

7. Before you make a promise, you'd better chew it over.

8. The insurance company should pick up the bill for the damaged ship.

9. In this developing country, the problem of women's social position exists side by side with the problem of children's education.

10. If you don't know of the local culture and customs, you will often get into difficulties.

V. 1. d 2. b 3. a 4. c 5. a 6. a 7. c 8. a 9. d 10. c 11. b 12. d 13. a 14. b 15. d

>>>>>Extended Activities

A. Function and Structure

I. 1. (*in the library*)

Kate: <u>Would you mind</u> if I use your dictionary?

Sue: <u>Not at all.</u> Please do.

Kate: Thank you very much.

Sue: You are welcome.

2. (*In Mr. Nelson's office, Mr. Hamilton's beeper sounds.*)

Mr. Hamilton: Uh-oh. It's probably my wife. <u>I should like to make a phone call here,</u> if you don't
          mind.

Mr. Nelson: <u>I'm sorry, you can't.</u> It's an interphone. You can use my cell phone.

Mr. Hamilton: Thanks a lot.

3. （*A student is talking to Professor Smith.* ）

David: Professor Smith, I'm a student majoring in Business Administration, but I'm very
          interested in English Literature. <u>Do you have any objection</u> if I attend your lecture on
          it?

Prof. Smith: <u>I can't see any objection to</u> your attending the lecture.

David: That's very kind of you.

4. (*Outside the house of Miss Stone, who is a well-known movie star.*)

Jenny: <u>Any chance of</u> taking a photo with Miss Stone? I'm a great fan of hers.

The guard: <u>No, I'm afraid not.</u>

Jenny: In that case, <u>can I speak to her</u>, please?

The guard: <u>I'm sorry, you can't.</u>

Jenny: I really adore her very much. <u>May I</u> see her for a minute?

The guard: <u>Sorry, out of the question.</u>

5. Bill: <u>Will you allow me</u> to use your car tonight? I have to drive my sister to the station.

Jack: <u>Feel free to do that.</u>

Bill: Many thanks!

B. Special Use

1. wait ... make	2. finishes	3. was seated	4. worked
5. is	6. don't go ... do ... prefer	7. is believed	8. went
9. moves	10. make/makes	11. read ... was	12. visited ... went .. met
13. touches	14. lay ... slept	15. was given ... drove	16. take ... place
17. doesn't sell	18. was		

C. Practical Reading

1. a   2. c   3. b   4. d   5. c   6. a   7. d   8. b   9. b   10. a

D. Additional Vocabulary

1-7;   2-13;   3-20;   4-16;   5-11;   6-1;   7-12;   8-19;   9-3;   10-18;

11-2;   12-4;   13-17;   14-5;   15-14;   16-6;   17-15;   18-8;   19-9;   20-10

Unit 9
Telephone Calls

Teaching Aim （教学目的）

1. Cognitive Information （认知信息）: Making a Telephone Call;

   Phone Call Etiquette

2. Language Focus （内容重点）

   — **Key Words:** I. address, horrid, instrument, clamor, spoil, justifiable, rude, canned music, indignity, office hour, time zones, handle, lurk, ignore, tax, accusation, connection, consideration, confront, surrender, party, offense, bother; II. adequate, antiquate, surcharge, alternative, booth, fade, patience, telecommunication, readout, dial, expire, switch, guess work, token, code, capacity, efficiency, assign, deposit

   — **Phrases:** I. devote ... to, shut up, put ... on hold, subject ... to, suspect ... of, get out of, in agreement with, at the mention of, be confronted with; II. scratch off, be similar to, in exchange for

   — **Useful Structures:** *conj.* + V-ing phrase

                          without + V-ing phrase

                          be a must

   — **Grammar:** Perfect Tenses of Verbs

3. Communicative Skills （交际技能）

   — **Expressions:** Making Telephone Calls

   — **Reading:** Yellow Pages

Lead-in 导入

>>>>> Listening Comprehension Tasks

Difficult Words & Expressions

1. procedure: a series of steps taken to accomplish sth. 步骤

2. put sb. on the spot: 使某人处于困境

3. step out: 暂时离开一下

4. help out: 帮忙

5. upcoming: occurring soon; forthcoming 即将到来的

6. conference: a formal meeting 正式会议

Passage Script 1

If you are answering the phone at a job, your employer may have a specific way he would like you to answer the phone. If your company doesn't have any standards for telephone procedures, follow the same standards that you would if you were answering the phone at home. Speak clearly, be polite, and offer to take a message or help out if you are answering the phone for someone else.

Here are some common practices that will make you sound polite, whether talking on the phone to a friend, customer, potential employer, or complete stranger.

1. Answering the phone

Some people like to let callers know who they've reached as soon as they pick up the phone. Companies and some individuals may answer the phone "You've reached the John Smith Corporation" or "Hello, this is John Smith." Sometimes a simple "Hello" or "Hello, this is John" will do. Unless your employer asks you to answer the phone in a particular way, choose a style that's comfortable for you and polite to others. Just avoid answering the phone in a way that may make the person on the other end feel uncomfortable or put him on the spot, such as "What?" or "Who is this?"

2. Taking messages

If you answer someone else's phone or answer for someone who is not around, you should always offer to take a message. Again, this can be as simple as saying "I'm sorry, Ann's stepped out. May I take a message?" or "I'm sorry, she's busy at the moment. May I take your name and number and have her call you back?"

If the person who is calling asks you to help out instead and you don't feel comfortable or don't know the answer to their questions, it is always polite to say, "I'm sorry I don't know, but I'd be happy to pass the message on to Ann." Just remember to pass the message on! If someone leaves a message, be sure to write down his name, phone number, time he called and the message — then be sure to give the message to the person he was calling.

3. Interrupting others on the phone

Wait until someone has finished his phone conversation before talking to him. If it's urgent and you need to use the phone or talk to someone who is on the phone, don't pick up the line and start talking. Instead, say "Excuse me! May I talk to you for a second?" or "I'm sorry, but I need to make an urgent call. Do you mind if I use the phone?"

Passage Script 2

Telephone Talk Phrases

1. Hello, you've reached Marina Smith at ABB Company. I'm sorry I'm not available to take your call. Please leave a message and I'll call you back as soon as I can. Thank you.

2. I'm sorry, I'm losing you. Can you call me back?

3. Hello, this is Marina Smith calling to follow up regarding your order with ABB Company. Can you please call me back at 999-344-3344.

4. Hi, it's John again. Sorry I lost you. My cell phone dropped the signal.

5. Hello, you've reached John Block at ABC. It's Monday, May 22, and I will be out of the office all day. I will be checking my voice mail from time to time and will return all urgent calls. Thank you.

6. Hello, this is John Block from ABC. I'm calling regarding the upcoming conference in Miami. I'll try you again later today.

7. We're breaking up. I'm having trouble hearing you. Let me call you back later.

8. Hello, this is Marina Smith at the ABB Company. I will be on vacation from Friday, May 12 through Monday, May 22. Please leave a message, and I'll call you back when I return. Thank you.

9. I can barely hear you. Let me call you back on my other phone.

Key

II. 1. b   2. d   3. b   4. c   5. b   6. d   7. a   8. d   9. b   10. c

IV. 1. Phrases for leaving a voice mail: 3, 6

2. Phrases for recording a voice mail message on your machine: 1, 5, 8

3. Phrases for cell phone calls when the signal is not good enough: 2, 4, 7, 9

>>>>>Spot Dictation

Mr. Bennett works in a <u>store</u>. His telephone number is <u>278-9536</u>. He is not in his office <u>at the moment</u>. There are <u>two calls</u> for him. A clerk <u>answers</u> the phone and takes the following <u>messages</u>.

> A Mr. Smith called to <u>inform</u> that <u>300 kilos</u> of flour <u>ordered</u> by Dr. Bennett had been <u>ready</u>. The flour cost <u>32 cents</u> per <u>kilo</u> and <u>300 kilos</u> was <u>$96</u>. They would be <u>delivered</u> to the door <u>at 10 am</u> the next day.
>
> A Ms. <u>White</u> called to ask <u>whether</u> Dr. Bennett still wanted <u>5 boxes</u> of chocolate and the <u>total</u> price was <u>£ 57.5</u>. If he <u>wanted</u> them, he could <u>give</u> her a call on <u>398-4071</u> or <u>dial</u> the <u>order number</u> on <u>GJ 404</u>.

Background Information（背景知识）

1. History of telephone

Probably no means of communication has revolutionized the daily lives of ordinary people more than the telephone. Simply described, it is a system that converts sound, specifically the human voice, to electrical impulses of various frequencies and then back to a tone that sounds like the original voice. A practical telephone was actually invented independently by two men working in the United States, Elisha Gray (1835—1910) and Scottish-born Alexander Graham Bell (1847—1922). Incredibly, both men filed for a patent on their designs at the New York Patent Office on February 14, 1876, with Bell beating Gray by only two hours! According to the famous story, the first fully intelligible telephone call occurred on March 6, 1876, when Bell, in one room, called to his assistant in another room. "Come here, Watson, I want you." Watson heard the request through a receiver connected to the transmitter that Bell had designed, and what followed after that is a history of the founding of the Bell Telephone Company (later AT & T), which grew to be the largest telephone company in the world.

2. Basic telephone tips

In our hi-tech world of computers and laser printers, the telephone is still most businesses' primary point of contact with customers. Clearly, the telephone is not a business tool to be overlooked or underestimated. Proper telephone technique involves some basic common sense which everyone who works for a company should use. Here are some basic tips:

> *Making the call*

When making a business call, be sure to first identify yourself and your company. If you're routed to a receptionist or operator, also include the name of the person you're trying to reach. Be prepared with one or two sentence explanation of the purpose for your call. When you are connected with the person, state the purpose of your call and then be sure to ask if you are calling at a convenient time. If you get shunted to a receptionist and he or she asks why you are calling, give a concise but informative statement that can be easily relayed. Do not, however, assume that your message will be communicated; when you speak directly with the person you are trying to call, repeat your message in your own words.

> *Answering the phone*

Telephone calls usually lead to some action to be taken, so make sure your first vocal impression is a good one by trying to answer the phone as pleasantly and professionally as possible. Identify yourself and your company when receiving an incoming call. If you work at a large corporation with many departments, it may also help to include your department or section name. If you must put someone on hold, ask first and — most importantly — wait for their answer. If someone expresses reservation about being put on hold, calmly explain why it is necessary. Remember to keep the person on hold updated on the status of his or her call every 30 seconds.

> *Voice mail and messages*

If you have to leave a message or voice mail for someone, make it short and to the point. Speak clearly and slowly and leave your name, phone number, and a brief message. Say your name and number at the beginning and again at the end of the message, especially if you don't know the person you're calling. Returning messages promptly is always appreciated. It's customary to return telephone calls within 24 hours. If you cannot attend to the caller's needs within that time, briefly phone the person to say when you will be available.

> *Your own voice mail*

The message you leave as your outgoing message is an important business tool. Information is critical. The best messages communicate several key things to the person calling you: your name, the organization and/or group you're in, the current date (this tells them you are checking your messages), whether you are in the office or not that day, when to expect a call back, whom to contact if the call is urgent, and how to get to that person.

> *Taking messages*

Record the time and date the call came in. Verify the caller's name, company name, and phone number. Get a short statement about the caller's intent. Take telephone messages completely and accurately. If there's something you don't understand or can't spell, such as a person's surname, ask the caller to repeat it or spell it for you. Then make sure the message gets to the intended recipient.

3. Telephone etiquette

> When speaking on the telephone, proper etiquette is just as important as when you meet someone in person.

- Keep business conversations to the point.
- Do not keep someone on hold more than 30 seconds.
- Always leave your phone number if you ask for someone to call you back.
- Maintain a phone log to refer back to for valuable information.
- Listening is essential whether in person or on the phone.
- Make sure your voice mail is working properly.

> The Phone

- Always return calls. Even if you don't yet have an answer to the caller's question, call and explain what you're doing to get the requested information, or direct them to the appropriate place to get it.

- If you're going to be out, have someone pick up your calls, or at a minimum, have your answering system tell the caller when you'll be back in the office and when they can expect a call back.

- When you initiate a call and get a receptionist or secretary, identify yourself and tell them the basic nature of your call. That way, you'll be sure you're getting the right person or department and the person you're trying to reach will be able to pull up the appropriate information and help you more efficiently.

- When you're on the receiving end of a phone call, identify yourself and your department. Answer the phone with some enthusiasm or at least warmth, even if you ARE being interrupted. The person on the other end doesn't know that!

- Personalize the conversation. Many people act in electronic media (including phone, phone mail, and e-mail) the way they act in their cars. They feel since they're not face-to-face with a person, it is perfectly acceptable to be abrupt, crass, or rude. We need to ensure that we make best use of the advantages of these media without falling headfirst into the disadvantages.

Language and Culture Focus (语言文化要点)

>>>>Reading I

1. Or suppose you happened to be entertaining guests, doing business, taking a bath, listening to a symphony or any combination of those activities and were forced to stop everything and devote your full attention to anybody who chose to address you.

【译文】或假设你碰巧在招待客人、办正事、洗澡、听交响乐或同时在做上述的数件事情，却被迫要中止所有事情并将全部注意力转到要和你说话的人身上。

2. devote to: to set apart for; give completely to. 把……专用于；把……贡献于；专心致力于

【例句】He has devoted his life to helping the poor.

I don't think you should devote so much time to this question.

Several pages of the newspaper were devoted to an account of this event.

【相关词】

devoted *adj.* 忠实的；热爱……的；专用于……的

【例句】a devoted father/friend

devoted to music/football

He is very devoted to his wife.

devotion *n.*

1) 深爱；挚爱

【例句】a mother's devotion to her child

2) 献身；忠心

【例句】devotion to duty 忠于职守

a teacher's devotion to his task

our devotion to our leader

3. address: to direct speech or writing to a person or group. 向……讲话；给……写信

【例句】The educator had to address a hostile crowd of teachers.

4. horrid: very unpleasant; nasty. 极令人厌恶的；极不友好的

【例句】Don't be so horrid to me!

5. instrument *n.*

1) a small tool used in work, such as science or medicine, where very careful movements are necessary. （指用来进行细致工作的）器械；器具

【例句】surgical/teaching instrument

2）musical instrument. 乐器

【例句】stringed instrument 弦乐器

wind/brass instrument 管乐器

【相关词】

instrumental *adj.* be important in making sth. possible. 对……重要的；有帮助的

【例句】Wilson was instrumental in introducing new methods of production.

6. clamor: ［for］to express a demand continually, loudly, and strongly. 大声疾呼；强烈要求

【例句】The people were clamoring for his execution.

The children were clamoring to be fed.

7. shut up

1）(to make sb.) stop talking. （使）闭嘴

【例句】Shut up! I'm trying to think.

Can't you shut that dog up?

He was going to tell the newspapers, so we offered him $1, 000 to shut him up.

2）to keep enclosed; confine. 把（某人/某物）关起来

【例句】He shut himself up in his room and refused to come out.

3）to make (a place, esp. a shop at the end of a business day) safe before leaving by locking doors, etc. （尤指商店）下班；关门；打烊

【例句】Business was slow so we shut up early for the day.

8. justifiable: *adj.* done for good reasons. 有正当理由的

【例句】justifiable anger

Is abortion justifiable when the child is unwanted?

【相关词】

justified *adj.* 有合理解释的；有正当理由的

【例句】I think your conclusions were fully justified.

be justified in doing sth.

【例句】Under the circumstances, the principal was justified in expelling the student.

9. rude: speaking or behaving in a way that is not polite and is likely to offend or annoy people. 不礼貌的；粗鲁的；讨厌的

【例句】Don't be so rude to your father!

I didn't mean to be rude, but I had to leave early.

【相关搭配】

It is rude to do sth.

【例句】It's rude to stare.

10. put...on hold:

1) to make sb. wait to be spoken to on the telephone. 接电话时让人等

【例句】The caller is on hold. 那个打电话的人正等着通话。

Put him on hold (=make him wait).

2) to be delayed; to be in a state in which no action is taken for a time. 暂缓；推迟；搁置

【例句】We've put the project on hold for a month.

11. subject ... to: to cause to experience or suffer. ［常用被动语态］使遭受（痛苦）；使接受（某种经历）；使蒙受……

【例句】We were subjected to a good deal of ill-mannered abuse.

They were subjected to torture.

The scientists subjected the products to a number of rigorous tests.

No one would willingly subject himself to such indignities.

Police subjected him to hours of questioning.

12. canned music: music recorded in advance and having an unoriginal or artificial quality. 事先录制好的音乐

canned laughter: 事先录好的笑声

【例句】It's interesting to hear canned laughter on a TV comedy show.

13. indignity: a state or situation that makes one feel ashamed or feel loss of respect. 侮辱；轻蔑

【例句】I suffered the indignity of having to say I was sorry in front of all those people.

14. Two people who keep different office hours, either because of their jobs or their time zones, may easily spend days leaving messages for each other-even more days than it takes to send a letter.

【译文】两个因工作或时区不同而有不同办公时间的人，很可能要花数日才能把电话留言传到对方，甚至比传递一封信所花的天数更多。

15. handle *vt.*

1) to deal with; to be responsible for or in charge of sth. 对付；控制

【例句】It was a difficult situation but he handled it very well.

She really knows how to handle a fast car.

Ms. Brown handles the company's accounts.

I decided to let John handle the situation.

You don't have to come. I can handle it.

2) to buy, sell, or deal with in business. 经营；经销；处理

【例句】We do not handle that sort of book.

This branch office handles grain exports.

This travel agency handles British Airlines business.

16. What is the proper number of rings a caller should wait before hanging up?: In this sentence, attention should be given to "before hanging up", a structure formed by "conjunction ＋ V-ing". When this is the case, the logical subject of the *V*-ing is generally the subject of the sentence, as the word "caller" in the above sentence.

【例句】 While working in the office, he received a call from his mother.

After meeting the guest, he returned to his office.

Before finishing the task, they went out for supper.

17. hang up: to finish a telephone conversation by putting the receiver back. 挂断电话

【例句】 It's a bad line; hang up and I'll call you back.

I was so angry that I hung up on her.

18. lurk *vi.*

1) to exist unseen. 暗藏；潜伏着

【例句】 Danger lurks in that quiet river.

Doubts that lurking in my mind haunted me.

2) to move or wait quietly and secretly, as if intending to do sth. wrong and not wanting to be seen. 潜行；埋伏

【例句】 The photographer lurked behind a tree, waiting for her to come past.

There's someone lurking about outside.

19. get out of: to leave a room or a place. 离开

【例句】 Mary screamed at me to get out.

She went for a walk just to get out of the house.

If you don't get out of here now, I'm going to call the police.

20. ignore: to take no notice of; refuse to pay attention to. 不顾；不理；忽视

【例句】 My advice was completely ignored.

The government would be unwise to ignore the growing dissatisfaction with its economic policies.

【相关词】

ignorance *n.* ［of］lack of knowledge, information, or esp. sth. one ought to know about. 无知；愚昧

【例句】 Ignorance of the law is no excuse.

The workers were kept in complete ignorance of the company's financial situation.

ignorant *adj.* ［of］lacking knowledge, information, or esp. something one ought to know about. 无知的；无学识的；愚昧的

【例句】 He is ignorant even of the simplest fact.

244

I'm afraid I'm rather ignorant about computers.

21. be in agreement with: to conform to, be in accord with. 和……相一致

【例句】In this respect it is in agreement with those theorists.

I found myself in agreement with the lawyer, for once.

22. tax ... with: to charge (sb.) with sth. bad or doing wrong. 指责

【例句】He was taxed with neglecting the safety regulations.

23. accusation: (a statement) accusing someone of doing wrong or of breaking the law. 控告；告发；指责

【例句】How do you answer the accusation that your policies have caused high unemployment?

You shouldn't make wild accusations without any evidence.

24. a bad connection: not clear. 不清楚，不清晰

【例句】I phoned Ann, but we had such a bad connection that we gave up trying to talk.

connection: the way in which two facts, ideas, events, etc. are related to each other, and one is affected or caused by the other. 联系，关系   **synonym: link**

【例句】There is a connection between pollution and the death of trees.

Mr. O'Hara had no known connection with terrorist activity.

Williams apparently has no connection to the case.

Students often see little connection between school and the rest of their lives.

He demonstrated the close connection between social conditions and health.

25. at the very mention of it: just as/the moment one mentions it.

【例句】He got angry at the very mention of it.

A roar of laughter went up at the very mention of such a thing.

26. without ＋ V-ing phrase:

【例句】How dare you do such a thing without consulting me?

Without looking at the target, he shot the arrow.

27. consideration *n.*

1) careful thought and attention. 斟酌；考虑

① **under consideration** 在讨论中；在考虑中

【例句】There are several amendments under consideration.

② **due/long consideration** 充分考虑

【例句】After due consideration, I have decided to tender my resignation.

③ **take sth. into consideration** 考虑到某事

【例句】Your teachers will take your recent illness into consideration when marking your exams.

2) the quality of thinking about other people's feelings and taking care not to upset them. 体谅;体贴

① **out of consideration for** 为……着想

【例句】The murdered woman's name has not been released, out of consideration for her parents.

② **show consideration for** 体谅……

【例句】He never shows any consideration for his mother's feelings.

28. confront *vt.*

1) to face bravely or threateningly. 勇敢地面对;对抗;正视;遭遇

【例句】Students should not be confronted with too much information in one lesson.

They have confronted the problem of terrorism with great determination.

2) to be faced with and have to deal with; meet. 面临;遇到

【例句】He prepared answers for the questions he expected to confront during the interview.

【相关词】

confrontation *n.* [with] 对抗;对峙

confrontational *adj.* 对峙的;对抗的

【相关搭配】

confront sb./sth. with sth.: 使不得不面对,使不得不承认

【例句】When he was confronted with the evidence of his guilt, the suspect had no choice but to confess at once.

The current development in the field of social science confronts us with quite a few new problems.

29. surrender

1) *vt.* to give up under pressure or from necessity. 交出

【例句】You will have to surrender your passport at the hotel desk.

I hereby surrender all claims to the money.

2) *vt.* [to] to give up or give in to the power, as a sign of defeat 投降;自首;屈服

【例句】After three days, the hijackers surrendered themselves to the police.

The government has surrendered to the pressure of big business and lowered interest rates.

3) *n.* giving up or giving in under pressure or from necessity. 投降;屈服;让步

【例句】This is by no means an unconditional surrender. 这绝不是无条件投降。

The statement made by the government amounted to a surrender to the forces of evil.

政府的申明无疑是向恶势力屈服。

30. party: a person who is concerned in some action or activity. 一方;当事人

【例句】Are you a party to the agreement?

We know he is the guilty party, because we saw him take the money.

31. offense: hurting of one's feelings. 冒犯;伤害感情

【例句】to give/cause offense to sb. 得罪某人

I hope you won't take offense（不要见怪）, if I ask you not to smoke.

Don't be upset by what he said — he meant no offense（没有冒犯你的意思）.

32. **bother**: *vt.* to cause trouble, worry, or annoyance to. 打扰；烦扰；使苦恼

【例句】Don't bother me with foolish questions.

Henry never bothers his brains about what to do next.

Will it bother you if I turn on the radio?

>>>>>Reading II

1. the Far East: a collective term indicating the countries of East Asia, including China, Japan, South Korea, North Korea, and sometimes adjacent areas（远东）. This term is used according to the view that Europe is the center, and the names of other places are determined by their distance from Europe. Therefore the Middle East（中东）and the Far East.

2. In some developing countries, however, phone systems are antiquated, and the simple act of making a local call could be nightmarishly difficult.

【译文】一些发展中国家的电话系统陈旧过时，一次简单的本地通话可能带来梦魇般的麻烦。

3. adequate: just enough for the purpose.

【例句】adequate parking facilities

a country with adequate, steady rainfall

The city's water supply is no longer adequate.

Are transport systems adequate to deliver the food to remote areas?

4. antiquated: old-fashioned, not suited to modern needs or conditions.

【例句】antiquated laws 过时的法律条文

antiquated air-conditioner

antiquated machinery

5. nightmarishly: like a terrible dream, extremely terrible. 恶梦般的

It's noun is "nightmare", which refers to a terrible dream, or something that is terribly frightening and unpleasant.

【例句】the nightmare of a nuclear war

Driving on that ice was a real nightmare.

In his nightmare, he burned his own house.

My first day of school was a nightmare.

6. surcharge: an extra amount of money in addition to the usual payment. 附加费

【例句】an import surcharge 进口附加税

We have to pay a fuel surcharge on our airlines tickets because of the sudden increase in the cost of oil.

The government is imposing a 15% surcharge.

If you are surcharged on something, you have to make an extra or additional payment after the original payment is made.

【例句】He was surcharged on the parcel.

7. charge: to ask in payment.

【例句】How much do you charge for a double room?

They charge a heavy tax on imported wine.

The shop doesn't charge for delivery.

They tried to charge me £80 for a room for one night.

The bank charges me 25% interest on the loan.

8. alternative (to): sth. that one can choose or decide between two possibilities.

【例句】We had to fight. There was no alternative.

I'm afraid I have no alternative but to report you to the police.

The ministry will have no alternative but to raise our rates.

The preposition "to" usually follows "alternative".

【例句】There are several alternatives to your plan.

Are there alternatives to prison?

9. phone booth: (also phone box) a small enclosure or shelter in the street, station, hotel, etc., where there is a telephone for use by the public.

【例句】public phone booth 公用电话亭

10. a different looking phone: a phone that looks different from other phones.

different looking: We may put an adjective before "looking" to form a compound adjective.

【例句】different looking 看起来不一样的

good looking 相貌英俊的

ordinary looking 相貌平常的

extraordinary looking 相貌非凡的

11. instructions: (usually with -s ending) clear and detailed information on how to do sth. 操作指南，用法说明

【例句】I didn't follow the instructions printed on the box, and broke the machine.

Read the instructions before you switch on the engine.

12. fade: to lose brightness, color or freshness, and become paler gradually.

【例句】fading photographs

　　　　an old man in a faded blue shirt

　　　　The wallpaper has faded.

　　　　Flowers soon fade when they have been cut.

　　　　These curtains were once bright green but the sun has faded them.

　　　　How can I stop the sun from fading the carpet?

13. scratch off: to remove sth. from a surface by rubbing it with sth. sharp. "away" can be used with "scratch" in this sense.

【例句】I scratched off/away a little of the paint with my fingernail.

　　　　The dog has scratched some of the paint off the door.

14. Patience is a must: You must be patient and keep calm rather than get annoyed. Here "must" is a noun, which refers to something that is absolutely necessary or very important to have or experience.

【例句】Warm clothes are a must in the mountains.

　　　　Rubber gloves are a must if your skin is sensitive to washing powders.

patience: the ability to keep calm and control one's feelings so as not to be made annoyed.

【例句】You need patience if you want to get served in this shop.

　　　　It took a vast amount of patience not to shout at him.

　　　　I've lost all patience with you.

15. newsstand: a stall on a street or in a station, from which newspapers， magazines and books are sold. 书报摊，书报亭

16. vary: to be different; to change.

【例句】The price varies according to the season.

　　　　The quality of their products never varies. It is always excellent.

　　　　The screens will vary in size depending on what one wants.

　　　　The sums they receive vary from individual to individual.

17. telecommunication: communication by satellite, cable, telegraph, telephone, radio or TV. 电信

18. receiver: the part of the telephone that you hold near to your ear. 听筒

【例句】She picked up the receiver and dialed the number.

19. dial tone: sound heard on the telephone showing that one can begin to dial the number. 拨号音

20. different than: different from.

21. insert: to put in.

【例句】insert a key in a lock

insert the peg into the hole

insert an amendment into the contract　在合同中加入一项修正条款

She removed the sheet of paper on which she had been typing and inserted a new one.

22. **digital:** If something is digital, its information is represented or displayed in the form of changing electrical signals.

【例句】digital sound recording 数码录音

digital watch

digital camera　　　　　　　　　　digital computer

23. **readout:** showing of information from a memory or storage device that has been processed by a computer.

【例句】Using this program, you can get a readout of all the areas where sales have increased.

24. **dial:** to make a telephone call by moving the circle on the front of a telephone.

【例句】How do I dial Paris?

Put in the coin before dialing.

Jim dialed his home number.

She dialed the operator to ask about a taxi.

25. **accordingly:** in a way suitable to what has been said or what has happened. 相应地

【例句】Please inform us of your decision, and we will act accordingly.

He wanted to be treated like any other star entertainer and be paid accordingly.

Sometimes the press went so far and suffered accordingly.

26. **Phones will often tell you when your card is almost expired, and will give you a chance to switch cards without breaking the call.**

【译文】电话会自动告诉你电话卡何时到期，并在不中断通话的情况下，为你提供换卡的服务。

27. **expire:** to come to an end, to reach the end of the period of time for which sth. is valid or during which sth. is allowed to exist.

【例句】The trade agreement between the two countries will expire next year.

The car broke down two days after the guarantee had expired.

"Expiry" or "expiration" is the noun form.

【例句】What is the expiry date on your library book?

The French licenses have no expiry date.

The president can be elected again at the expiration of his first four years.

28. **switch card:** to change card. Here "switch" means "to change".

【例句】The wind has switched from north to east.

Let's switch positions.

He got tired of teaching and switched to writing stories.

29. **guess work:** the attempt or process of trying to guess or estimate sth. without knowing adequate information or facts.

【例句】She arrived at the right answer by pure guess work.

This is pure guess work at this stage, of course.

30. **be similar to:** to be like or alike; to be of the same kind or to share the same features.

【例句】My opinions are similar to hers.

My problems are very similar to yours.

31. **long distance:** to or from a distant place between two people or places that are far apart.

【例句】long distance call 长途电话

32. **operator:** a person who works at a telephone exchange or switch board. 电话接线员

【例句】Operator! I've been cut off.

He dialed the operator.

33. **in exchange for:** If you give a person something in exchange for something else, you give it because he is giving you the other thing.

【例句】He gave me an apple in exchange for a piece of cake.

They were given food, shelter, and clothes in exchange for two years' labor without wages.

They sold chemicals and textiles in exchange for agricultural products.

34. **token:** a piece of paper or card or metal that is worth a particular amount of money and can be used instead of coins for goods. 金属代币, 代币券

35. **place an international call:** make an international call.

36. **code:** (also called dialing code or area code) part of a telephone number that represents a particular town or country and is dialed before someone's personal number in order to be connected to the right area, town, or village. 电话区号

【例句】a code book 电话区号号码簿

What's the code for London?

The code for Shanghai is 021.

international access code: the code needed to dial into another country.

access: means of entering, reading or obtaining sth.

【例句】The only means of access to the building is along a muddy track.

They attempted to gain access through a side entrance.

Students need easy access to books.

Her ex-husband has access to the children at weekends.

I demanded access to a telephone.

37. in addition (to): besides.

【例句】In addition, there were parallel meetings with trade unionists.

They eat, in addition to leaves, a great deal of fruit.

In addition to giving a general introduction to computers, the course also provides practical experience.

38. specific: We can use "specific" to refer to a particular fixed area or subject, etc.

【例句】Education should not be restricted to any one specific age group.

Let's look at a specific area of public policy.

There's a specific tool for each job.

39. *the Global Road Warrior:* This is a book created by World Trade Press, a developer and publisher for the international trade community. This book provides the premier source of business travel information on business practices, society, communications, culture, climate, commerce and transportation in 175 countries. It also adds extra sections on things like business customs and how to do business, where to stay, customs and immigration issues, local transportation, weather, tipping, and much more. It also includes a map and basic country information such as population, language, etc.

40. guide: a book which gives advice, or instructions to do sth. or offers information about sth. 指南；手册

41. domestic: of or within a particular country; not foreign or international.

【例句】domestic policy

domestic flights

domestic news

The company needs to acquire domestic sources of oil and natural gas.

42. additional charge: the extra price that one has to pay for a service or for sth. one buys.

【例句】Additional charge is made for repairs.

43. add...to...: to put together with sth. else, so as to increase the number, size, degree or importance.

【例句】Please add a few more names to the list.

Would you like to add anything to what I've said?

The decision to buy this weapon will add at least $25 million to the defense budget.

44. undoubtedly: certainly, unquestionably.

【例句】This is undoubtedly true.

Undoubtedly, many families are victims of bad housing.

A personal chauffeur is undoubtedly a symbol of social status.

45. simply: We use "simply" to give emphasis to sth. that we are saying.

【例句】I simply can't believe it.

We simply must face the fact.

I don't like driving. I do it simply because I have to get to work every day.

46. **capability:** the ability or quality, or a way in which someone or sth. has the power or skill. 能力，性能

【例句】nuclear capability 核力量

the capability of society to meet the needs of people

a computer with a good graphics capability 制图性能好的电脑

Some jobs are still beyond their capabilities.

No one doubts her capability for the job.

The engineer explained the plane's technical capabilities (技术性能).

47. **efficiency:** the quality of being able to do a task successfully without wasting time or energy.

【例句】improve the efficiency of reading

efficiency in developing ideas

business efficiency

It would improve our efficiency if we used more up-to-date methods.

48. **assign:** to give.

【例句】I've been assigned the job of looking after the new students.

They assigned the job to me.

She kept calling him to assign some new tasks.

Boys are assigned chores in the garage.

She had been assigned to work in the fields for six months.

They assigned someone to watch me 24 hours a day.

49. **returnable deposit:** money that you have to pay in advance before renting sth., such as a car or a flat, and will be returned to you if no damage is done. Here it refers to the sum of money you deposit before using the phone at a post office. 可退还的押金

deposit: 押金

【例句】When you return the bottle, we'll return your deposit.

You may have to pay a deposit to open an electricity account, but if you pay your bills promptly, they will return it to you.

50. **limited:** not very great in amount, range, power or degree.

【例句】student of limited ability/intelligence

limited time/funds/resources

Seating is limited to 500.

The choice was very limited.

>>>>>Extended Activities

A. Function and Structure: Making Telephone Calls

1. The differences between Chinese and Britons in phone calls

When a Briton answers a phone call, he or she may tell the caller his or her name first, while in China the caller speaks first and asks the receiver whether a certain person is available for the phone call. In Chinese phone calls people always say "I'm...", but this is not appropriate in English. The correct expression is "This is sb. (speaking)" or just "sb. speaking".

2. How to practice phone calls in English

Learning how to communicate well on the telephone is one of the top priorities for many students who need to use English at work. Learning the common phrases that are used on the telephone helps students know what to expect. However, what students often need most is more practice. Telephoning requires special skills, as there are a number of difficulties that arise when telephoning. The first and foremost difficulty is not being able to see the person you are communicating with. This lack of visual communication often makes students, who can communicate quite successfully in other situations, nervous and thereby hinders their communicative abilities. So the most important thing about practicing telephone conversations is that you shouldn't be able to see the person you are speaking to on the phone. You may ask, "How can I do that if I am practicing with a friend or another classmate?" Here are a few suggestions for practicing phone calls without looking at your partner:

If you are in the same room — Put your chairs back to back and practice speaking on the phone, you will only hear the other person's voice which will approximate a telephone situation.

Use the telephone — This is pretty obvious, but really not used that often. Give your friend a call and practice various conversations （role plays）.

Tape yourself — If you are practicing alone, tape standard answers and then practice using the tape recorder stopping and starting to simulate a conversation.

Real life situations — Businesses are always interested in telling you about their products. Find a product you are interested in and research it over the telephone.

B. Special Use: Perfect Tenses of Verbs

1. 现在完成时

1) 现在完成时的未完成用法

现在完成时表示过去开始的动作或状态持续到现在。例如：

He has been in the army for two years.

We have waited all day.

He has lived here all his life.

2) 现在完成时的完成用法

① 表示过去开始的动作到说话时刻已经结束。例如：

I haven't seen you for ages.（现在我看到你了，not see 的状态已经结束。）

It has been very cold lately but it's just beginning to get warmer.（现在不冷了，冷的状态已经结束。）

② 表示过去发生、但与现在有关联或对现在有影响的事件。例如：

Return all the books you have borrowed.（借与还有关联。）

I have written several letters to them.（因为写过了，所以现在不用写了。）

③ 表示过去的经历。例如：

We have met each other before.

I have been to Beijing twice.（去过已经回来。）

比较：He has gone to Beijing.（在路上，或还在北京，没有回来。）

2. 现在完成时与一般过去时的区别

1) 现在完成时强调过去的动作现在仍在持续；而一般过去时强调过去的动作已经结束。例如：

His father was an English teacher all his life.（他父亲已经死了。）

His father has been an English teacher all his life.（他父亲仍然活着。）

He lived in Shanghai for 20 years.（他现在不住上海了。）

He has lived in Shanghai for 20 years.（他现在仍在上海。）

He smoked for six months.（他以前抽过 6 个月的烟，但现在不抽烟了。）

He has smoked for six months.（他已经抽了 6 个月的烟，现在还抽烟。）

He was in the army for ten years.（他现在不在部队里了。）

He has been in the army for ten years.（他现在还在部队里。）

2) 现在完成时强调过去动作对现在的影响，而一般过去时强调该动作与现在没有关系。

Who has taken my dictionary?（现在不见了，找不到了。）

Who left the door open?（门现在可能已经关上了。）

Who has left the door open?（门现在还开着。）

He had a bad car crash.（该事件已经过去，对现在没有影响。）

He has had a bad car crash.（他现在可能在医院。）

The lift broke down.（电梯以前坏过，但对现在没有影响，现在已经好了。）

The lift has broken down.（电梯坏了，我们只能走上楼了。）

I washed the car.（过去洗的，对现在没有影响，可能现在又脏了。）

I have washed the car.（该动作对现在有影响，现在车子看上去还很干净。）

Someone broke the window.（窗子现在已经修好。）

Someone has broken the window.（窗子现在仍然没有修好。）

3) 一般过去时能与确定的过去时间如 yesterday, last night, just now, two minutes ago 等连用，而现在完成时没有这种用法，它只能与 already, just, yet, before, ever, never, recently, lately, so far, up till now, for, since 等时间状语连用。例如：

I have just finished my homework.

I finished my homework just now.

Have you had breakfast yet?

Did you have breakfast before you left the hotel?

I have already read the instruction.

I read the instruction last night.

Have you ever fallen off a horse?

I have never been late for work.

Has he been here recently?

She has been abroad lately.

① 请注意在对话中完成时与过去时的转换。

— Have you read the book?

— Yes, I have.

— When did you read it?（when 暗示过去的具体时间，所以用过去时。）

— Last month.

又例如：

— Have you seen my stamps?

— Yes, I saw them on your desk a minute ago.

— Have you had breakfast?

— Yes, I had it with Mary.

② for 后面跟的是一段时间。例如：

We have lived there for ten years.

③ since 后面跟的是时间点。since 可以作介词、副词和连词。例如：

We haven't heard from each other since 1989.（介词）

I have never seen him ever since.（副词）

You haven't changed much since we last met.（连词）

如果 since 后跟的是从句，从句通常用过去时。例如：

Since I went to school, I have written with my left hand.

④ It is ... since ... 句型。

该句型表示"自从……以来已经有……时间了"，it is 也可以用 it has been。例如：

It is thirty years since he joined revolution.

It's a long time since I saw him.

It has been two years since he left his motherland.

⑤ 用现在完成时的句子中如果有 for 和 since 结构，谓语动词必须是状态动词或表示可持续动作的动词，这时谓语动词不能用瞬间动词。例如：

He has been dead for five years.（不能说 He has died for five years.）

He has been out for ten minutes.（不能说 He has left for ten minutes.）

I have kept the book for two weeks.（不能说 I have borrowed the book for two weeks.）

⑥ already 常用于肯定句；而 yet 常用于否定句和疑问句。

⑦ 当 once 表示"曾经"时，我们通常用一般过去时；当 once 解释"一次"时，我们通常用现在完成时。例如：

I once lived in a thatched hut.

I have been there once.

⑧ 现在完成时与形容词最高级、序数词以及 only 等的搭配。例如：

This is the best book I have ever read.

This is the worst film I have ever seen.

This is the easiest job I have ever done.

This is the first time I have seen such a great man.

This is the only book he has written.

3. 过去完成时

1) 过去完成时经常与"by ＋ 过去时间"或"by the end of ＋ 过去时间"搭配。例如：

By last year, he had written 10 novels.

By the end of last month, we had finished 10 units.

2) 过去完成时可表示过去某一时刻之前发生的动作或经历，也称为"过去的过去"。例如：

He arrived at 2∶30. He had been asked to wait in the VIP room.（在到之前接到通知。）

When she had sung her song, she sat down.（先唱歌，后坐下。）

When he had shut the window, we opened the door of the cage.（先关窗，再打开笼子。）

When he had seen all the pictures, he said he was ready to leave.（先看再说。）

所以，当两个过去动作一前一后发生，后面的动作是过去时，则前面的动作为过去完成时。又例如：

He looked pale. He had been ill for a long time.

He told me he had been to London twice.

I had just poured myself a glass of coffee when the phone rang. When I came back from answering it, the glass was empty. Somebody had drunk the coffee or thrown it away.

但如果上述例子是按照事件发生的先后顺序的, 就不需要用过去完成时。例如:

She saw empty glasses and cups and realized that three people had been in the room. (在她发现的时候, 人已经走了。在她发现之前房间里有三个人。)

He arrived at 2 : 30 and was asked to wait in the VIP room. (先到, 再接到通知。)

3) 与过去完成时搭配的固定结构。

与过去完成时搭配的固定结构有: had no sooner...than...; had hardly...when...; 以及 had scarcely...when...。这三个结构都是 "一……就……" 的意思。例如:

I had no sooner left the room than the telephone rang.

I had hardly left the room when the telephone rang.

I had scarcely left the room when the telephone rang.

上述结构也有倒装用法。例如:

No sooner had I left the room than the telephone rang.

Hardly had I left the room when the telephone rang.

Scarcely had I left the room when the telephone rang.

C. Practical Reading

关于电话服务信息, 其主要内容有地点/地址、电话号码、服务时间、服务内容、商品名称、服务方式、服务机构、顾客等。要回答阅读材料后的问题, 可以将以上项目快速扫读后归类, 特别是服务机构和产品等最关键的项目应该是重点归类的对象。然后再根据题目中的要求 "按图索骥" 即可。例如: 通过大致归类, 我们可以知道这里的服务有 Coffee; Western beef; Indian Curry; Italian Dishes; seafood; STEAK; no reservation needed 等服务内容。

题目中的 7 至 10 题都与以上内容有直接关系, 通过 "对号入座", 我们就可以迅速找到相应的答案。

Teaching Tips（教学提示）

1. Lead-in   本单元导入部分安排了听力理解和听写填空两项任务。听力理解部分既有语篇又有习语的听音训练, 共设有 4 项听力练习。听力练习的编排和以往各单元一样, 第一和第三项练习均属预听活动, 主要目的是在进行精听训练之前, 让学生对听音内容的主旨(Gist)有所了解, 初步把握听音和理解上的难点所在, 为接下来的听力活动做好词汇和心理上的准备。语篇部分介绍了一些常用电话礼仪技巧：如何有礼貌地接听电话，为他人传递讯息，以及打断对方谈话等。语篇所配精听练习则为最常见的多选择题（Multiple-choice Questions），要求学生选择最合适的选项补全句子，侧重考察学生理解、辨析语篇细节和关键信息的能力。在听音前，教师可以鼓励学生快速浏览各个句子以及各选项，根据语篇主题以及自己的常识对将要听到的内容进行积极的预测和推断。如时间许可，还可以让学生双人结对，对他们预测的答案进行简短的讨论。听音时则引导学生侧重对自己的预测进行检验和确认，以提高他们听音的兴趣。习语部分列出了九句电话用语，要求学生分别按场景归类：1）Phrases for leaving a voice mail 要求给对方留语音讯息；2）Phrases for recording a voice mail message on your machine 要求来电方在你的机器上留下语音讯息；3）Phrases for cell phone calls when the signal is not good enough 手机信号不佳时的用语。听音前，教师可以结合扩展性练习中 Function & Structure 部分的内容对学生进行 warming-up。如教师可以从 Function & Structure 部分提供的电话常用习语中随机挑选一些读给学生听，不让学生看书，让学生自己来归纳，这些习语分别用于什么样的场景。听写填空（Spot Dictation）注重数字，打电话常用的动词，订单的词语，可以作为导入活动安排在 Reading II 课文讲解之前进行。

2. Reading I Brainstorming　全班学生通过自由讨论的形式，列出他们所知道的在商务活动中常用的沟通方式和工具。教师可向学生指出：1）随着现代科技的发展，新兴的沟通方式和通讯工具层出不穷，但电话仍是日常商务活动中最重要、最常用的工具。商务英语专业的学生必须掌握一定的电话使用技巧并学习基本的商务电话用语和礼仪；2）商务活动中有外部沟通（external communication）和内部沟通（internal communication）之分。内部沟通指公司内部上司和下属之间（superior & inferior）、员工之间（colleagues）的沟通和交流；而外部沟通指的是公司与客户（customers）、公众（the public）、媒体（media）、政府机构（government agencies）等其他社会实体之间的信息传递和交流。教师可请学生在他们列出的沟通方式和工具中挑选哪些适用于公司的内部沟通，哪些适用于公司的外部沟通。当然，电话是一种同时适用于内、外部交流的重要商务工具。

3. Reading I Pairwork　学生双人结对讨论与本单元主题 Telephone 相关的话题。Question 1 教师还可请学生谈谈在公共场合使用手机应注意些什么，如：上课时能否接听手机？ Question 2 建议教师从以下不同角度对学生进行一定引导：电话的发明对人类生活的正、负面影响；电话和其他通讯工具（如：信函 Correspondence、传真 Fax、电子邮件 e-mail 等）相比较有何优势和缺陷。

4. Reading I 练习 IV　Question 1 中 talk show, 指"访谈节目"（a television or radio show in which well-known people, such as authorities in a particular field, participate in discussions or are interviewed and often answer questions from viewers or listeners）。在英国，talk show 也被称为 chat show。

5. Reading I Post-reading　设有两项任务。任务 1 列出了课文中提到的 5 个使用电话中经常碰到的场景，要求学生根据课文内容，归纳并填写 Miss Manners' Advice 一栏；Your Response 一栏则由学生根据其平时使用电话的经验和想象填写完成。任务 2 学生分组活动，讨论在电话使用中必须遵循的一些规则和礼仪。关于 telephone etiquette, 在本教师用书 Background Information 部分和学生用书 Business World — Twelve Telephone Tips 中均有涉及。教师还可结合下面的补充材料一起使用。

Telephone Tips: Do's and Don'ts

Do's

Do speak clearly. Remember, the caller can't see you to read lips, facial expressions or body language. He or she can only hear you. Take the time to speak clearly the first time, and you won't waste time repeating yourself.

Do use your normal voice. If you have to raise your voice because of poor cell phone reception or a noisy environment such as a restaurant or building site, be aware that the listener may not be experiencing similar problems and may misinterpret your response as anger, frustration or hostility. Advise the person on the other end that you are having difficulty and either leave the restaurant or call back later.

Do remove gum, pencils, cigarettes or anything else from your mouth while talking on the phone. Put the coffee cup down. The sounds of chewing, slurping and clicking are not attractive or professional.

Do address the caller by the proper title, Mr., Ms., Mrs. or Dr. as indicated. If uncertain as to marital status, business or academic level, use Mr. or Ms. If uncertain as to the gender of the individual you are calling, use the entire name, as in, "May I speak to Pat Smith?" Then revert to using Mr. or Ms. Maintain a polite formality, especially on initial contact.

Do avoid poor language habits and using filler words, such as "you know", "you guys", "like" or "ummm".

Do identify yourself not only when speaking directly with a person, but also when leaving messages with others or on answering machines. Give your name and contact number both at the beginning of the message and at the conclusion so the listener will not have to replay the message for the information.

Do ask if you can put a person on hold and then wait for them to reply. Not everyone delights in being put on hold. Either do not interrupt the original call or, if you think this may be the call you've been waiting for all morning, excuse yourself, tell the first caller you will call back in a few minutes and allow them to get on with their day.

Do listen to the caller. Pay attention to what they are saying so that you can answer the question they ask, instead of the one you thought they were going to ask. Write down important information as they are talking.

Don'ts

Don't speak too fast. People sometimes speak too fast because they are in a hurry or they are bored and not paying attention. Remember, although you may say the name of your company or your own name dozens of times in a day, for many callers, this is the first time they may be hearing it.

Don't speak too softly or breathy trying for an effect. This does not sound sexy, rather it sounds childish and people may not take you seriously.

Don't talk with your mouth full. Do not eat your lunch and try to make a sales presentation at the same time. It's irritating and impolite. No one will be interested in why you are calling, and they will just want you off the line.

Don't say "uh-huh" and "unh-unh". These vague grunts can easily be misunderstood and they also give the impression that you are not paying attention to the speaker.

Don't express a false familiarity and address a new caller by his or her first name. Americans tend to be very informal in addressing others. However, not every one appreciates a stranger saying, "Hey, Bob, this is Bill and I'd like to talk to you about ..." For many cultures, this is actually considered rude.

Don't leave long garbled, wandering messages that no one can understand or that take six replays to get the information. No one is going to listen to a message multiple times. Use written notes to help you be brief and to the point.

Don't keep someone on hold more than few seconds, not minutes. Seconds feel like minutes if you are the one on hold and rarely does anyone really like the taped music selections. If you think the interruption will take more than one minute, end the call, and call back later.

Don't engage in side conversations while trying to talk to someone on the phone. Unable to actually see or participate in what is happening around you, your caller will feel ignored and resentful. Be respectful of your listener's time.

6. Reading II Vocabulary Question 2 中 the express company 指 "快递公司"。

7. Reading II Translation Question 1 中 "公关" 系 "公共关系 Public Relations" 的简称。下文是关于 PR 的一些常识。

> **Public relations** (PR) is internal and external communication (use of symbols and symbolic acts) to inform or influence specific publics using writing, marketing, advertising, publicity, promotions, and special events. Some public relations specialists work as full-time employees of companies, politicians, nonprofit organizations, or governments; while others work for PR agencies or as free-lance PR consultants that contract their services to clients (usually corporations, wealthy individuals or other special interests) who pay for their expertise at keeping them in or out of the spotlight, whichever is necessary. According to the Public Relations Society of America (PRSA), one of the profession's leading trade associations, public relations has been defined in many widely differing ways. The earliest definitions emphasized the roles of press agentry and publicity, since these were major elements from which modern public relations grew. More recently, the PR industry has pushed to redefine itself as a management function. The practice of public relations is often disparaged using terms such as "spin", and public relations practitioners are sometimes characterized as "spin doctors" or "flacks".

8. Reading II Cloze

Question 3　此处选 c. directory, 指 "通讯录, 姓名地址目录 a book containing an alphabetical or classified listing of names, addresses, and other data, such as telephone numbers, of specific persons, groups, or firms"。而选项 b. catalogue 指 "（商品）目录，（商品）价目表 a list or itemized display, as of titles, course offerings, or articles for exhibition or sale, usually including descriptive information or illustrations"。

Question 4　此处选 a. code, area code 指 "电话地区号"。下文中也有 "New York City has one area code"一说。Code 意为"代码, 密码 a system of symbols, letters, or words given certain arbitrary meanings, used for transmitting messages requiring secrecy or brevity", 如: bar code 条形码, zip code 邮政编码; 而选项 b. zone 指"地区 a section of an area or a territory established for a specific purpose, as a section of a city restricted to a particular type of building, enterprise, or activity", 如: a residential zone 住宅区; 选项 c. digit 指"10个阿拉伯数字符号从0到9中的任意一个 one of the ten Arabic number symbols, 0 through 9", 如: The number 2001 contains four digits; 选项 d. number 指"号, 号码 a numeral or a series of numerals used for reference or identification", 如: telephone number, apartment number。

Question 6　　此处选 b. does, "so does the whole state of Oregon" 意思是 "The whole state of Oregon also has one area code"。

Oregon is a state of the northwest United States in the Pacific Northwest. It was admitted as the 33rd state in 1859. Claimed by the United States after Capt. Robert Gray explored the mouth of the Columbia River in 1792, the area was further explored by Lewis and Clark in 1805 and was soon the site of fur-trading posts. The Oregon Country, a region encompassing all the land from the California border to Alaska and the Pacific Ocean to the Rocky Mountains, was held jointly by Great Britain and the United States from 1818 until 1846, when the international boundary was fixed at the 49th parallel. In 1848 the Oregon Territory was created, including all of present-day Washington and Idaho. The state's current boundaries were established in 1853. Salem is the capital and Portland the largest city. Population: 2, 853, 733.

Question 7　　此处选 c. state, 因为 Oregon 是美国的一个州。下文是关于 Oregon 州的简介。

Question 11　　此处选 d. booth, phone booth, 固定搭配, 指"电话亭"。

Question 15　　此处选 a. receiver, 特指"电话听筒", 如: The part of a telephone you speak into and listen at is called a receiver。选项 b. acceptor 和 d. receptor 均可指"接收器, 感收器"; 选项 c. receptionist 指"接待员, 办公室职员, 主要被雇来接待来访者并接电话 an office worker employed chiefly to receive visitors and answer the telephone"。

Key（练习答案）

>>>>>Reading I

Pre-reading

I.

Business Communication Types	Business Communication Tools
brochures, pamphlets, posters, various forms of advertising, contact letters, faxes, telephone calls, news release, press conference, web sites, e-mails, newsletters, meetings, instant messaging, memos, notes, notices, messages, formal and informal discussions, presentations...	telephones (standard/fixed/wireless/mobile), pagers (beepers), facsimile machines, intercom, notice board, Personal Digital Assistants (PDAs), computers (desktop/laptop/notebook) and Internet... Auxiliary tools: digital camera, scanner, printer, wireless transmission...

II.

4.

Situations	What You Will Do
If you are not the person the caller wants	Ask the caller to hold the line and fetch the person wanted.
If the line is busy	Hang up and redial.
If you get a wrong number	Tell the caller it's a wrong number and ask him or her to dial again.
If the person you are calling is away	Leave a message.
If the person you are calling is busy at the moment	Call back sometime later.

Exercises

II. 1. c   2. b   3. b   4. d   5. c

III. 1. address   2. whiny   3. complain   4. lurk   5. ignore

     6. tax   7. consideration   8. confront   9. offense   10. oblique

     11. apply   12. unmannerly   13. surrender   14. party

IV. 1. was put on hold   2. devoted ... to   3. subjected ... to   4. is suspected of

5. taxed ... with   6. shuts up   7. was confronted with   8. surrender

9. to complain of   10. to get out of (=escape from)

V. 1. To tell the truth, I am in agreement with what they say.

2. He was so angry that he left us without saying a single word.

3. Helen hung up before Jack finished what he wanted to say.

4. Can you shut the dog up?

5. At the mention of what he was going to do, he seemed very excited.

>>>>Reading II

Exercises

I. 1. F   2. T   3. F   4. T   5. T   6. F   7. T   8. NM   9. T   10. T

III. 1. d   2. b   3. a   4. d   5. d   6. a   7. c   8. b   9. b   10. c

IV. 1. The public relations girl was devoting her full attention to her work so that she didn't notice someone coming in.

2. Our opponents were shut up by our arguments because their conclusion was incorrect.

3. This product specialist is subjected to ridicule, criticism and satire, but people have to admit that the factory can't exist without him.

4. As far as this problem is concerned, I am quite in agreement with what the production inspector has said.

5. He used to feel angry at the very mention of rising prices.

6. As soon as the murderer entered the room, he was confronted with a policeman pointing a gun at him.

7. I scratched some paint off the door as I was getting out of the car.

8. Our sales are very similar to theirs, so it is not easy for either of us to control the market.

9. The overseas student from Japan is giving Mary Japanese lessons in exchange for English lessons.

10. The bank's manager did his job without complaining for fifty years, but he was suspected of corruption and bribery.

V. 1. a   2. c   3. c   4. a   5. d   6. b   7. c   8. b   9. b   10. a

11. d   12. c   13. b   14. c   15. a

>>>>>>Extended Activities

A. Function and Structure

I. 1. Telephone-answering

machine: Hello. This is Nancy Henderson 567-9320. I'm sorry I'm not in at the moment. Please leave your name and number after the tone and I'll get back to you as soon as possible.

John: Hi, Nancy. This is Peter speaking. I'm ringing to find out whether you are free tonight. I have two tickets for tonight's concert. Could you ring me back? I'll be home until 2 pm. Bye.

2. Operator: Good morning, Universal Toy Company.

James: Can I speak to Mr. Simon Fraser, Manager of Design Center?

Operator: Who's calling, please?

James: James Turner.

Operator: Hold the line, please. I'm connecting you.

(*Phone rings in Mr. Simon Fraser's office.*)

Mr. Simon Fraser: Hello, Simon Fraser here.

James: Hello, Mr. Fraser. This is James Turner speaking. I need to talk to you about our latest design...

Mr. Simon Fraser: I'm sorry, but I'm at a meeting at the moment. I wonder if I could ring you back later.

James: No problem. You can get me on 645-32718 all afternoon.

3. Mr. Perkins: Please put me through to extension 2121.

Operator: Extension 2121, OK. Hold the line, please.

Mr. Perkins: Hello! Could I speak to Mr. Johnson, please?

Mr. Harper: Sorry, Mr. Johnson is not available at the moment. I'm his assistant, Jacob Harper. Can I take a message?

Mr. Perkins: Ah, yes. This is Harry Perkins. I'm calling to tell Mr. Johnson that our L/C is issued by the Bank of Scotland, No: M1218907NS00018.

Mr. Harper: Sorry. It's quite noisy here. I didn't catch what you said. Could you repeat that?

Mr. Perkins: I call to say that our L/C is issued by the Bank of Scotland, No: M1218907NS00018. Please ask Mr. Johnson to call back. I want to talk with him over the packing instructions and labelling regulations. I'm on 46378421 until 6 pm.

Mr. Harper: I see. <u>Thanks for calling</u>.

4. A: Hello.

B: Hello, Jay?

A: I'm sorry. <u>There's no Jay here</u>.

B: Is this 786-0234?

A: No, it isn't. I guess <u>you've dialed the wrong number</u>.

B: Oh, sorry.

A: That's all right.

5. Mary: Mary, here. <u>Who is it speaking</u>?

Betty: Hi, Mary, This is Betty speaking. <u>Could you get</u> Tom <u>for me</u>, please?

Mary: I'm sorry. He's not in right now. <u>Do you want to leave a message</u>?

Betty: Yes. Please ask him to call me at 567-4327 as soon as he comes back.

Mary: OK. <u>I'll tell him that you called</u>. Goodbye... Oh, wait a minute. He is back. Tom, <u>you are wanted on the phone</u>.

Tom: Hello, this is Tom speaking.

6. Mr. King: Hello, <u>James King is calling Ms. Carter</u>.

Secretary: <u>Hold the line, please.</u> (*through intercom*) Ms. Carter, I have a Mr. King on the line. Can I put him through?

Ms. Carter: I'm on another line. Tell him I'll call him back in a minute.

Secretary: Sorry, Mr. King. Ms. Carter is on another line at the moment. She asked <u>if she could call you back in a minute</u>.

Mr. King: I don't think she needs to call me back. <u>Could you take a message for her</u>?

Secretary: Certainly.

7. Mrs. Smith: Hello.

Jane: Hello, Mrs. Smith. This is Jane.

Mrs. Smith: Hello, Jane. How are you? I haven't seen you for a long time.

Jane: Fine. Thank you. I'm busy with my term papers. May I speak to Jessica?

Mrs. Smith: Oh, Jessica has just gone to the store. She'll be back soon. <u>Can I take a message</u>?

Jane: <u>Would you tell her I rang</u>? I just call to say hello to her and to you all.

Mrs. Smith: Thank you. Come by if you're free. <u>I'm so glad you have called</u>.

8. Joan: Joan here. <u>Who is it speaking</u>?

Tim: Hello, Joan. This is Tim. <u>Could you get Dick on the phone</u>?

Joan: Dick, <u>this is for you</u>.

Dick: Hello.

Tim: Hello, Dick. It's Tim here. Look, the reason I'm calling is to ask if you're free this evening. I've got two tickets for the theater and Caroline is on a business trip. Would you like to go with me?

Dick: I'm awfully sorry. I'm afraid I can't. I have to babysit tonight.

Tim: What? <u>I don't quite follow you.</u> You have to...

Dick: I have to babysit.

Tim: Babysitting? Where's Joan then?

Dick: She's going to an evening class. She enrolled in an adult computer course and she has classes every evening, so I have to take care of little Jimmy.

Tim: Well, that's too bad.

Dick: Anyway, <u>thanks for calling</u>.

B. Special Use

1. had (we) reached ... began	2. have traveled	3. got ... has been
4. arrived ... had already taken	5. left	6. Have (you) been invited
7. has always wanted	8. left ... had learned ... learned	9. met ... haven't seen
10. have ... met	11. have lived ... died	12. died ... had reigned
13. made ... has been ... has been	14. set out ... had left ... hadn't returned	
15. used ... rode ... have had	16. did ... bought ... had made	

C. Practical Reading

1. 1213 North Duke.

2. 419-2084.

3. From 11 : 00 am to 12 : 00 pm. Monday through Thursday. From 11 : 00 am to 1 : 00 pm Friday and Saturday.

4. 419-3701.

5. Great prices, good meals.

6. Villa Dinner Theatre; 410-2308.

7. President's Room; 30 Yancey Street.

8. Captain Eddie's.

9. No.

10. Pizza Place; 2107 Willowhaven Road.

D. Additional Vocabulary

1-4;   2-5;   3-14;   4-1;   5-10;   6-23;   7-19;   8-15;   9-26;   10-2;

11-17;   12-18;   13-22;   14-3;   15-8;   16-16;   17-11;   18-12;   19-7;   20-27;

21-28;   22-13;   23-6;   24-30;   25-29;   26-9;   27-20;   28-21;   29-25;   30-24;

Unit 10
Air Travel

Teaching Aim（教学目的）

1. Cognitive Information（认知信息）: Air Travel

         Reserving Flight Tickets

2. Language Focus（内容重点）

— **Key Words:** I. determine, stroll, justice, reward, punish, ulcer, to the bone, round, guy, abuse, wimp, saunter, fuss, crush, conspiracy, ultimate, counter, hurry, tumble, guts, snap; II. reservation, available, opening, book, supersaver, tentatively, penalize, fare, rate

— **Phrases:** I. take off, to the bone, pay off, make a fuss, on board, on top of, show up, make it, out of breath, in advance, argue over; II. as for, be eligible for, prior to

— **Useful Structures:** be about to do

        do sth. three/...times

        no matter how/whether/what etc.

        have the guts（to do）

        so long as...

        what if...

— **Grammar:** Continuous and Perfect Continuous Tenses of Verbs

3. Communicative Skills （交际技能）
— **Expressions:** Booking Flight Tickets
— **Reading:** Flight Schedule

Lead-in 导入

>>>> **Listening Comprehension Tasks**

Difficult Words & Expressions

1. captain: the officer in command of a ship or aircraft 机长（船长）

2. board: to enter or go aboard (a vehicle or ship or aircraft) 登机(车、船)

3. chief purser: 乘务长

4. crew: all personnel operating or serving aboard an aircraft in flight 全体机务人员

5. tray table: 小桌板

6. take off: 起飞

7. permit: to allow the doing of sth. 允许

8. fasten: to attach firmly to sth. else 系紧

9. turbulence: violent air flow 强气流

10. window shade: 遮光板

11. degree centigrade: 摄氏度

12. overhead bin: （飞机机舱里位于座位上方的）行李架

13. emergency: a serious situation or occurrence that happens unexpectedly and demands immediate action 紧急情况

14. life jacket: 救生衣

15. strap: a thin, flat metal or plastic band used for fastening 绑带

16. inflate: to fill sth. with air or gas so as to make it swell 充气

17. tab: a small flap on a garment （衣服上的）小垂片

18. vest: a waist-length, sleeveless garment worn for protection 防护衣

19. oxygen mask: 氧气面罩

20. air pressure: 气压

21. infant: a child in the earliest period of life 婴幼儿

22. buckle: a clasp for fastening two ends 搭扣

23. unfasten: to separate the connected parts of 解开，松开

24. refer to: 查阅，参考

Passage Script 1

Ladies and gentlemen,

Welcome board Air France AF116 from Paris to Shanghai. Your flight is under the command of Captain Anderson. I am the chief purser Sophie. In addition, we have 12 cabin attendants, 4 from China, who will be available through the flight to serve you. Please let us know if you need assistance. Thank you.

Ladies and gentlemen,

The crew member of Air France has the pleasure of welcoming you aboard. Would you please put your seat in the upright position, fasten your seat belt and lock your tray table in place. We will be taking off in a few minutes. You are reminded that smoking and telephone-operation are not permitted at any time during flight. Please use your "call button" if you require assistance. Our crew will attend to your needs. We hope you enjoy a pleasant flight and thank you for choosing Air France.

Ladies and gentlemen,

We will be taking off shortly. Please make sure that your seat belt has been securely fastened. Thank you.

We are now passing through turbulence. For your own safety, please remain seated and fasten your seat belt. Thank you.

Ladies and gentlemen,

We will soon be landing at the Shanghai Pudong International Airport. Would you please put your seat in the upright position, fasten your seat belt, lock your tray table in place and pull up the window shade. Thank you.

Ladies and gentlemen,

We have landed at the Shanghai Pudong International Airport. The present outside temperature is 13 degrees centigrade, and the local time is 6:37pm. Please remain seated until the "FASTEN SEAT BELT" sign is turned off and the airplane has come to a complete stop. Please don't forget to take along your personal belongings. When opening the overhead bins, please take care to ensure the luggage does not fall out. Once again, we would like to thank you for flying with Air France and hope to serve you again soon. Thank you and good-bye.

Passage Script 2

Ladies and gentlemen,

For your safety, this aircraft is fully equipped with emergency equipments. We will explain the location and method of use. There are ten emergency exits located on the left and right sides respectively. They are identified by the exit signs. Life jackets are under your seats. In case of emergency, put the jacket over your head, and then bring the straps from behind you to the front as the attendant is demonstrating. Fasten the straps and pull tight. The jacket will be automatically inflated by pulling the two red tabs at the bottom. There are two mouth pieces inside the life jacket which can be used to inflate the vest by blowing air into them if the jacket hasn't been inflated enough. The oxygen masks are in panel over your head. If there is any change in the air pressure, the masks will fall automatically. The masks are as shown. When the masks fall, pull one of them to your face. Cover your nose and mouth and then breathe normally. Place the strap over your head to keep the mask in place. If you have an infant, put your mask on first, then put the infant's mask on. Each seat is provided with a seat belt. Please keep it fastened whenever seated. Just pull the buckle to unfasten it. Your cabin attendants have just demonstrated the proper method of using the life jacket and oxygen mask. Please refer to the emergency instruction card in the seat pocket for more information. Thank you.

Key

II. 1. a　2. b　3. c　4. d　5. c　6. c　7. a　8. d　9. d　10. c

IV. 1. c　2. b　3. a　4. e　5. d

V. 1. The procedure of putting on the life jacket should be **c, e, a, d, b, g, f**.

2. The procedure of taking the oxygen mask should be **d, b, c, a**.

>>>>>Spot Dictation

(Mr. and Mrs. Smith are <u>taking</u> a flight to London. They arrived at the airport just <u>in time</u>.)

Mrs. Smith: Come on! I don't want anything to <u>go wrong</u>.

Mr. Smith: Let me <u>take care of</u> everything, all right? Now, let's go to the <u>check-in counter</u>.

Airline Clerk: May I see your <u>tickets</u> and <u>passports</u>, please?

Mr. Smith: Here they are.

Airline Clerk: Have you got any <u>check-in baggage</u>?

Mr. Smith: Two bags.

Airline Clerk: Would you put all your baggage <u>on the scale</u>, please? OK. Here are your <u>boarding passes</u>, which show your <u>boarding</u> time of <u>11:30</u> and <u>boarding gate</u>, which is <u>Gate 15</u>.

Mr. Smith: All right.

(Mr. and Mrs. Smith go to the <u>lounge</u> at the airport to have a cup of coffee.)

Mr. Smith: (*Upstairs at the <u>lounge</u>.*) What did you order for me?

Mrs. Smith: Black coffee. <u>What do we do now</u>?

Mr. Smith: Let me <u>finish</u> this coffee and then we will go to <u>Gate 15</u>. Listen, they<u>'re announcing</u> our flight.

Ladies and gentlemen,

We <u>regret</u> to announce that <u>due to</u> severe weather <u>conditions</u> Heathrow airport has been <u>closed</u>. Flight <u>LO123</u>, <u>scheduled</u> to leave <u>for</u> London at <u>12:15</u>, has been <u>cancelled</u>. We regret to <u>announce</u> that Flight <u>LO123</u> to London <u>has been cancelled</u>. Will all passengers <u>for</u> this <u>flight</u> please go to <u>the information desk</u>?

Background Information（背景知识）

1. History of flight

During the late 1700's, people made their first flights into the air using balloons, which were an early form of airship. After the first balloon flights, inventors tried to develop a heavier-than-air flying machine. Some inventors experimented with gliders (engineless planes). They studied birds' wings and discovered that the wings are curved. By building gliders with curved wings instead of flat ones, they could make the vehicles fly hundreds of feet or meters. But long-distance flight in a heavier-than-air machine did not become possible until the invention of an engine light enough but powerful enough to keep a plane in flight. The first such engines were four-stroke gasoline engines, developed during the 1880's and initially used to power bicycles, boats, and carriages. In 1903, the brothers Orville and Wilbur Wright — two American bicycle makers — made the first successful powered airplane flights in history near Kitty Hawk, North Carolina. After the Wright brothers' success, pilots and inventors worked continually to improve airplane design. By the late 1950's, passenger planes with jet engines had brought all countries within easy reach of one another, and the world seemed much smaller than it had been just a few years before.

2. Impact of air travel on human life

For all of history, humanity had seen the world from the ground. It had relied solely upon transportation that moved across the ground and over or around its obstacles. When Orville and Wilbur Wright flew history's first airplane for 120 short feet（36 and 1/2 meters）in North Carolina in 1903, the significance of their new invention was of course not yet apparent. The first passenger planes, barely 20 years later, did little to change that view. In 1927, Lindbergh's transatlantic flight captured America's imagination. Further developments during World War II sped the development of commercial aviation. Airplane manufacturers Douglas and Boeing built new airplanes with pressurized and heated cabins. Suddenly airplanes could fly above bad weather and mountains. In 1940, three million Americans flew. By 1956, 55 million flew. The first jet airliner, the Boeing 707, was introduced in 1959. It cut flying time between New York and London from twelve hours to six hours. But by the 1960s, air travelers were still mostly wealthy people and business people on expense accounts. Ordinary people could not afford to fly, to see their loved ones in other cities, or visit exciting vacation spots. However, by 1990, more adult Americans had flown than owned a car. Along with highways, the Internet, and cable and satellite television, widely available air travel has helped connect people with the world outside of their own communities. Air travel has had a profound impact, both material and social, on our life. It has affected the way we live, the way we view ourselves and the world around us, and the way we do business. Although difficult to measure, aviation's history suggests that it has contributed to widespread awareness of and connection to people and places very different from one's own.

3. Airline industry in China

Airline industry in China developed very rapidly over the last 50 years, as domestic routes increased from 12 to 1, 115 and international routes increased from nine cities in five countries to 64 cities in 34 countries. Until 1979, air travel was still quite rare. During the last two decades, more than 40 new airports were built and more than 60 were upgraded and expanded. In 1978, China ranked 32nd among ICAO-covenant countries in passenger volume and ranks 6th today. It is estimated that the passenger volume of China's air transportation will grow at an average annual rate of 8.5% between

2000 and 2019, reaching the annual volume of 438.7 billion kilometers. China is a permanent member of the International Civil Aviation Organization (ICAO), an agency of the United Nations established in 1947 to assist in the planning and development of international air transport, and is a party to many other intentional aviation conventions. Fifty-seven air companies from 43 countries operate air services in 13 Chinese cities. Prior to 2001, China had 31 international, regional, and domestic carriers, most of which were small and inefficient. Since mid-2001, the three newly formed groups (China Southern, China Eastern, and Air China) have become the dominant players and collectively command 80.5% of the passenger and 84.7% of the freight markets. These three major competitors have developed brand loyalty and are selected as the preferred carriers by the Chinese traveling public. One of the major limitations to the airline industry's growth is the lack of availability of airports and the related infrastructure that is required for the airlines to provide the air transportation services. Since 1987, Chinese government spent RMB 39.2 billion (US $4.72 billion) in constructing air infrastructure. Airline industry (airline companies and airports) has also been instituting significant changes to improve the infrastructure, especially to help customers acquire tickets and make informed decisions.

4. Air travel tips

Air travel today isn't as easy as it used to be. There are more questions, options, and concerns than ever. Will you be able to get an affordable seat? How many carry-ons can you bring on the plane? How long should you expect to be detained at security? What kinds of identification are absolutely required for domestic and international travel? To make air travel less intimidating, we've outlined some of the things to consider:

- ☐ Confirm flight times and dates for all portions of your trip to make sure that it matches up with your information.
- ☐ Make copies of your air travel itinerary and leave a copy with your workplace and family members or friends.
- ☐ Provide your travel agent or airline with phone numbers where you can be reached during your travels, in addition to giving these phone numbers to your workplace and family or friends. Also include hotel addresses and contact numbers.
- ☐ Make sure that your passport is valid for at least six months beyond your return dates of travel.
- ☐ When traveling internationally make sure that you have any visas that may be required. Verify if there are business or tourist visas and which one best suits the purpose of your travel.
- ☐ Do make photocopies of your passport, visas and any other pertinent travel documents. Pack copies in your luggage as well as leaving copies with your workplace, family and/or friends.

☐ Bring a copy of your medical history with you. This could simply involve listing any medical conditions, blood type, etc.

☐ If you are traveling internationally, try to have key phrases written in the local language such as "help", or "I need to see a doctor/the police".

Language and Culture Focus (语言文化要点)

>>>>>Reading I

1. determine *vt.*

1) to find out the exact details or facts about sth. 找出；测定；确定

【例句】Your parents' income is used to determine your level of financial aid.

The purpose of the excise is to determine where we want to go from here.

2) to have a strong influence or effect on sth. 决定；支配

【例句】Usually the size of the practice will determine the number of doctors.

3) to officially decide sth. 确定；规定

【例句】The date of the court case was yet to be determined.

4) to form a firm intention to do sth. 决心（做某事）

【例句】We determined to leave at once.

2. stroll: to walk a short distance slowly or lazily, esp. for pleasure. 散步；溜达；漫步

【例句】We strolled in/around the park for an hour or so.

The manager was furious when the new trainee strolled into work two hours later.

"Stroll" can also be a noun.

【例句】Let's go for a stroll.

3. be about to do: If someone is about to do something, or if something is about to happen, they will do it or it will happen very soon. 将要，正打算

【例句】We were just about to leave when Jerry arrived.

Work was about to start on a new factory building.

The meeting is about to start.

The empire was about to collapse.

He was about to leave when he heard his name called.

比较 not be about to do sth.:（*informal*）used to emphasize that you have no intention of doing sth. 不打算

【例句】I've never smoked in my life and I'm not about to start now.

4. justice: the quality of being just; fairness. 正义；公正；合理性　　**antonym: injustice**

【例句】They have at last received compensation for their injuries, so justice has been done.

He claimed — with justice — that he had not received his fair share.

I wouldn't dispute the justice of his remarks.

【相关搭配】

bring someone to justice 将某人绳之以法

【例句】The police must do all they can to bring criminals to justice.

a court of justice 法院；法庭

5. reward:〔for/with〕to give a reward to for an action. 酬报；酬谢；报答；奖赏

【例句】He was generously rewarded.

They rewarded the student with a dictionary for his good performance in the speech contest.

How can I reward your kindness?

【相关词】

rewarding *adj.* worth doing or having; giving satisfaction. 有益的；值得做的；可喜的

【例句】Nursing can be a very rewarding career.

6. punish: to make someone suffer because they have done sth. wrong or broken the law. 处罚；惩处

【例句】Some people believe that smacking is not an acceptable way to punish a child.

In some countries women who have abortions can be punished by imprisonment.

【相关词】

punishment *n.* 惩罚；处罚

【例句】a harsh/severe punishment

You know the punishment for treason, don't you?

We are determined that the terrorists will not escape punishment.

7. ulcer: a sore area on the surface of an organ or outside of the body 溃疡

【例句】stomach ulcer 胃溃疡

8. to the bone: This phrase is always used together with other words to emphasize the extreme or minimum degree.

【相关搭配】

be chilled/frozen to the bone: to be extremely cold. 冻僵

【例句】By that time I was chilled to the bone, exhausted from the traffic.

I swear you are frozen to the bone.

close to the bone: 露骨的

【例句】Some of his jokes were a bit close to the bone.

cut something to the bone: 把（成本或服务等）削减到最低程度

9. do sth. three/four... times: "... times" is used as the adverbial to express frequency of activities. 做某事三次/四次

【例句】He made no answer until the teacher called his name three times.

He did it many times, but every time he failed.

We usually say "do sth. once/twice", instead of "do sth. one time/two times".

10. round: a round of events is a series of related events, which are part of a longer process. （一轮）

【例句】a third round of peace talks

the Government's latest round of expenditure cuts

In the text, it refers to one (drink) for every one. （斟）一巡（酒）

【例句】We will have another round of drinks before we get down to work.

11. guy: (*informal*) a man. ［非正式］男人；家伙

【例句】Dave's a nice guy when you get to know him.

【相关词】

pal *n.* ［非正式］密友；好友

【例句】We just weren't pals anymore.

buddy *n.* ［非正式］朋友；伙伴

【例句】We're good buddies.

fellow *n.* ［过时］朋友［用于友好地称呼男人］

【例句】Hello, my dear fellow!

fellow workers/students/countrymen: 同事/同学/同胞

12. abuse

1) *n.* wrong use. 滥用；妄用

【例句】the abuse of power/drugs

2) *n.* bad or cruel treatment. 虐待

【例句】child abuse

3) *vt.* to rude things to or about; to put to wrong use; use badly. 滥用；妄用

【例句】He abused his power.

13. wimp: coward; person with no courage. 懦夫

【例句】Don't be such a wimp! 别那么窝囊！

14. saunter: to walk in an unhurried way, and esp. in a confident manner. 溜；散步   **synonym: stroll**

【例句】He sauntered in the forest, listening to the chirping of the birds.

15. pay off

1) to pay and dismiss sb. 付钱打发人走

【例句】His work was most unsatisfactory, so we paid him off at the end of the week.

2) to pay the whole of (a debt). 付清（债务等）

【例句】I just paid off my debt and had no more money for investment.

16. make a fuss

1) to complain or become angry about sth., especially when this is not necessary. 大惊小怪；小题大做

【例句】I don't know why you're making such a fuss about it.

Don't make so much fuss over losing a pen.

2) to protest. 抗议；抱怨

【例句】I'm going to have to make a fuss about the service in this hotel.

17. on board: on a ship, plane, or spacecraft（在船/机上）**synonym: aboard**

【例句】There are 12 children on board the ship.

18. And when we finally take off, all us wimps know that not only will that late luggage be the first off the plane, but it is probably sitting on top of our luggage, crushing our shirts.

【译文】当我们最终起飞了，我们这群懦夫明白那个迟到的行李不仅会先下飞机，而且此时可能正骑在我们的行李上，压皱着我们的衬衫。

19. on top of: rest on, above. 在……上

【例句】There was a pile of books on top of (=on) the table.

Put the letter on top of that pile of books, where it can be seen easily.

They've finally got on top of the situation (=They have control of it).

The bird sat on the top of the tree.

There were flags on the tops of many of the buildings.

20. show up

1) to arrive as expected or arranged.（按预期或安排）到达或出现

【例句】Did everyone you invited show up?

2) to make clear the unpleasant truth about. 揭发

【例句】I intend to show up this deception/show up this man for the liar he is.

21. crush: to press sth. so hard that it breaks or is damaged. 压碎；压坏；压扁

【例句】His leg was crushed in the accidents.

Two people were crushed to death in the rush to escape.

【相关搭配】

crush a rebellion/uprising/revolt 镇压叛乱/起义/反叛

crush sb's hopes/enthusiasm/confidence 使某人的希望/热情/信心破灭

22. no matter how/whether/what etc.: used to say that sth. is true or that sth. happens whatever the situation is. 无论, 不管 Here "no matter" introduces an adverbial clause of concession (让步状语从句).

【例句】Feeding a baby is a messy job no matter how careful you are.

I'm determined to visit England no matter what it costs.

I'll finish the job, no matter how long it takes.

I'll follow you no matter where you go.

23. conspiracy: *n.* an evil plan; the act of making such a plan. 阴谋

【例句】a fraud conspiracy 诈骗阴谋

a conspiracy to smuggle drugs into that country

The men were found guilty of conspiracy to murder.

【相关词】

conspire *vi.* 密谋; 共谋; 搞阴谋

【例句】The criminals conspired (together/with each other) to rob a bank.

conspirator *n.* 阴谋家; 共谋者

24. ultimate

1) *adj.* greatest; better or worse than any other. 最大的; 极限的

【例句】To look for the gas leak with a lighted match really was the ultimate stupidity.

With a top speed of 200 miles per hour, this is the ultimate sports car.

2) *adj.* final. 最后的; 最终的

【例句】Their ultimate destination is London.

Their ultimate objective is the removal of all nuclear weapons.

The ultimate aim of their efforts is to establish peace and security in the world.

3) *n.* ［in］ the highest point. 终极; 顶点; 极限

【例句】the ultimate in stupidity/luxury

【相关词】

ultimately *adv.* 最终; 终于; 最后

【例句】Ultimately, the success of the product depends on good marketing.

25. counter: *n.* a narrow table or flat surface on which goods are shown in a shop, bank, etc. 柜台

【例句】I'm sorry. This counter is closed now.

【相关词】

over the counter (OTC): drugs, medicines etc. that are bought over the counter are ones that you can buy in a shop without a prescription from a doctor. 非处方药

26. make it: be successful.

【例句】If you work hard, you will make it.

At one point I was so exhausted and weak that I didn't think I was going to make it.

Even though he couldn't swim, he managed to make it to the riverbank.

27. out of/short of breath: breathing very quickly (e.g. after running fast); panting hardly. 上气不接下气

【例句】He arrived at the airport, out of breath.

28. stumble: to fall suddenly or helplessly; roll over or down quickly or violently. 倒下；跌倒；摔倒；绊倒；翻滚

【例句】The little boy tripped and stumbled down the stairs.

Stock market prices stumbled (=fell sharply) after rumors of a rise in interest rates.

29. guts: the courage and determination you need to do sth. difficult or unpleasant. 胆量；决心

【例句】It takes guts to start a new business on your own.

【相关搭配】

have the guts to do sth.: have the courage to do sth.

【例句】The writer didn't have the guts to put a name to it!

30. snap: ［at］to speak or say quickly and usually in an annoyed way. 急促地说；厉声地说

【例句】"Shut up!" snapped Mr. Smith to cut short Tom's long and pointless report.

He tends to snap at people when he's got a headache.

He snapped out an order.

31. After a lifetime of arguing over whether I really have to pack 24 hours in advance and set the alarm clock four hours ahead, I have learned one other fact about early-airport people and late-airport people: They always marry each other.

【译文】在经历了一辈子的纠结是否真的需要提前24小时打包，并设定闹钟提前4小时响，我明白了另一个有关早去机场与晚去机场人的事实：他们是天生的一对。

32. argue

1) *vi.* ［over/with/about］to express disagreement in words, often with strong feeling; quarrel. 争辩；争论；争吵

【例句】Do what you are told and don't argue with me.

They are always arguing about/over money.

The children were arguing over which TV program to watch.

2) *vi./vt.* to provide reasons for or against sth., esp. clearly and in proper order. 辩论

【例句】We could argue this point for hours without reaching any conclusions.

He argued for/against the proposed tax cut.

I would argue that sending men to the moon is a waste of money.

【相关词】

argument *n.* 争论；争辩；争吵；论据；理由；辩论

33. in advance: before something happens or is expected to happen. 事先

【例句】 I should warn you in advance that I'm not a very good dancer.

▶▶▶▶▶ Reading II

1. reservation: an arrangement made in advance to have sth. kept for you, such as a room in a hotel, a table in a restaurant, a seat in the theatre or on a plane. 预定

【例句】 a hotel reservation

Have you made the reservations for our holiday yet?

I will make the reservation for seven thirty.

reservationist: the person who arranges reservations for customers.

2. available: able to be obtained or used. 可得的；可利用的

【例句】 I'm sorry, sir. Those shoes are not available in your size.

Every available ambulance rushed to the scene of the accident.

Details of the competition are available from our head office.

Is the new timetable available yet?

We want to make our products available to a wider market.

More information becomes available through the use of computers.

3. momentarily: in a very short time; very soon. 很快；马上

【例句】 We will be landing at the airport momentarily.

4. North Northern Airlines: an airline in the United States.

5. line: telephone line. 电话线

6. recording: a performance, speech, piece of music or other sound that has been recorded. 录音

【例句】 some recordings of early Russian music

a new recording of the Second Symphony

They made a recording of her voice.

We are listening to his latest recording.

Very few recordings of Picasso's voice exist.

7. Ithaca: a city in the south of New York at the south end of Cayuga Lake. 伊萨克市

8. New York: Here it refers to New York State, located in the northeast of the United States with Albany as its capital. 纽约

9. Boston: a seaport and capital of Massachusetts in the eastern part of the United States. 波士顿

10. opening: vacancy. Here it refers to "flight available". 空位

11. Philadelphia: a city in Southeast Pennsylvania, on the Delaware River. 费城

12. Syracuse: a commercial and manufacturing city in central New York State. 锡拉丘兹市

13. book: to arrange in advance; to reserve. 预定

【例句】 to book seats on a plane

to book a table in a restaurant

I'm afraid these seats are already booked.

Go to the Youth Hotel and book yourself a place for the night.

He booked a ticket to London.

Before leaving the airport, he booked himself on the next afternoon's flight.

Book early to avoid disappointment.

14. Buffalo: a commercial and industrial city in the west of New York State on Lake Erie. 布法罗

15. "**You are not eligible for the supersaver, since you are not booking nine months in advance, and since you are not staying overnight in Boston on a Saturday, Tuesday, Wednesday, or Thursday. The fare is 497.50 dollars. I can book you tentatively now. And if you change your mind, you will not be penalized so long as you have not purchased your ticket and you are not holding a supersaver reservation, or so long as more than seven days remain prior to departure.**"

【译文】 您无法获得特惠票，因为您没有在 9 个月前预订，也没有于周六、周二、周三或周四晚上在波士顿过夜。机票是 497.5 美元。我可以试着帮您订订看。如果您想变更，只要您还没有付款购票，也没有预订特惠票，而且是在出发的七天之前，都不会被扣款。

16. be eligible for: If someone is eligible for something, he or she is able or qualified or allowed to do it. 是附含……条件的

【例句】 Is she eligible for maternity leave (产假)?

Students on a part-time course are not eligible for a loan.

You may be eligible for the grant.

Not all applicants are eligible for the post.

17. supersaver: ticket that costs much less than usual price. 超级优惠票

18. fare: the price that you pay for a journey you make, such as in a bus, train, taxi, or plane, etc. 票价

【例句】 pay one's train fare

How much is your bus fare home?

He spends fifty pounds a month on fares to work.

In English there are a variety of words you can use for what you have to pay:

辨析 **cost:** the amount of money you have to pay for services, activities, or things you need all the time, such as food and electricity.

【例句】We'll make sure you have the operation, whatever the cost.

Price: the amount of money you have to pay for something that is for sale, especially in a shop.

【例句】There's a great new clothes store on Main Street, and its prices seem very reasonable.

charge: the amount of money that you pay for a service, or for being allowed to use something.

【例句】There's no charge for telephoning the operator.

fee: the amount of money that you pay to someone for a professional service, or the amount that you pay in order to do something.

【例句】Some actors can ask a fee of around $1, 000, 000 a movie.

rate: the usual cost of a service or job.

【例句】We are able to offer a whole range of services at very reasonable rates.

hourly/weekly/daily rate

Our shop assistants are paid an hourly rate of £5. 50.

toll: money that you have to pay in order to drive over some bridges or roads.

【例句】You have to pay tolls on many of the major roads in France.

toll bridge/road/lane (=one that you have to pay to use）

rent: the amount of money that you pay to live in or use a place that you do not own.

【例句】She pays £350 a month rent for a one-bedroomed apartment.

rental: the amount of money that you pay to use a car, television, tools, etc. over a period of time.

【例句】The rental on the TV includes maintenance and repairs.

19. **tentatively:** If you do something tentatively, you do it cautiously or without much confidence because you are not sure and you want to see what will happen. 试验性地；谨慎地

    【例句】She raised her hand and waved, tentatively.

    He gave his reply tentatively.

20. **penalize:** to punish. 惩罚；处罚

    【例句】The council will be penalized for spending too much last year.

    You will be penalized if you don't answer all the questions.

    The referee penalized the English player for wasting time.

21. **so long as:** (also as long as) if, on condition that. 只要

    【例句】You can go out, as long as you promise to be back before 11 o'clock.

    Our profits will be good so long as the dollar remains strong.

    Detergent cannot harm a fabric, so long as it has been properly dissolved.

    You couldn't turn the heat off so long as the system was operating.

22. **departure:** the act of leaving a place or starting a journey. 出发,离开

    【例句】What is the departure time of the flight to New York?

She packed her suitcase ready for departure.

There are several departures a day for New York.

23. **What if...:** What will happen if... 若是……又会怎么样

1) used to ask what you should do or what the result will be if something happens, especially something unpleasant or undesirable.

【例句】What if this plan of yours fails?

What if there is no one at home?

What if I miss the train?

2) used to make a suggestion.

【例句】What if we moved the sofa over here? Would that look better?

24. **Albuquerque:** a city in central New Mexico. 阿尔布克市

25. **Mexico City:** a city and the capital of Mexico, in the central part of the country. 墨西哥城

26. **as for:** This structure is used when you are starting to talk about someone or something new that is connected with what you were talking about before; concerning. 至于；关于

【例句】Kitty's got so thin. And as for Carl, he always seems to be ill.

You can ask the others, but as for myself, I'll be busy in the office.

You can have a bed; as for him, he'll have to sleep on the floor.

Mary's diet required an unusually big effort on her part. As for myself, I had a glass of juice three times a day.

That's the answer. As for the cause, how do I know?

27. **Pocatello:** a city in the southeast of Idaho. 波长特洛市

28. **Fairbanks:** a town in central Alaska, on the Tanana River. 费尔班克市

29. **Alaska:** a state of the United States in Northwestern North America, with Juneau as its capital. （美国）阿拉斯加州

30. **Special Spring Flyaway rate:** discount ticket offered by an airline to passengers who take flights in spring time. 春季特价票

rate: a charge or payment fixed according to a standard scale. 率（与特定数额或数量有关的费用或收费）

【例句】the rise in the mortgage rate

They are demanding higher rates of pay.

The big banks have put up interest rates for borrowers to 15%.

31. **"We have one opening left on all the same flights departing Boston Sunday, April 24. And the supersaver fare is 1, 597.50 dollars."**

【译文】4 月 24 日星期天从波士顿出发的所有同样航班我们都留了一个空位，特惠价是 1 597.5 美元。

>>>>>**Extended Activities**

A. Function and Structure: Booking Flight Tickets

1. Classes of air transportation

According to rules of I.A.T.A. (International Air Transport Association), all places in the plane are divided into three classes: First, Business and Tourist class. Availability of First and Business classes varies depending on route, aircraft type and air company. In First and Business classes respective fares are used. All discounted fares are used for the transportation in Tourist class and all discounts apply to full tourist class fare. The cheaper ticket you would like to have, the more limitations the fare has, such as advanced purchase, limitations of minimum and maximum time of ticket validity, restrictions of rebooking, cancellation penalties, etc. Passengers that travel in First and Business class may carry 40 and 30kg respectively free of charge. Tourist class passengers are allowed to take 20kg only.

2. Booking tickets online

More and more frequent travelers are booking their airfares online, but it pays to shop around and know some tricks to finding the best deals. Your best approach will likely depend on how flexible your travel plans are, but regardless of your situation, there are a variety of ways to save money. Airlines tend to offer the lowest prices on 21-day advance tickets. However, advance purchase fares can often be secured in as little as 14 or 7 days ahead of your departure date. If you wait until fewer than 7 days, you're unlikely to find a good deal. If you have the flexibility, consider including a Saturday stay. Although some airlines are doing away with this practice, most tend to reserve the lowest fares for itineraries that include a Saturday night stay. Savings can easily be 50%. If you can't change your dates, consider changing your flight times. Most travel sites have an "anytime" option for your preferred flight times, and that might turn up cheaper flights at less popular times of the day.

B. Special Use: Continuous and Perfect Continuous Tenses of Verbs

英语中的进行形式包括现在进行时、过去进行时、现在完成进行时、过去完成进行时和将来进行时等。所有这些进行时态,都具有一些基本的特征:

1. 表示正在进行的动作。例如:

Why are you sitting on my desk?

He is interviewing an applicant.

He was having breakfast at seven.

When I arrived, Tom was talking on the phone.

They were building the bridge this time last year.

2. 表示动作的持续、没有间断或反复发生。例如:

Someone is knocking at the door. （有人在不停地敲。）

He is jumping with great joy. （他一直在不停地跳。）

I was reading the book day and night during those days.

I have been waiting for an hour and he still hasn't turned up.

She has been staying at home all afternoon.

He has been scoring plenty of goals this season.

I had been looking for it for days before I found it.

The telephone had been ringing for two minutes before it was answered.

He was tired. He had been working all day.

He is always working. （他一直在不停地工作。）

有时, 进行时的这种用法与 always, constantly, continually, forever 等词连用, 含有一定的感情色彩, 通常含有不满、抱怨的意味。例如:

She is constantly complaining about the house. （她老是不停地抱怨这房子——表示不满。）

Tom is always going out after dinner. （Tom 吃好饭后老是要出去——表示不满。）

He is always finding fault with me. （他老是要挑我的刺——表示不满。）

Jane was always coming late. （简总是迟到——表示不满。）

3. 进行时表示缓慢的过程; 一般时强调动作的突发性和瞬间性。例如:

The building falls down. （房子突然倒下了。）

The building is falling down. （房子正在慢慢倒下。）

所以一般时可用于动作迅速变化的体育项目的直播评论; 而动作较慢的体育项目直播评论用现在进行时。例如:

George swings a right at Mike — he ducks and it glances harmlessly off his shoulder. （用于拳击比赛中, 表示快速的动作。）

Oxford are rowing well. They are catching up. Ah, Cambridge are increasing their pace. （用于划船比赛, 表示相对较慢的动作。）

4. 强调说话时刻暂时的情形。例如:

The bucket is leaking. （桶正在漏。强调现在的情形。）

I'm enjoying the seaside. （强调此刻正在海边度假。）

The bucket leaks. （这个桶漏。强调一般事实, 但不一定正在漏。）

I enjoy the seaside. （强调一般的喜好。）

5. 表示动作的未完成性。例如:

Now I'm remembering. （我现在开始想起来了。……但还没有完全想起来。）

The sky is clearing. （天空正开始放晴。……但还没有完全变晴。）

The roses are just coming out. （玫瑰花正开始开放。……但还没有完全开满。）

I'm finishing. （我就要结束了。……但还没有结束。）

He is dying. （他就要死了。……但还没有死。）

The bus is leaving. （公共汽车就要开了。……已经起动, 但还没有离开这儿。）

The helicopter is landing. （直升飞机正在着陆。……从飞行状态到停止状态, 但还没有停止。）

The bus is stopping. （公共汽车正在停下来。……从行驶状态转为停止状态, 但还没有停下来。）

I was reading the book last night. （未读完。）

I read the book last night. （已读完。）

The old man was dying. （还没有死。）

The old man died. （已经死了。）

The boy was drowning. （还没有淹死。）

The boy drowned. （已经淹死了。）

I have been polishing the car. （动作可能还未完成。）

I have polished the car. （动作已经完成。）

He had been repairing the engine before his wife returned. （活可能还没有干完。）

By six o'clock, he had repaired the engine. （活已经干完。）

6. 进行时更具描绘性, 可以用于描写, 作为背景介绍。但若是叙述事件的发生先后, 我们用一般时。请注意下面例句中的过去进行时和一般过去时的搭配。

It was snowing as the medical team made its way to the front.

A wood fire was burning on the hearth, and a dog was sleeping in front of it. Mother was knitting and singing softly to herself. Suddenly, there was a knock on the window. Mother stopped knitting. The dog woke up.

7. 表示委婉的语气和殷切的心情。例如:

I'm looking forward to your coming.

I'm hoping you will have lunch with me.

I was hoping you could lend me a hand.

8. 与进行时搭配的时间状语 this time yesterday, at ten yesterday morning等是过去进行时的标志。例如:

He was watching TV this time yesterday.

They were having a meeting at ten yesterday morning.

this time tomorrow, at three tomorrow afternoon等是将来进行时的标志。例如:

He will be playing soccer at three tomorrow afternoon.

She will be writing a letter this time tomorrow.

在while引导的时间状语从句中，主句和从句的动词可以同时用过去进行时，表示两个动作同时进行，并含有对比意义。

While I was working in the garden, my wife was cooking dinner.

9. 进行时与动词的搭配

1) 状态动词一般不用于进行时。状态动词除了be动词之外，还包括感官动词，如feel, hear, see, smell, notice, taste等；情感动词，如hate, like, love, want, wish等；观点动词，如agree, believe, think, suppose, expect等；所属关系的动词，如belong, own, possess, owe, have等；其他动词如appear, seem, matter, keep, hold等。状态动词通常表示静止的状态，一般不用于进行时。连系动词通常也是状态动词。例如：

He has been in hospital since the accident.

I have a big family.

The weather feels cold.

Don't you feel the house shaking?

The milk smells sour.

The coffee tastes bitter.

He looked tired.

What do you think of it?

It appears out of question.

It doesn't matter.

2) 表示结果的动词通常不用于进行时。例如：

I saw him leave the house.

I can't see it clearly.

He has finished his work.

3) 但上述动词也有例外的情况：

① be动词用于进行时可以表示暂时的状态。例如：

You are not being very polite.

（你此刻不是很有礼貌。……暂时的状态，平时不是这样。）

比较：You are not very polite.（你一贯不讲礼貌。……经常如此。）

② have作动词时，表示吃饭、上课等意思，可以有进行时。例如：

They are having a class.

I'm having dinner now.

③ feel表示"用手摸"时，有进行时，此时feel为及物动词。例如：

The doctor was feeling his pulse.

He was feeling for the keyhole in the dark.

He is feeling the surface of the ice.

④ smell、taste 表示 "闻味道"、"尝味道" 时, 有进行时。此时 smell 为及物动词。例如:

Why are you smelling the milk?

She was tasting the pudding to see if it was sweet enough.

⑤ look 用于进行时能与比较级连用, 强调过程。例如:

He was looking paler and paler.

⑥ think 表示 "思考, 考虑" 时, 有进行时。例如:

What are you thinking about?

Tom is thinking of emigrating.

⑦ appear 表示 "出现" 时, 有进行时。例如:

The actress is appearing on the stage.

10. 完成进行时与完成时、进行时的比较

完成进行时包含了完成时的基本用法, 与完成时的 "未完成" 用法相仿, 表示某一动作从过去一直持续到现在。所以有时完成进行时和完成时可以互换。例如:

We have lived here for ten years.

We have been living here for ten years.

How long have you learned English?

How long have you been learning English?

He has slept for ten hours.

He has been sleeping for ten hours.

但完成进行时还带有进行时态的持续性、暂时性和未完成性的含义, 更强调动作的持续不断或反复发生。例如:

I have been working in the garden all day. （强调一直在不停地工作。）

He has been writing this letter for three hours. （强调一直在不停地写信。）

It has been raining for weeks. （强调这几周一直在不停地下雨。）

Mr. Williams has been teaching English for 20 years. （强调20年来一直在进行英语教学, 从未间断。）

Catherine has been seeing Mary on and off recently. （强调动作的反复发生。）

You have been watching too many horror films these days. （强调动作的反复发生。）

虽然现在进行时和过去进行时也表示动作的持续不断和反复发生, 但它们只强调现在或过去某一孤立的时间点上动作的状况, 而完成进行时将动作的过去与现在联系起来, 强调动作从过去到现在持续的过程。

Bob has been working on the paper for the last six months. （强调一直在写论文, 而且是从6个月前一直写到现在。）

He has been lecturing for two hours. （强调一直在讲, 而且从两个小时前一直讲到现在。）

I have been cooking since 8 o'clock this morning.（不仅仅指现在正在做菜；更强调从8点开始一直做到现在。）

因此，完成进行时实际上是完成时和进行时的合二为一。

C. Practical Reading

通过阅读诸如航班日程等实用性文体材料，利用阅读中获取的信息解决商务活动中的实际问题，这是外语学习者应该掌握的基本技能之一。本练习并不难，但要求回答准确无误。因为任何一个看似细小的地方，可能就是商务活动中的关键一环，要提醒学生千万不可以大意。

航班日程的内容一般包括：航空公司名称、航班号码、飞行日、出发地、目的地、起飞时间、到达时间等信息。其中飞行日用阿拉伯数字1234567分别表示周一至周日。航班号码一般由航空公司的首字母缩写加阿拉伯数字构成。如UA838，其中UA代表United Airlines。时间的表示法要完整，例如8点整，不能简单地写作8，而应该是08：00。

要解决本阅读中的题目，只要将航班日程中的各个项目仔细对照一下即可找出答案。其中第二大题中的3、4两题需要根据实际需要来选择航班，主要考虑的问题就是航班的时间问题。答案也比较容易找到。

Teaching Tips（教学提示）

1. 在本单元开始时教师可针对学生的兴趣爱好，结合背景知识1（航空的历史）、背景知识2（航空对人类生活的影响）和背景知识3（中国航空业的发展历程），用先提问后补充的方式帮助学生了解与单元主题相关的一些信息。背景知识4（航空旅行的小贴士）可以留到Reading I结束后讲解，作为复习，帮学生再回顾总结一下搭乘飞机旅行的一些相关小常识。

2. Lead-in　本单元导入部分安排了听力理解和听写填空两项任务。听力理解部分包含两个语篇，共5项听力练习。两个语篇都属Announcement。第一篇听力是航空公司乘务人员在飞机起飞、飞行途中和降落时向乘客所作的播报；第二篇听力则是乘务人员对乘客如何正确使用飞机上紧急安全救生设备的指导。听力练习的编排和以往各单元一样，第一和第三项练习均属预听活动，主要目的是在进行精听训练之前，让学生对所听语篇的主旨（Gist）有所了解，初步把握听音和理解上的难点所在，为接下来的听力活动做好词汇和心理上的准备。第二项练习为多项选择题（Multiple-choice Questions），侧重考察学生理解、辨析语篇细节和关键信息的能力。第四项练习为图片配对题，第五项练习为排序题，要求学生列出穿着救生衣和机上氧气面罩使用过程的正确顺序。在听音前，教师可以就飞机安全事宜作简单的背景介绍。如：

飞机其实是最安全的交通工具，但是，由于各种客观原因，旅客仍有必要了解机上各种安全设施的使用常识。

安全带是保证旅客在飞机发生剧烈颠簸时不被碰伤的安全设备。一般只有在遇到气流时机长才告知旅客系好安全带，但建议旅客除了上洗手间之外，尽量坐在座椅上并一直系好安全带。

氧气面罩是在机舱失密或机舱内因故出现有害烟雾、气体时保证旅客正常供氧需求的设备。氧气面罩一般"藏"在座位的上方，每个座位配备一个，在需要使用时，会由机组人员操纵自动落下。在旅客座椅上方，有氧气面罩应急手动释放字样，有"推"的标记。推开后，氧气面罩自动下放到旅客面前。在释放板上，有怎样使用的图形和文字说明。旅客应按照说明正确操作。旅客遇到紧急情况，切忌慌乱，应轻轻拉过距自己座位最近的套在头上，不要乱抓乱抢，特别是不要越过座位去拉邻座的，以免拽断输氧管。另外还要记住，应在先戴好自己的面罩后再帮助别人。

救生衣是飞机在海上迫降时使用的救生用品，置于每个座位的下方，一旦需要使用时，只需坐在座上方弯腰伸手掏取，也不要取邻座的，以免发生混乱。救生衣设计都是一次性的，在没有必要使用时，切忌取出和充气。救生衣是用尼龙材料做成上下两个气囊，起到了双保险的作用。附件中有左右各一的两个高压气瓶，只要分别拉两边的红色把手，即可在2秒钟内自动充气；两边的口吹管还可人工充气以增加浮力。

安全门是飞机在机场以外的地面或水面迫降后疏散机上旅客的出口。门上有明显标记，其把手为红色。安全门一旦开启，便会有一条连接地面（或水面）的滑道自动展开并充气。所以，在正常情况下，不论是空中还是地面，安全门都是不允许打开的。

Flight Safety Instructions

If you've ever flown on a commercial airliner, you probably remember how, just before takeoff, the steward or stewardess stood in the aisle and reviewed the flight safety instructions, demonstrating how to fasten a seat belt, how to use an oxygen mask, and pointing to the aircraft's emergency exits, among other things.

Stowing Luggage

The flight safety instructions begin with some information on luggage. Passengers are directed to stow their luggage in the compartments above them. They are also reminded to make sure that the compartments are securely shut, since luggage can shift around during the flight. If there isn't room in the overhead compartments, passengers are instructed to stow their bags beneath the seats in front of them.

The Exit Rows

Flight safety instructions typically continue with information regarding the exits. In case of an emergency landing, certain rows lead to the designated exit points. These rows are pointed out. Those sitting in the exit rows are almost always adults, since they are expected to open the exit doors in the event of a crash, as well as help others to them. The option is usually given to an exit-row passenger to switch with someone else if he doesn't feel comfortable with these responsibilities.

Electronic Devices

Electronic devices are not to be used during takeoff and landing. Some electronic devices are barred from use throughout the duration of the flight; this includes cell phones. Laptops, CD players, MP3 players and iPods are permitted after takeoff and before landing. The reason typically given for these restrictions is that some of these devices can interfere with on-flight equipment.

Oxygen Masks and Life Vests

In the event that the oxygen level in the main cabin becomes unstable, oxygen masks will drop in front of every passenger. Passengers are to take them, secure them to their heads using the elastic band and breathe through the masks normally. Passengers are instructed to make sure their masks are on first before assisting other passengers or children. In the event that a life vest might be necessary, passengers are told that underneath each seat is a life vest, which can be inflated by pulling a colored tab. The vests double as flotation devices when needed.

Other Odds and Ends

Passengers are typically instructed not to smoke during the duration of the flight and are reminded that they are prohibited from tampering with smoke detectors in the restrooms. Passengers are shown how to buckle, tighten and unbuckle a seat belt. Passengers are additionally instructed to obey the "Fasten Seat Belts" sign. When it is lit, seat belts are to be fastened. As a general rule, passengers are encouraged to fasten their seat belts whenever they are seated.

听写填空(Spot Dictation)是一对夫妇在伦敦希思罗机场的经历,包括一段对话和一段航班误点的通知,主要使学生知道一些机场的信息和常用词语,可以作为导入活动安排在阅读Ⅱ课文讲解之前进行。

3. 在本单元开始时教师可选择讲解背景知识1、2、3点,而将背景知识4留到课文结束后再讲。

4. Reading I Brainstorming　学生通过自由讨论的形式,列出他们所知道的关于空中旅行的词汇。教师可用下列方式对学生予以一定的引导:让学生设想他们即将进行一次空中之旅,从准备工作起到旅行结束的整个过程中,他们会做些什么,碰到什么,看到什么,听到什么,需要什么等,以此把一些常用的关于空中旅行的词汇按顺序串起来,便于学生理解和掌握。当然教师也可根据其他线索对相关词汇进行分类。如:在空中旅行时经常会用到的名词、动词等。Reading I Pairwork 学生双人结对讨论一些搭乘飞机旅行的小常识。鉴于有些学生可能没有相关的经验,教师可请学生课前查找并阅读相关材料。讨论题2),教师应向学生指出,一般乘客最为关注的无外乎安全、价格、便利、服务等问题,有着不同旅行目的的乘客会对以上几项内容各有偏重。讨论题4)的着重点是在business上,教师可请学生设想一下business traveler和一般的traveler对航空公司的服务会有什么不同的要求。譬如说,business traveler可能对机场和飞机上的通讯设施会有所要求,以便及时掌握商务讯息,而一般乘客可能就没有这方面的需求。讨论题5),一般航空公司在飞机起飞前2~3小时开始检票,飞机起飞前半小时或1小时关闭检票口。

5. Reading I Post-reading　中设有两项填表任务。任务1)的目的是检查学生对课文的理解。有些内容可直接从课文中概括归纳得到,有些则需要学生动动脑筋,从课文的字里行间找寻线索,并通过自己的想像来完成。教师也可请学生说说为什么他们会得出这样或那样的推断。任务2)要求学生对4种最普遍的交通方式加以比较。教师可建议学生先确立比较的标准或角度,如安全(safety)、速度(speed)、成本(cost)、舒适性(comfortableness)等。尽管许多人觉得搭乘飞机旅行很不安全,但目前最为安全的交通方式还是首推空中旅行。此外,学生可能普遍认为空中旅行费用最昂贵,但随着国内航空业竞争的加剧,各大航空公司大打价格战,有些线路出现了机票比火车票还便宜的现象(见下文)。教师可向学生指出,对交通方式的选择取决于对以上一系列因素的权衡和考虑,而这些因素本身也处在不断的变化中。

> Since the train has long been the travel vehicle of choice in China, airline companies, to combat this long lasting traditional means of travel, have resorted to extreme price reductions to woo travelers, especially those among eastern cities. At times an air ticket was cheaper than a train ticket between the same two cities. For

example, during July 2001, an air ticket from Beijing to Ji'nan was priced as RMB 180 (USD 22) while the train ticket cost RMB 200 (USD 24).

6. Reading II是关于电话购票的经历，对售票员推销机票的迂回手法进行嘲讽。在讲解Reading II 课文时，最好准备一张美国地图，让学生根据课文一一标出飞机起飞和降落的地点，从而对课文中的嘲讽含义有更深的理解。

7. Reading II Vocabulary

Question 2　Karaoke /kəˈrɑːəukeɪ/ Karaoke is a Japanese form of entertainment in which people take turns singing the lyrics to prerecorded background music. Karaoke can be a very funny form of entertainment as the audience gets to watch and listens to the performances.（卡拉OK, 自动伴奏）

8. Reading II Cloze

Question 6　选 d. flight, 指 a scheduled airline trip, 飞机飞行的航程。

journey 应用范围很广，泛指"陆上、水上或空中的单程长、短途旅行"，一般来说，它着重指"长距离的陆上的旅行"。如: He will want his supper straight away after this long journey.

trip 为一般用语，指"任何方式的, 从事业务或游览的旅行", 往往着重于"短途旅行"。在口语中, 可与journey 互换。如: He always goes on business trips abroad.

tour 指"以游览、视察、购物等为目的的旅行", 常含有"最后回到原出发点"的意思, 如: He is going to make a round-the-world tour.

voyage 主要指"乘船作水上旅行"。如: He got seasick during the voyage.

cxcursion 指"娱乐性的短途旅行"。如: He went on an excursion to the Great Wall.

expedition 指"有特定目的的远征或探险"。如: They're going to make an expedition to the South Pole.

Question 13　此处选a. on, 是由前文effects要求的。effect 指the power to produce an outcome or achieve a result; influence "影响, 效用", 常和 on 连用。如: Alcoholic drink can have a bad effect on your body. The drug had an immediate effect on the pain. The government's action had no effect on the trade imbalance.

Question 14　此处选c. menu, 因为前文有dishes一说, 明显是指"菜单"。

Question 15　此处选a. light, 作形容词用, 表示"清淡的; 容易消化的"。

Key （练习答案）

>>>>>>Reading I

Pre-reading

I.

airline	airport	air terminal	air fares	air ticket
aircrew	pilot	airhostess	steward	stewardess
land	arrive	fly	take off	depart
tourist class	first class	economy class	business class	cabin
board a plane	get into a plane	get off a plane	miss the flight/plane	cancel the flight

II. 2. Air travel safety and security, service, airfare, convenience...

4. air-miles awards for frequent flyers/valet service airport parking/double baggage allowance/priority status at check-in/exclusive business lounges/advanced seat selection/business class selection/comfortable seating/wider, fully reclining seats/in-seat phone or fax facilities/in-flight catering or free drinks/free newspapers and magazines/in-flight entertainment/on-board duty-free sales/scheduled flights...

Exercises

II. 1. c   2. b   3. a   4. c   5. b

III. 1. embarrassment   2. stumble   3. snap   4. saunter   5. figure
6. conspiracy   7. justice   8. ulcer   9. wimp   10. guts

IV. 1. made a fuss   2. made it   3. was about to   4. out of breath   5. to show up
6. on top of   7. to the bone (= all the way through)   8. in advance   9. had the guts
10. arguing over

V. 1. Mrs. Baker required the new tenant to pay his first two months' rent in advance.

2. Things are looking bad, we might have to pay off more workers.

3. Don't lose heart! Keep trying and you will make it.

4. Aunt Lucy always makes a fuss of small matters.

5. The porter put the trunk down and stood there with a meaningful smile, which reminded me that I should pay him off first.

6. I ran as fast as I could, reaching my office quite out of breath.

Post-reading

Task 1

Situations	Early-airport People	Late-airport People
packing luggage	pack 24 hours in advance	luggage may not get packed until the taxi is waiting at the door
going through Customs	luggage always carefully examined by the Customs officers	luggage examined in a hurry since there is little time for it
luggage on plane	first on board but last off the plane	last on board, but first off the plane
getting a seat on a plane	get to the airport much early to get the best seat but always dissatisfied	never worry about it but always seem to have no trouble getting a good seat
several minutes before the plane takes off	have settled down in their seats for a long time and wait anxiously	walk unhurriedly into the airport/have another drink in the airport bar
preparing for a test	begin studying for the test three or four weeks before	burn the midnight oil the night before examination/may memorize something even on his way to the exam room
choosing a marriage partner	a late-airport person	an early-airport person
having an appointment	arrive at least 15 minutes before the appointment	arrive at the appointed time or a bit late

>>>>>Reading II

Exercises

I. 1. T 2. F 3. F 4. T 5. F 6. F 7. T 8. NM 9. F 10. T

III. 1. b 2. a 3. d 4. a 5. b 6. a 7. c 8. c

IV. 1. He is fully aware that a recognized university degree in business or an MBA is very advantageous to him.

2. What he hates most is his employees' making a great fuss about nothing.

3. When all the passengers are on board, the plane will take off immediately.

4. The president did not show up in the board meeting, for he was on a business trip to Europe.

5. No matter how great the risks are, we've made up our minds to do our best to succeed.

6. I had hoped to attend the lecture, but I found at the last minute that I couldn't make it.

7. What if it rains and there is no place nearby for us to shelter from the rain?

8. It's impossible to know in advance whether their investment plan will yield a profit of $500, 000.

9. As for his ability to lead the company to success, I have no doubts that he is qualified for the task.

10. So long as you work hard, you'll have training opportunities abroad and excellent career prospects.

11. Only postgraduates are eligible for this research project.

V. 1. d   2. a   3. c   4. c   5. b   6. d   7. b   8. a   9. c   10. d
   11. b   12. b   13. a   14. c   15. a

>>>>> **Extended Activities**

A. Function and Structure

I. 1. Caller: Hello, is that Air France information desk?

    The man on the information desk: Yes, can I help you?

    Caller: I'm calling to <u>find out how much it costs to fly to Paris from Shanghai</u>.

    Man: $799 for first class and $549 for economy.

    Caller: Thanks.

    2. (*in the booking office*)

    Man: Hello, United Airlines, booking office.

    Caller: Hello, this is Mr. Bill Collins. <u>I'd like to confirm my reservation</u>.

    Man: Yes, please wait a moment. Mr. Bill Collins, three first singles to St. Francisco, UA837, on Sept. 12th.

    Caller: That's right. By the way, <u>do we have to change planes</u>?

    Man: Oh, UA 837, you needn't. It's a non-stop flight.

    Caller: <u>How much luggage can we take with us</u>?

    Man: Ten kilos each person. You are required to pay overweight if you carry more.

    Caller: I see. Thank you very much.

3. (*a man on the information desk*)

Man: Good morning, this is Kennedy International Airport.

Caller: Good morning, <u>are there any flights to Cairo on Sunday</u>?

Man: I'll find out for you. Yes, there are two flights to Cairo on Sunday — EA 343 and PA 513.

Caller: <u>When do they take off</u>?

Man: EA 343 takes off at 9 : 30 am and PA 513 takes off at 3 : 30 pm.

Caller: I see. Thank you very much.

4. (*in the booking office*)

The woman in the booking office: Can I help you?

Mr. Smith: <u>What flights are there from</u> Shanghai to Moscow for tomorrow?

Woman: Wait for a moment, please. SU526 takes off from Putong International Airport at 15 : 35.

Mr. Smith: <u>What time is the plane due to arrive</u> in Moscow?

Woman: The plane is due at 20 : 20.

Mr. Smith: Good. <u>I'd like to book a seat</u> on flight SU526 to Moscow. <u>How much is the fare</u>?

Woman: First class or economy?

Mr. Smith: <u>I want a first class ticket to Moscow</u>.

Woman: $439 in that way.

5. (*at a travel agency*)

Tourist: <u>Could you tell me about flights</u> to Budapest (布达佩斯) please?

Agent: Certainly, sir. There's a Finnair (芬兰航空公司) flight that leaves Helsinki (赫尔辛基) at 9 : 20 via Copenhagen (哥本哈根) arriving in Budapest at 12 : 20.

Tourist: Does that go everyday?

Agent: No, only on Mondays and Fridays.

Tourist: I would like to go in the middle of the week. <u>Is there a non-stop plane</u> to Budapest?

Agent: Yes, on Mondays and Thursdays there is a Hungarian Airlines (匈牙利航空公司) flight nonstop to Budapest.

Tourist: <u>When does the plane take off</u>?

Agent: It leaves at 18 : 00 and arrives at 19 : 35 local time.

Tourist: Is that first class?

Agent: No, I'm afraid not, only economy class.

Tourist: <u>How much does it cost</u>?

Agent: $599 single and $749 for a round trip.

Tourist: Well, I think that would suit me. <u>I want an economy class single on that flight</u>.

Agent: Yes, an economy class single ticket. I'll see to it.

Tourist: Thanks a lot.

B. Special Use

I. 1. have been longing

2. was feeling

3. will be playing

4. are... doing, Making, ... am showing/am going to show

5. was cooking

6. is happening ... is crying ... are quarreling

7. has been playing

8. will have been working

9. had been studying

10. had been waiting

11. was rushing ... were driving

12. is (constantly) complaining

13. was running

14. has been digging

15. had been overworking

II. 1. will be cleaned: will have been cleaned

2. has made: has been made

3. being signed: signing/to be signed

4. has been resulted: has resulted

5. be increased: increase

6. were not agreed: didn't agree

7. was put: was put forward

8. being repaired: is being repaired

9. encouraged: was encouraged

10. would be set: (should) be set

C. Practical Reading

I.

Airlines	Day	Destination	Flight	Departure	Arrival
United Airlines	1234567	Tokyo	UA838	10 : 20	14 : 10
Dragon Air	123567	HK	KA805	14 : 20	16 : 40

（续　表）

Airlines	Day	Destination	Flight	Departure	Arrival
Asiana Airlines	1234567	Seoul	OZ3345	11：45	14：40
Aeroflot Russian	3	Seoul	SU525	08：50	11：40
Northwest	1357	Los Angeles	NW5983	17：00	13：30

II. 1. 3.

2. They are OZ3345, OZ3285 and SU524.

3. OZ3345 and OZ3285 fly from Shanghai to Seoul daily and SU524 once a week.

4. They are KA802 (10：45) and NH155 (11：30).

5. Flight NH920 of All Nippon Airways, departing at 15：15 and arriving at 18：50.

6. Yes. She can fly KA808 of Dragon Air, which arrives in Shanghai at 18：50.

D. Additional Vocabulary

1-9;	2-36;	3-38;	4-2;	5-7;	6-16;	7-3;	8-12;	9-17;	10-4;
11-15;	12-14;	13-40;	14-11;	15-10;	16-19;	17-34;	18-21;	19-1;	20-27;
21-35;	22-26;	23-30;	24-31;	25-25;	26-33;	27-13;	28-18;	29-20;	30-5;
31-24;	32-23;	33-6;	34-39;	35-29;	36-32;	37-37;	38-22;	39-8;	40-28

Appendix

WORD STUDY

Unit 1

risk	perform	replace	limit	share

Unit 2

maintain	project	fit	launch	range

Unit 3

admire	realize	associate	assume	complain

Unit 4

Involve	content	advance	present	initiative

Unit 5

taste	rush	contain	lose	choose

Unit 6

value	affect	differ	prefer	estimate

Unit 7

concern	lack	relieve	claim	reflect

Unit 8

behave	roll	blow	illustrate	establish

Unit 9

spoil	apply	suspect	insist	spell

Unit 10

suffer	aware	miss	embarrass	figure